# Attachment Theory for Social Work Practice

**Also by David Howe**

SOCIAL WORKERS AND THEIR PRACTICE IN WELFARE
  BUREAUCRACIES
AN INTRODUCTION TO SOCIAL WORK THEORY
THE CONSUMERS' VIEW OF FAMILY THERAPY
HALF A MILLION WOMEN: Mothers Who Lose Their Children by
  Adoption (*with Phillida Sawbridge and Diana Hinings*)
ON BEING A CLIENT: Understanding the Process of Counselling and
  Psychotherapy

# Attachment Theory for Social Work Practice

David Howe

*School of Health and Social Work*
*University of East Anglia*
*Norwich*

Consultant Editor: Jo Campling

LEARNING RESOURCES
CENTRE
Havering College
of Further and Higher education

palgrave
macmillan

Published by
PALGRAVE
Houndmills, Basingstoke, Hampshire RG21 6XS and
175 Fifth Avenue, New York, N.Y. 10010
Companies and representatives throughout the world

PALGRAVE is the new global academic imprint of
St. Martin's Press LLC Scholarly and Reference Division and
Palgrave Publishers Ltd (formerly Macmillan Press Ltd).

ISBN-13: 978–0–333–62561–3 hardback
ISBN 10: 0–333–62561–7 hardcover
ISBN-13: 978–0–333–62562–0 paperback
ISBN 10: 0–333–62562–5 paperback

This book is printed on paper suitable for recycling and made from fully
managed and sustained forest sources. Logging, pulping and
manufacturing processes are expected to conform to the environmental
regulations of the country of origin.

A catalogue record for this book is available
from the British Library.

20 19 18 17 16
11 10 09 08 07

Printed in China

# Contents

*Acknowledgements*                                                    vi

1   Social work and social relationships                              1
2   Becoming a social being                                           9
3   The development of social understanding                          27
4   Attachment theory and social relationships                       45
5   The organisation of experience                                   71
6   Ainsworth's attachment classification system                     78
7   Disturbed social relationships                                   96
8   Relationships with parents and family                           105
9   Relationships with peers                                        116
10  Relationships with self                                         131
11  Relationships with society                                      144
12  Relationships with partners                                     151
13  Relationships with children                                     160
14  Resilience and the development of protective
    mechanisms                                                      178
15  Assessment                                                      188
16  Responses                                                       208

*Bibliography*                                                      224
*Name index*                                                        238
*Subject index*                                                     242

# Acknowledgements

My interest in attachment theory and the nature of social relationships in human affairs has been steadily nurtured over the years by my friend and colleague, Diana Hinings. I have lost count of the number of conversations we have had about people and cases, theory and practice, reason and emotion. Her influence pervades every page of the book and I owe her a considerable debt of gratitude. I should also like to take this opportunity to thank Jo Campling. Without her timely prompting and continued encouragement, this particular book would not have been written.

DAVID HOWE

The author and publishers would like to thank a number of publishers for their kind permission to reproduce extracts from the following: *The Making and Breaking of Affectional Bonds* by John Bowlby (Tavistock Publications, 1979); *A Secure Base: Clinical Applications of Attachment Theory* by John Bowlby (Routledge & Kegan Paul, 1988); *Mate and Stalemate* by Janet Mattinson and Ian Sinclair (Blackwell Publishers, 1979); *Developing Minds: Challenge and Continuity Across the Life Span* by Michael Rutter and Marjorie Rutter (Penguin Books, 1993) copyright © Michael Rutter and Marjorie Rutter 1993; *Developing Minds: Challenge and Continuity Across the Life Span* by Michael and Marjorie Rutter (Basic Books/ HarperCollins Publishers Inc., 1992) copyright © Michael Rutter and Marjorie Rutter 1992; *Relationship Disturbances in Early Childhood* edited by Arnold J. Sameroff and Robert N. Emde (Harper-Collins Publishers Inc., 1989) copyright © Basic Books Inc. 1989. Every effort has been made to trace all the copyright-holders, but if any have been overlooked the author and publishers will be pleased to make the necessary arrangement at the earliest opportunity.

# 1

# Social work and social relationships

**Introduction**

This is a book about relationships and the part they play in our psychological development, social competence and personal well-being. Many aspects of our personality form during childhood as we experience a constant round of close relationships with parents, family and friends. The kind of adult into which we grow is not only a product of our biological nature, it is also the result of the myriad interactions we have with those around us throughout the formative years of our psychological development.

For the majority of us, the quality of our relationships with other people remains the most important area of experience and the yardstick by which we measure happiness and contentment. Throughout our lives we enjoy being in close relationship with others. Many of our most intense experiences occur in intimate relationships. We are fascinated by the experience of love and the strong and powerful feelings that can develop between people. All over the world there is a vast outpouring of poetry, literature, film, music, drama, journalism and television devoted to the themes of love, courtship, sex, family life, the growth of intimacy, the breakdown of relationships, the way we view others and the way others view us. We live our lives in a constant weave of good, bad and indifferent relationships.

Because relationships are so important, the quality of social life can be measured in terms of the quality of our social relationships. Disturbed relationships, hostile relationships, the loss of relationships and the absence of relationships not only cause individual pain and unhappiness, they also produce ripples in the social fabric that make such personal experiences a public concern. Children raised in emotionally fraught families can become angry, confused and diff-icult. Women in relationships with impulsive, insecure and jealous men may find themselves the victims of violence. And those who feel unsupported and unloved can feel lonely and depressed.

Social workers become involved with people who either experi-ence distress or cause distress. Practice in this field operates in a world of strong feelings and deep emotions. When marriages break down or children are under suspicion of being abused, when very elderly parents with Alzheimer's disease are cared for twenty-four hours a day by tired sons and daughters or when teenage boys play truant, steal cars and break into houses, social workers are likely to find themselves in situations in which feelings are running high and people's behaviour is in a heightened state.

Working effectively and appropriately with people at such times demands a good knowledge of the human condition and a sound understanding of how and why people behave as they do under stress. Without such knowledge and understanding, the best laid plans can easily go astray. Although there is an increasing predilec-tion in social work for establishing relationships with others based on grounds which are seen as rational, systematic, logical and legal, to ignore the irrational, emotional and psychological in human relationships is to limit severely the scope of practice.

## Human beings and social relationships

Our background concern will be about the development of social understanding and the formation of personality. Three claims will be made: (i) the kind of person or 'self' we become forms and arises in social relationships; (ii) the type of self which forms depends largely on the *quality* of those social relationships; and (iii) the way the self handles present social relationships depends on the self's experiences of past social relationships. To help us develop these claims, it will also be necessary to render some of the major lines of thought that are currently taking place in developmental psychology and other social sciences. These disciplines are exploring the idea that *to be a human being* and *to become a social being* involve one and the same process. It is fundamental to human development that we grow up *in relationship* with other human beings. Without such relationships, not only would we be socially incompetent, we should also be less than fully human. It is becoming clear that in order to understand individuals, we have to recognise the fundamental role that relationships play in their psychological development. In the words of Sameroff (1989: 32), 'The study of the linkage between a child and his or her experience contains the recognition that no individual can be understood apart from the relationships in which he or she lives.'

In order to understand children and adults, we need to recognise the constant dynamic that takes place between their personal characteristics and the types of social environment in which they find themselves. The connections run both ways: the quality of relationships will influence the kind of personality that forms, and the emerging personality will affect the kind of relationships experienced. Natural differences in temperament, humour, argumentativeness, self-confidence, and intellectual curiosity will form in, react to and provoke different social responses and so create different social environments for each individual to handle (Dunn 1993: 14). For example, natural levels of openness or humour might be enhanced or undermined in different family environments and social contexts.

Dunn (1991: 380) observes that, 'no measure of an individual's behaviour at a particular point in time can be assumed to be independent of that individual's previous history of relationships'. Rigid fathers, loving mothers, involved grannies, jealous sisters, caring teachers – the individual exists in relation to a complex and shifting array of people. Babies enter the world, observes Bruner (1983), ready to interact and relate with other human beings. In the words of Fraiberg (1977): 'If we take the evidence seriously we must look upon a baby deprived of human partners as a baby in deadly peril. This is a baby who is being robbed of his humanity.' But the social world in which a particular baby finds himself or herself will vary widely in terms of language, culture, meaning, parenting, family life and economic wellbeing. 'It is clear,' states Dunn (1993: 1), 'that perception and classification of experience are profoundly affected by the cultural world in which individuals grow up, and such cultural influences are mediated chiefly through differences in relationships.'

## Past and present relationships

It is the ability to cope with other people that makes us human. And in order to become socially competent, and therefore fully human, developmentally we need to experience being in relationship with other people. However, the corollary of this claim is that the quality of those relationships will have a direct bearing on an individual's social competence, emerging personality and burgeoning identity. For example, research has shown that many women who were sexually abused or emotionally exploited as girls by their fathers have low self-esteem, lack confidence and behave submissively (Smith 1991; Burkett 1985 cited in Sroufe 1989b: 103 and 123).

We might note, then, that: (i) social workers are people who become heavily involved in the assessment of relationships (including their own dealings with clients), and (ii) the character and quality of these relationships are the product of people's earlier relationship experiences. It is therefore incumbent on those who deal with people who are not coping and who may be experiencing difficulties in their relationship with others (children, partners, parents, teachers, social workers, doctors, health visitors, officials) to understand the nature, significance and origins of people's personalities and relationship styles. To this extent, assessing the quality and character of people's relationships is basic to the practice of good social work.

**Social relationships and developmental psychology**

Social work approaches which are informed by a developmental perspective accept uncertainty as not only an inevitable feature of human relationships but also understand that the nature of those uncertainties will indicate the character of the various personalities involved in that relationship. Therefore, one way to gain your bearings in demanding relationships is to try and *understand* and *explain* what is going on. Why is this man behaving so aggressively? What are the reasons for this woman staying with her violent partner? Why does this client always turn up late for appointments? In this approach, we need to understand (i) *what* people are feeling; (ii) *what* they are doing and with whom; and (iii) *why* they have these feelings and *why* they do what they do.

Social workers, health visitors and general practitioners will be all too familiar with the type of families who dominate their caseloads and absorb vast amounts of their time. Typical are the Bolt family who live in a three-bedroomed council house in a very run-down part of the city. The five children range in age from ten months to thirteen years. Mr Bolt is unemployed and has spent several short periods in prison for a variety of offences including car theft, burglary and handling stolen goods. The couple seem to row constantly. One or the other of the parents is usually on the point of leaving. There are no set mealtimes and family life seems very disorganised and confusing. The younger children repeatedly suffer a series of minor medical complaints and accidents. Mrs Bolt is a regular visitor to both the local doctor's surgery and the city's hospital accident and emergency unit with children who have either drunk household cleaning fluid, spiked themselves on railings, or contracted a bad eye infection. The older children attend school erratically, the girls tending to stay at home with their mother while the boys roam the streets getting into trouble shoplifting, vandalising property and sniffing solvents. There is a constant stream of social workers, police officers, health visitors and housing officials to the home.

The social work and police departments are currently investigating an allegation that Mr Bolt is taking pornographic photographs of his wife and children. The electricity supply has been cut off for non-payment of bills but Mr Bolt has somehow managed to wire the television set to the outside supply. He sees himself as something of a 'do-it-yourself' expert. However, his recent attempts to knock down a dividing wall 'to make more room' for his newly acquired pool table nearly resulted in the house falling down. The housing department reacted critically and quickly. They are currently in the process of removing the temporary supports and rebuiding the missing wall. The pool table is out in the garden and is not surviving the heavy rains too well. Every week finds the family battling against a fresh crisis. The latest has seen Mrs Bolt being rushed off to hospital after she fainted in a busy department store, hit her head on a counter and suffered concussion. And in spite of calling all social workers 'interfering bastards who do nothing to help you', Mrs Bolt makes frequent visits to the social work office asking for help, advice and sympathy.

## Understanding people and their relationships

The human self and the development of mind, consciousness and sociability form within a social context. There is a social basis to human individuality. And as the social context is essentially a world of language, meaning and endless interpretation, any notion of the self is necessarily seen as a fluid, changing, and culturally informed thing. These developments represent a shift in thinking from regarding individuals as essentially discrete psychological entities to understanding them as products of their social history and context. We cannot generate psychological understandings of people without taking note of their current and past social contexts. Who we are and what we do is based on a lifetime of relationship experiences. Social competence, therefore, is not simply the result of some inborn trait but rather it is 'an emergent property of relationships' (Dunn 1993: 117).

It is because human selves and personalities form within social relationships that the quality of social relationships, particularly during childhood, is so important. There are five particular reasons, then, why social workers might wish to study and understand people's emotional development and those psychological theories which consider the significance of social relationships in human development.

1. Those who work with families may have an interest in understanding children and their development and so may wish to strengthen their assessment skills in this sphere. Understanding the behaviour and developmental needs of children can guide practice and decision-making. Although psychological wisdom is employed, in such cases it is often put to statutory use and helps the social worker make procedural decisions.

2. Social workers might also wish to assess the behaviour and personality of parents insofar as these things affect their ability to care for children and meet their developmental needs. Such assessments might throw much light on the way parents deal with their children's needs and how they cope under stress. They might also reveal how parents typically deal with their children, social workers, and all the other officials who wander in and out of their lives.

3. The parents' own history of relationships can help the social worker understand how they relate with each other as well as their children. Parents and their personalities produce particular social environments and relationship patterns. It is within these parentally generated environments that children develop.

4. Exploring and appreciating theories of the relationship can help social workers understand both their own and other people's

seemingly irrational, unpredictable and disorganised behaviour. Practitioners who have an intense and disciplined curiosity about what other people say and do, are less likely to be surprised, thrown or angered when, for example, they find themselves faced with someone who demands that the social worker take away their three-year-old son or who decides to stay with an aggressive, jealous partner. The ups and downs, the to-ings and fro-ings of people's relationships with others lies at the very heart of the social worker's concern for other people and their wellbeing. A developmental perspective helps practitioners to make sense of people and the quality of their relationships, no matter how turbulent or disturbed they might be. To fail to understand such matters is to cut yourself off from key dimensions of practice. A developmental perspective also allows practitioners to increase their tolerance, patience, concern, compassion, curiosity and resilience when faced with difficult people and troubled situations.

5. A sound understanding of relationships and the personalities which arise within them can give the social worker ideas about how to react, what to say and what to do.

To be 'interested in people' may be cliche or even twee, but it remains fundamental to professions which either offer a personal social service or are required to make sense of human behaviour in a social context. An intense curiosity and interest in the feelings, thoughts and behaviour of oneself and other people is likely to produce practices which are more effective, accurate and humane. It is therefore neither an indulgence nor an irrelevance for those who work in the fields of health and social welfare to become ardent students of personal experience and social relationships. To the extent that social workers are interested in people, the tide of ideas about our social development which is rising throughout many of the human sciences promises an invigorating prospect for the profession and its practices.

## The theory and practice of social relationships

The argument that social workers need to understand the significance of people's past and present relationship experiences will be built up over a number of stages. These stages will form the main chapters of the book.

We shall begin by considering the unique importance of the social environment in human development (Chapter 2). Out of this arises the idea that the development of social understanding underpins the growth of psychological integrity and social competence (Chapter 3). Attachment theory has offered a particularly stimulating set of ideas which have made original and far-reaching links between psychological development and the quality of social experience. Although Bowlby's original formulations have been revised, attachment theory is proving to be a particularly robust and adaptable intellectual outlook for understanding social development. It continues to trigger a vast amount of research into the development of mind, personality and social understanding (Chapters 4–6).

An examination of successful and less successful developmental pathways then leads to an extended discussion of the nature and significance of disturbed relationships for social workers and their practice (Chapters 7–13). Although childhood adversity is highly correlated with poor developmental outcome, there are children who manage to resist the damaging impact of disturbed social relationships. The concept of 'resilience' is introduced and the characteristics that seem to allow some children to emerge relatively unscathed from bad experiences are identified (Chapter 14).

Attachment and theories of the relationship are then used to guide the assessment process (Chapter 15). Assessments which employ a developmetal perspective have a distinct and wide-ranging character. They are particularly valuable for those who practise in social work's more difficult and demanding areas. And finally, the assessment process also suggests what kinds of practical responses are available to social workers and which are likely to be appropriate as well as effective (Chapter 16). Such responses include understanding people, skills training, personal support, family support, social support, counselling, psychotherapy, and economic help.

# 2

# Becoming a social being

In this chapter we shall look at how our personalities and concept of self form within the close social relationships experienced throughout childhood. The processes involved are wonderfully subtle; they turn biological entities into social beings and admit us into the full panoply of interpersonal life. However, the development of high levels of social competence and emotional security depend heavily on earlier experiences of good quality social relationships. Those unlucky enough to suffer disturbed or deficient social relationships during childhood often find social life and the management of personal relationships difficult and stressful. We shall follow the first part of the story from biological inclination to personal awareness in a social context.

## Genes and experience

Talk of attachment behaviour and social relationships forms part of the debate about the relative significance of (i) biology, and (ii) culture in human development. This is the nature-nurture debate – the relative weight that genes and experience play in the growth of personality. The issue revolves around the extent to which human behaviour is either biologically *innate* or socially *learned*, genetically *inherited* or *culturally* acquired.

The biological version sees the child's behaviour as genetically determined and developing along prescribed lines. In contrast, the version which emphasises learning believes that experience plays the major part in human growth and development: the child's sense of self and personality forms as she responds both to her physical and

9

social environment. In order to gauge where this debate is now pitched, I shall briefly outline the main features of human development seen, firstly, in terms of nature and, secondly, in terms of nurture.


**Nature**

From this perspective, individuals enter the world already programmed to react and cope in the right ways at the appropriate times. Determined by their genes, people develop along specified pathways laid down in their genetic blueprint. We contain within our make-up the rules for our own development. We develop autonomously; the social environment plays only a supporting role.

Whatever skills, talents or personality traits we eventually display, they are essentially a product of our genes and not our experience. For example, there is evidence that affectional qualities such as cheerfulness or shyness are probably genetically determined (Rutter and Rutter 1993: 88). Anti-social problems and alcohol abuse in biological birth parents have been used to predict the increased incidence of antisocial personality and alcohol abuse in adoptees (Cadoret *et al.* 1985a and 1985b; Cadoret 1986). More schizophrenic disorders have been identified in the biological relatives of schizophrenic adoptees than have been found in control groups (Kety *et al.* 1978; Rosenthal *et al.* 1971; Tienari *et al.* 1990). Autistic children continue to have autistic characteristics throughout life. Autism appears to have a physiological base and experience has little impact on the underlying condition.

As individuals grow and develop, there is an unfolding of their inherent properties. Experience acts merely as a trigger for the release and emergence of our various behaviours and potentialities. At most, the environment helps us work out what is already implicit in our innate biological make-up (Hamlyn 1978: 28–9). Therefore, behaviour and character come *with* experience but not *from* experience. Indeed, in broad operating terms, our inherited characteristics define what we experience rather than what we experience defining the way we are. Individuals remain at the centre of their experience. They make sense of the world using structures and dispositions which are the property of their biology and not of the world which they experience.

**Nurture**

In contrast to the idea of a genetic programme which prescribes both development and outcome, other theorists emphasise the part which *experience* plays in influencing behaviour and development. As we experience the world of things and people, so our knowledge and understanding grows and develops. It is in coping with experience and trying to make sense of it, both physically and socially, that we establish mental structures and outlooks which determine our personalities, abilities and aptitudes. The logic and order that is inherently present in the world imposes itself on us and not the other way round. We are products of our experience. Our character and operating style form within the family, the local community, the culture and the language environment in which we happen to find ourselves.

**Nature and nurture**

There is a third option which seeks to combine the two perspectives of nurture and nature producing a much more dynamic relationship between biology and experience. Current estimates suggest that genetic influences account for anything between 30 and 70 per cent of the variation between individuals (Dunn 1993: 111; Rutter and Rutter 1993).

Adoption studies of children who have been separated from their biological parents and reared by biologically unrelated people show that many behaviours have an inherited quality *but that the expression of those behaviours may be modified, supressed or enhanced by the quality of the social environment* in the adoptive home (see Cadoret *et al.* 1990). For example, there is evidence that the IQs of adopted children show higher correlations with those of their biological parents than with those of their adoptive parents. *But* research has also shown that adopted children reared in homes which were much more socially advantaged than the homes in which their non-adopted siblings were raised enjoyed anything up to a 12-point IQ advantage over their brothers and sisters. These two findings are not incompatible. They simply mean that although adopted children inherit their genes for intelligence from their parents, the environment in which they find themselves will also influence the extent to which intellectual potential will be realised. In short, biological maturation is influenced by experience (Rutter and Rutter 1993: 12 and 211).

In theories which propose a more dynamic relationship between nature and nurture, there is an assumed genetic predisposition for the individual organism to make sense of experience, but the sense which is made arises as the individual interacts and *relates* to his or her environment. The vastness and density of experience has to be regularised and ordered otherwise we should never be able to make headway in the world. As infants struggle to understand what is happening around them, they create models and cognitive structures to help them interpret the buzz of experience. These models help us to make sense of the world relatively quickly and efficiently. But they also do something else which is of great importance and consequence: they prefigure how subsequent experiences of that kind are to be interpreted.

Thus, experience helps generate the models and the models help us interpret and handle the meaning of those experiences. The *quality* of those experiences, therefore, becomes of considerable significance. With appropriate experience, infants become better at making sense of the things which are important to their survival at particular stages of their development.

On the whole, we cope better if we are able to regularise and systematise our experience. If our experience is inherently unpredictable or ambiguous, we find it more difficult to generate the mental structures which help us to order our experience. The world is experienced as a more confusing, less ordered place and we are never quite sure how to make effective sense of people and situations. So, there is a price to be paid for the potential benefits that experientially-based cognitive structures bring. There will be people whose mental models of how to understand the social and physical world will, as a result of poor quality earlier experiences, be weak. Such weak or incomplete models will fail to help people cope well with the kind of experiences which the model is meant to handle. For example, if a child receives inconsistent and erratic parental responses when he or she experiences anxiety, that child will fail to develop effective strategies for dealing with anxiety on future occasions.

Hinde offers many illustrations from his studies of animals as well as humans. Smiling, laughing and crying appear naturally in babies, suggesting that the development of these behaviours does not require imitation or learning from others. 'However, there are marked cultural differences in the situations that elicit these movements, in the extent to which they are enhanced or concealed and in the responses they elicit, indicating that their subsequent use is much affected by experience' (Hinde 1987: 58).

Individuals may also select or create social environments that suit their innate temperament and character. According to Rutter and Rutter (1993: 19–20) 'it is quite likely that genes do truly play a substantial role in determining the particular environments to which people are exposed'. So, for example, in *passive* correlations between genes and environment, parents may pass on certain genes as well as sponsor certain types of environment. Parents with high intelligence will not only transmit genes which affect intelligence, they are highly likely to offer homes and family life which stimulate intellectual development. Similarly, shy parents who produce genetically shy children, will also be providing them with a low-key environment as well as parental relationships which have a quiet, reserved quality. Furthermore, shy children may choose quiet friends and encourage gentle behaviour in others.

Genes may also *evoke* particular reactions from other people. Rutter and Rutter (1993: 20) give the example of a child with a cheerful disposition eliciting warm and friendly reactions, while a more difficult and miserable child tends to produce more irritable, snappish behaviour in others. And using an even longer time horizon, Robins (1966) has shown that anti-social boys who attended a child-guidance clinic were ten times more likely than a control group to be unemployed in adulthood and twice as likely to have been divorced. Caspi *et al.* (1990: 32) propose that interaction styles established early in life often persist into adulthood because they repeatedly provoke other people to respond in a way that confirms the individual's interactional style.

There is a third kind of correlation in which children *actively* select environments that suit their genetic predispositions. Sporty children will seek friends and places that allow them to practise and develop their athletic skills; extrovert children will enjoy and attend more social occasions than shy, introverted children.

However, as Rutter and Rutter (1993: 32–3) observe, even this formula has to be expanded. Those who have damaging early life experiences are more likely to behave in ways which tend to make other people react in such a way that more of the difficult or deficient behaviour is provoked. Our temperaments also appear to affect our social environment. Easily aroused, easily agitated children will quickly find themselves having to handle very different kinds of social relationships compared to their quiet, shy counterparts.

It is also the case that if the disturbed individual was fortunate enough to find himself or herself in a social environment (say a new family) that consistently reacted in such a way that the difficult or deficient behaviour was not provoked, then such a benign experience might modify subsequent behaviour. It just happens to be the case that most people remain in relationship with the same people – family and friends – over a long period of time. Thus, as Rutter and Rutter (1993: 33) conclude, people's behaviour shapes their environment and early experiences tend to determine later experiences. For example, adverse childhood experiences make people more vulnerable to later adverse experiences. The authors also suggest that people who have had problematic social relationships in the past are more likely to meet adverse social experiences in the future, including unsatisfactory relationships, having children when very young, stressful marriages, and divorce.

Hinde (1987: 63) therefore argues that we must reject both genetic determinism *and* the *tabula rasa* view that human development is entirely the result of experience. Children interpret experience as well as create experience (Sroufe 1978: 45). It is the dynamic combination of genetic programming, innate temperament and experience that produces each unique individual personality. 'The futility of a dichotomy between the biological and social aspects of human nature is now generally recognised' (Hinde 1989: 251). Human beings have organic brains and in the context of other people they develop minds. Biological approaches must encompass psychosocial influences; people are thinking beings and they are heavily influenced by the way they process the experiences which they undergo (Rutter 1991: 338).

## The biological and social origins of uniqueness

Thus, the two things that affect our developmental prospects are (i) the character of our genes, and (ii) the qualities of the social environment in which we find ourselves. The interaction of these two components guarantees the world an infinite variety of people and personalities. Each environment is made up of particular people in particular numbers, each with his or her own temperament and personality, each carrying a certain culture and language which in turn evolve over time and place, generating infinite meaning and endless interpretation. We are each born into a social environment that is unique to us. Our genes are programmed to react with and make sense of that environment which, as chance will have it, may or may not facilitate the brain's task of making sense and organising experience. So it is, then, that all human behaviour, including problematic behaviour, requires 'both a genetic liability and an environmental trigger' (Robins and Rutter 1990b: xvi).

## The formation of the self in social relationships

The success of human beings as a species turns on two evolutionary accomplishments. We can co-operate on a grand as well as a small scale. And in order to co-operate, we need to communicate and understand other people's thoughts and feelings, desires and beliefs, plans and intentions. We need to know other minds. These are huge accomplishments and in trying to appreciate them we need to consider a number of important and intimately linked phenomena.

If being a social animal is fundamental to being human, then being in relationship with other people is profoundly important. Relating with others is not only what we have to be able to do in order to *be* recognised as a competent human being, it is also the thing we have to do in order to *become* a human being. Both the self which forms and our consciousness of that self emerge as we find ourselves relating with and needing to understand other people. The established world of other people in which we find ourselves is both the problem to be solved and the occasion for its solution.

Until relatively recently, psychologists have been inclined to see the social environment – the world of other people and relationships – as a source of contamination for the proper study of the individual. 'The true object of psychology,' observes Ingleby (1986: 299), 'was the individual considered in abstraction from culture: the social was something which had to be stripped away to reveal this object.'

Somehow, the infant seemed to appear in the world as a pre-formed, discrete entity:

> The child – like the pilgrim, the cowboy, and the detective on television – is invariably seen as a free-standing isolable being who moves through development as a self-contained and complete individual . . . Impulses are in the child; traits are in the child; thoughts are in the child; attachments are in the child. (Kessen 1979: 219)

However, it is now being realised that not only are other people and the relationships we have with them influential in our development, but our experience of them is critical to the formation of a sense of self and the qualities of being human. This is a very radical notion. It is not that individual selves enter the world and proceed to interact with it. Rather, it is only by being in social relationships that we can actually form a sense of self and become human. We are constituted within the matrix of social relationships in which we find ourselves. Our psychological development is thoroughly embedded in our social relationships (Hinde and Stevenson-Hinde 1987: 3). Indeed, one of the most important things that we have to do as human beings is make sense of and understand what other human beings are thinking, believing, intending and feeling. This requirement is so basic it is possible to claim that if we are to survive, it is a biological imperative that we must learn to make sense of our social surroundings.

We have also to understand that humanity has evolved in culture, not outside it. Culture means that language, which carries culture and meaning, saturates all human endeavours. In the conduct of human relationships, verbal communication and attempting to understand the minds of others are fundamentally important. Self-disclosure and intimacy, for example, seems to be a prerequisite for the development of most close relationships.

The extreme case of growing up without social relationships would mean that psychologically the individual would hardly be recognisable as a human being. The several cases of children reared in the wild and the story of Genie who was locked up in an attic without conversation or social intercourse of any kind until the age of eleven provide stark examples of what happens when human beings are deprived of social experience. In order to understand ourselves, we need to understand others; and conversely, in order to understand others, we need to understand ourselves. The two processes go hand in hand and they take place as we relate to other people.

## Making sense of social experience

The formation of the self that needs to understand other people as well as *be* understood by other people arises out of the brain's pre-programmed need to handle, anticipate and make sense of social experience. Nature does not require the infant and her brain to enter the world with a blueprint of how things work, how they are to be explained and understood. Much more cleverly, the brain is simply programmed to try and make sense of whatever experiences come its way. As the developing infant becomes more accomplished at organising social experience there is a parallel increase in neurosphysiological organisation.

As the brain interacts with the world, it seeks to make sense of it by developing working models or some kind of internalised representation. These models are built out of the actual experiences which the brain seeks to understand. Of course, you have to have experience of those experiences if you are to develop the neuronal structures and cognitive models which will then be able to make sense of those experiences.

For example, cats, like us, are genetically programmed to make sense of visual experience – they *learn* to see by seeing. During the kitten's early development, there are critical and sensitive periods of brain development when it needs to experience the thing of which it needs to make sense. If it does not experience that stimulus at the critical time, the brain fails to develop the right kinds of neuronal structures and processing models. It therefore finds it difficult to make good sense of that experience when it is eventually met. Cats literally learn to see as their brains develop neuronal structures in response to visual stimuli. When cats who were raised in total darkness are eventually introduced to light, they cannot 'see'. Light enters their eyes and stimulates nerve impulses to the brain, but the right neurological structures to process and make sense of visual experience have failed to form. There is nothing wrong with the cat's eyes. It is just that the animal did not receive the right kind of good quality visual experience at the right time and therefore failed to develop either the correct neuronal structures to process light or the effective conceptual models to make sense of what is being seen.

Rutter (1988: 336) also discusses the notion of sensitive periods in human development in which it is critical for the individual to be exposed to the relevant experience if he or she is to gain that facility. He mentions the acquisition of binocular vision:

> If children do not gain binocular vision during the early years of life (as, for example, through their having a strabismus) it is unlikely that normal binocular vision will be acquired later. It is presumed that some sort of effect on neural organisation is involved.

The most important bit of the world in which the human brain finds itself is the *social* world – the world of people and relationships, language and culture, meaning and interpretation. The meaningfulness of human relationships and social experiences is not a personally defined thing. The potential meaningfulness of other people and the relationships we have with them is already present 'out there' in the language we use to understand and conduct social experience. The world of other people is therefore already socially meaningful. As the infant begins to generate mental structures out of the experiences met, the meaningfulness which is already externally present in language, social life and relationships will enter the internal models and representations that are forming to make sense of the meaning present in those very experiences.

So, with even greater subtlety and complexity, the external characteristics of the social environment help the brain construct internal mental models which then seek to make sense of that external social environment. This hermeneutical trick is as important as it is neat. So, although the brain is programmed to make sense, the particular social sense which it makes is the product of it finding itself in a particular social world already possessed of local meaning. The sense which the child develops of his or her social context is in part the sense which that social context already possesses. If the child is to cope with his or her social world, it is important that the meanings that inform external social life get on the child's mental inside. These meanings should help form and construct the inner working models that the child will need to use in order to make sense of people and relationships. The properties of the outer social world, therefore, help develop the properties of the inner psychological world.

In this way, the individual and his or her cognitive models become fine-tuned to the actual world in which they find themselves. The social 'outside' helps form the psychological 'inside' so that the individual cannot easily be dissociated from the particular cultural world in which she finds herself. It is no longer appropriate to see the individual as a psychologically discrete entity. The mind is not something which just appears *in* the world; mind is a direct product of the brain's 'making sense' propensity being *of* the world. By modelling what appears to be going on, we begin to develop a working sense of what is happening in terms of the characteristics of the social situation of which we need to make sense (Howe 1993: 180–2). As biology and experience relate dynamically, so we begin to understand and relate competently with our fellow men and women. Individuality, therefore, is socially based (Burkitt 1991: 2).

The very process of trying to understand social experience means that we are seamlessly woven into the fabric of social life. The history of our social relationships and the brain's need to make sense of them help explain why our psychological development is a thoroughly social affair. The picture emerging is one in which cognitive structures and psychological selves form as they seek to *make sense of social experience and recognise it as meaningful.* The generation of the self and self-awareness only becomes possible within a social environment. The experience of self can never be prior to society. We emerge out of the social flux as we interact with other people. Formed within the same broad matrix of language and culture, selves formed in particular times at particular places have the capacity to understand one another (Mead 1934). And as similar social 'outsides' help form personal 'insides', then to the extent that I know me I have the capacity to know and understand you.

## Experience and expectations

Having established mental structures to model experience in the light of that experience, future experiences of that kind will be made sense of in terms of the model held. A model not only helps me make sense of that experience, it also determines the *reality* of that experience for me. Models help shape the meaning of current experience and influence how they are to be interpreted. In this way, *past* experiences, of which the brain has sought to make sense, begin to influence the way *future* experiences will be understood and tackled.

As Klein (1987: 41) sees it, the brain develops more and more robust and efficient ways of modelling and ordering experience. Throughout the first months of life, the nervous system is rapidly building up ever more complex and subtle and regulated patterns of responsiveness (Fahlberg 1991: 50). Past experiences help generate current models. The more a particular cognitive structure is used and is found to be effective, the more likely it is that it will organise future experience. 'Just as water running down the side of a mountain will gradually cut a channel, which will subsequently serve as the preferred route, so will experience tend to increase the transfer efficiency at certain synapses and thus create favoured pathways for later nerve impulses' (Cotterill 1989: 74). The most important, regular and significant experiences, therefore, are dealt with with increasing efficiency by the mental models and neural pathways which have already become established. 'This is how the organism controls its own behaviour,' continues Klein (1987: 41), 'instead of being controlled by environmental stimuli only. Enduring changes in the pathways affect the reception and organisation of subsequent messages, more than these later messages affect the existing organisation.' The child's ability to interpret and determine the meaning of experience not only creates the perceived reality of these experiences, it represents a victory of the individual over the environment.

In similar vein, Leslie (1991) makes a distinction between 'primary representation' and 'metarepresentation'. Primary representations are the direct experiences of the world which the brain stores. The information is literal; it is not modelled or interpreted. It helps us act 'unthinkingly' and unreflectively and aids survival. For example, past experience tells us that boulders are big and heavy and that this is a boulder falling down the cliff face so best to run out of the way.

*Meta-representations* on the other hand help the individual organise the meaning of experience. The brain constructs models of the world; it abstracts common features; searches for rules. This allows both the physical and the social world to be anticipated and manipulated. Meta-representations are not so much a description of the world in the way that primary representations are. They are more a device for *organising experience* and representing possible situations, probable explanations and likely interpretations. We use meta-representation to develop theories about what lies behind other people's actions – what is in their minds; what they are thinking, feeling, meaning and believing. We model their actions and behaviour. Without the capacity for meta-representation, a child would not be able to make sense of all the subtleties and ambiguities in social life. The child would be socially inept. Meta-representations allow us to escape the constant immediacy of the present and locate ourselves and our actions along a past–present–future continuum. We become self-aware and self-reflexive and these give us huge evolutionary advantages in dealing with the world.

The first step, therefore, in being able to cope with and negotiate the social environment is to conceptualise it and make some sense of what you think is going on. The infant and her brain are then freed from having to respond afresh to each new social situation – situations *like this* have been met and provisionally modelled before. Action becomes increasingly planned and thought out in the light of past experience. As the richness and density of past experiences increases, so our maps and models grow more structured, sophisticated and versatile.

'Some critical aspects of the ability to step back and consider (one's own) cognitive processes as objects of thought and reflection is acquired by a minority of children by 3 years of age, and simple forms have been acquired by most (but not all) children by 6 years' (Main 1991: 134). Children begin to appreciate the relationship between their own mental states and their behaviour, and, equally important, they begin to recognise that there is also a relationship between other people's mental states and what they do. Therefore to understand other people's behaviour, children need to think about other people's thoughts, beliefs, intentions, hopes and desires.

## The quality of experience and mental representations

If the infant's mental representations of the self and others form within social relationships, the coherence, consistency and relative richness of those relationships will affect the quality and coherence of the child's mental representations. In normal development, a strong sense of self emerges well before the end of the first year:

Thus, a new level of organization has emerged by the end of the first year, and the flexibly organized, goal-directed quality of the infant's behaviour suggests considerable inner organization as well. *The infant responds to new situations in light of his or her past history and purposefully selects behaviors with respect to goals* . . . The working model of the infant at this time may be better described as a model of the relationship than of the self . . . To be sure, however, the self is nascent here. Numerous theoreticians have suggested that it is from the attachment relationship that the particular organization of the individual emerges. (Sroufe 1989a: 78–9; emphasis in original)

For children who enjoy secure, regular relationships with parents and caregivers, the models are continuously modified and updated with experience. The mental models and cognitive representations become both more complex and more flexible, more able to handle the uncertainties and ambiguities of social life.

However, the downside of the modelling process is that initially we try to fit all new experiences of social relationships into old models. We appraise current experiences in terms of the way we understood and dealt with similar events in the past. There will be occasions when the new experience cannot be understood using the old concepts. In these cases the old models should be refined or modified in the light of the new experience. But with well-engrained, previously successful models, such revisions are not always easy to make. This is particularly the case when cues are ambiguous. We tend to see what we expect to see.

We are influenced by the other person's reputation, gender and social standing, and by our overall view of the situation. If we feel generally ill done by, innocent remarks and actions are more likely to be seen as hostile, mocking or rebuffing. Also, however, negative experiences are likely to leave behind feelings of self-blame, inadequacy, helplessness and low self-esteem. An important aspect of personality comprises the developement of cognitions about ourselves, our relationships and our interactions with the environment. (Rutter and Rutter 1993: 100)

There are also people whose formative experiences have taken place within insecure and unresponsive caregiving relationships. They will have found it difficult to develop effective working models of other people and social relationships. New social experiences therefore tax the usefulness of the models held. If people and situations continue to puzzle or confuse individuals, they will feel unable to control their understanding of the situation and so their level of anxiety will rise.

This analysis has serious implications. The more limited, incomplete or distorted the social experience, the less adequate or coherent will be the models for making sense of social experience. If the models are weak, then the individual's ability to make sense of experience and *cope with it* will be impaired. Not being able to make sense of and cope with particular experiences is confusing, frustrating and stressful. Stress and confusion make people feel anxious and anxiety inhibits people's constructive behaviour. New experiences are less easily accommodated and understood. Exploration of the new, therefore, remains a potentially distressing experience for these individuals and so there is a reluctance to pursue strange, potentially interesting and possibly stimulating encounters.

> In the case of the anxiously attached child . . . this gradual updating of models is in some degree obstructed through defensive exclusion and information. This means that the patterns of interaction to which models lead, having become habitual, generalised, and largely unconscious, persist in a more or less uncorrected and unchanged state even when the individual in later life is dealing with persons who treat him in ways entirely unlike those that his parents adopted when he was a child. (Bowlby 1988: 130)

**Coping with social life**

Throughout the life cycle, our relationships with others may cause either pleasure or pain. 'Intimate attachments to other human beings,' said Bowlby (1980: 442), 'are the hub around which a person's life revolves, not only when s/he is an infant or a toddler, but throughout adolescence and the years of maturity as well and on to old age.' So, for example, social relationships that are experienced as warm, caring and supportive ensure safety and survival during infancy; they promote good health, both physical and psychological; they protect against some of the more damaging consequences of stress and trauma; they ward off depression; and they allow us to handle ourselves appropriately and competently as we negotiate the social world. Attachment and intimacy remain important throughout life. They continue to play a key role in the development and experience of close relationships with friends, lovers and children (Rutter and Rutter 1993: 142).

In broad terms, if attachment relationships during childhood were experienced as secure, future relationships are more likely to have a positive quality. On the other hand, if attachment relationships were experienced as insecure, future relationships with friends, lovers and children are more likely to contain serious negative elements. For example, mothers report that the way their mothers related to them when they were infants affects the way they look after and relate to their own babies (Main *et al.* 1985; Ricks 1985, cited in Sroufe 1989b). Parents who quarrel and row excessively are more prone to produce children who misbehave and get into trouble (Rutter and Garmezy 1983; Patterson and Dishion 1988). Wherever we look, the evidence suggests that the quality of our social environment during development has a direct bearing on our current levels of social competence and emotional wellbeing. In short, some relationships strengthen people's ability to cope with life's ups and downs, while others, more disturbed and disordered, upset and confuse people's social competence.

## Summary and conclusions

In our development, what is on the social outside eventually establishes itself on the psychological inside. In this sense, relationships become internalised. It is in our relationships with others that the self forms, the personality takes on many of its characteristics, and we develop mental models which seek to make sense of people and social situations. The key features of this thesis are that the formation of the self and the individual's personality take place within a matrix of social relationships; that these relationships will vary in quality for each individual; and that the quality and character of the self and personality which emerge will therefore reflect the quality of that person's relationship environment. Individual differences in relationships, therefore, lead to different developmental experiences. 'The self,' says Sroufe (1989a: 71), 'should be conceived as an inner organization of attitudes, feelings, expectations, and meanings, which arises in the caregiving matrix.' It is the individual's history of relationships that gives rise to the organisation that is self. Distortions and inadequacies in early, significant caregiving relationships mean that the organisation of the self becomes distorted or incoherent. Problems in coping with other people and situations are most often experienced by those who have suffered disturbed and difficult social relationships.

Relationships are both the cause of many of our strongest feelings and the vehicle we use for handling and regulating them (Sroufe 1989b: 107). As attachment relationships to prime caregivers are a very important kind of relationship, we shall pay them particular attention. But researchers and theoreticians in this field increasingly recognise the importance of other types of relationship in the development of social understanding. Dunn (1993) and Rutter and Rutter (1993: 136) describe relationships of this kind as 'beyond attachment'. They include relationships with siblings and peers, as well as adults who are not primary attachment figures for that child. Children's relationships are therefore multidimensional (Dunn 1993: 113), and for each child the particular constellation of relationships experienced, in terms of number and quality, is *unique*. This is why no two siblings are alike (Dunn and Plomin 1990).

Dunn also reports that children are very sensitive to the quality of relationship between their parents and other children in the family. Such sensitivities to parental discrimination have a considerable developmental impact over time. For example, in her studies, Dunn (1993: 84) found that 'children who experienced less affection or more control than their siblings were more likely to be anxious or depressed'. They had a lower sense of self-competence and self-worth. It appears that sibling rivalries, jealouses and friendships are significant developmental experiences. It 'certainly seems probable,' observe Rutter and Rutter (1993: 49), 'that relative scapegoating within families is much more influential than is sometimes appreciated.' Four-year-old Jack, for example, was the son of his mother's first marriage. When she remarried and had another baby boy, Jack was neglected by his mother and disliked as a moody little boy by his step-father. The young child's initial attempts to show interest in his brother were rejected by his parents and Jack's subsequent displays of frustration, anger and sadness were punished. He began destroying all his toys and ripping up his books. His mother referred him to the local social services department saying she could no longer cope with him and that he was beyond her control.

The content and quality of relationships can be looked at in terms of the relative absence or presence of such things as intimacy and communication, warmth and mutuality, understanding and empathy, supportiveness and security, consistency and care, tolerance and acceptance. We might anticipate that good, consistent and attentive early relationships will produce coherent, well-integrated selves and organised personalities who are easily able to cope with social life.

In contrast, early relationships which are experienced as poor, inconsistent and uncaring produce incoherent, poorly integrated selves. The personalities which form are more likely to be weakly organised. They will find it harder to make sense of relationships and cope with other people. This sets up a vicious circle. Being less able to cope with many of the demands made by other people, they are more likely to react in ways which will seem socially incompetent. Social incompetence provokes adverse reactions in other people. Thus, those who are least well-equipped to handle stress and relationship difficulties are the people who are most likely to meet them.

3

# The development of social understanding

If we are to cope with other people and manage relationships it is vital that we develop social understanding. Although we are born with a strong predisposition to relate to other people, the ability to fully realise this potential depends heavily on our experiencing good quality social relationships with parents and family during the first years of life. In this chapter we explore how children develop social understanding and social empathy. Not only does this process allow children to make psychological sense of other people and social situations, it also binds them into the moral fabric of social relationships. Children who develop high levels of social empathy tend to be more co-operative, considerate and compassionate in their dealings with others. In short, their moral sensibilities appear to be well developed. But as we shall see, children unlucky enough to experience disturbed and deficient relationships fail to develop such a strong sense of social understanding and this adversely affects their ability to deal with family, friends and social situations.

**Children's theories of mind**

At the same time as the self forms within social relationships, a new psychological skill also begins to appear: social empathy and the ability to understand the thoughts and feelings of other people. This makes us social beings not just in the sense of being a product of the social environment but also in terms of being full, thoughtful and reflective participants in that environment. This skill also allows us to become moral creatures. To be a successful social being requires us to develop social empathy, to be able to see the world from the other's point of view and imagine their experience. This is more than simply acquiring some kind of emotional sensitivity. The ability to learn social understanding lies at the heart of our psychological and social development. Without social empathy, our attempts at social competence are weakened and our moral skills are severely limited.

Humphrey (1986) believes that the key to the success of human beings is our social intelligence. We attribute mental states to other people and recognise that their behaviour can only be understood with reference to what is going on in their minds. It is by understanding and explaining our own thoughts and feelings, says Humphrey, that we are able to understand those of other people. We can imagine what it is like to be them because we know what is like to be us (Humphrey 1986: 71).

On this argument, the more we can understand the nature and basis of our own thoughts and feelings, the more skilled we should become at understanding other people. 'In fact,' writes Humphrey (1986: 102), 'if psychology means survival, and experience means psychology, then experience means survival.' Experience is gained by exploration and exploration requires a secure base. Self-understanding needs a coherence of thought and a well-integrated sense of self. Certainly by the second year, it appears that children already have an advanced model of how their own mind works and once this is established the next step is to make sense of other minds. But those who have limited or distorted experiences during early chidhood will be less successful at knowing themselves and therefore understanding other people. To this extent they will be socially impaired; they will read social situations badly; and they will not handle relationships particularly well.

We need to know other minds if we are to manage social life. As individuals we are constantly interested in and preoccupied with the behaviour and mental state of other people – what is she thinking, how does he feel, why did she do that? To co-operate to the extent that we do as a species requires us to be able to communicate with and understand other people. It is therefore imperative that children develop sound and reasonably accurate social understanding. Those who fail to become socially competent in their relationships with others constantly struggle – they feel distressed, they fall foul of the law, they fail to sustain rewarding relationships, they feel depressed, they drift to the margins of society and beyond.

Babies join a busy and complex world of other people and social relationships. The minute they are born they become active participants in this world showing an intense interest in other people. Reciprocal interactions are a particular source of pleasure and stimulation. It seems that we are biologically predisposed to relate with others. But to be competent as well as active members of the social world, babies need to know what is going on and how to behave in a socially intelligible manner. Family life represents a complex social and emotional environment. Children quickly have to learn to make some sense of this world. 'It is extremely adaptive to be able to "read" and anticipate the feelings and actions of the people who share your family world – especially those with whom you compete for parental love and affection' (Dunn 1986: 103). Work on how children develop social understanding shows us that they are active and thinking members of their families from a very young age. Dunn's ethological studies which looked at children in their natural family settings:

> showed that in the course of the second and third year children demonstrated a growing ability to recognise and understand the feelings and behaviour of familiar others within their world. Their comforting behaviour for example demonstrated their understanding of the distress of others . . . their teasing showed their growing skill at deliberately provoking or exacerbating the annoyance or frustration of others. Most strikingly the observations provided evidence for children's understanding of the social rules of their world . . . [The research] suggested a model for the development of social understanding that sees *children's relationships*, and the emotional significance of those relationships, as centrally significant in those developments. The child begins to understand his world not solely because he possesses remarkable learning capacity and is in a familiar context, but because of the emotional power of the setting in which he interacts and watches other members of his world. (Dunn 1991: 385)

The rules of social relationships have to be understood if the child is to survive as a psychological being as well as a social being. But the rules will vary from culture to culture. For instance, in one society it might be expected that girls should be reserved and polite, while in another they might be encouraged to be talkative and expressive. But in whichever culture children find themselves, 'a sense of self-efficacy comes from managing a particular cultural world; all gain pleasure from their mastery of the difficulties – social and psychological – that face them, their own powers within that world' (Dunn 1988: 80).

By the time they are two or three, children show a great deal of interest in what other people are thinking and doing. They also have a useful and practical knowledge of how to read other people's minds and social situations. The 'theory of other minds' that a child develops allows him or her to recognise that there are links between what a person thinks and feels and what he or she does. In order to understand another person and respond appropriately and effectively one has to speculate about his or her cognitive and emotional condition and the kinds of behaviours those conditions are likely to sponsor. Theories are good things to have if you want to organise, distil and handle vast amounts of raw experience and undigested information.

But having a theory that other people have minds and that their mental state has to be known in order to make sense of what they say and do also requires the child to recognise that there is a similar relationship between one's own psychological state and what one says and does. Once again, we learn that 'The ability to make sense of other people is also the ability to make sense of oneself' (Frith 1989: 169). When we attempt to explain our own behaviour to ourselves and other people we invariably account for matters in psychological terms – 'I didn't feel too inspired today; my lecture must have sounded really dull'; 'I'm sorry I snapped at you but I am feeling very anxious about this job interview.' However, those on the receiving end of these brief accounts may not accept the explanation offered and might be thinking 'He wants me to say that his lecture was wonderful; he's really looking for reassurance'; 'Yes, you may be anxious, but you're also feeling guilty because if you get the job you'll have to move to another town and you know I shall be hurt.' Once we start theorising about each other's state of mind, asessment and counter-assessment begin to spiral.

In solving the problems of everyday social life – how can I get my mother's attention? Will she reject me if I cuddle her? I wonder what will make my peers like me? – and in developing an understanding of relationships, children also continue to refine their growing sense of self as that entity in which feelings are felt and actions are initiated.

Recognising that other people have feelings, moods, beliefs, desires and intentions is an extraordinary achievement even though it is absolutely necessary if children are to cope with social life. The ability to speculate about the possible relationship between a person's internal state of mind (wants, motives, desires, beliefs) and what they appear to be doing is known as 'mentalising'. Our social lives are saturated with such reflections and speculations: 'I think Gary was being so aggressive in that meeting because he knew he had made a mistake and he felt threatened by Neelam's obvious competence when she had to pick up the pieces.' A psychological interpretation of Gary's behaviour is made, and we do this kind of thing all the time.

## Other minds and shared understandings

The innate desire to communicate is seen in children from a very early age. Babies less than a year old will point to objects that they think are of mutual interest (Frith 1989: 146–7). The aim is to share attention. If the other person is the baby's mother, she may respond, smile and say 'Yes, that's your teddy.' Such mutual comprehension is as important as it is rewarding. It reveals that even from a very young age children are aware of other minds and that these minds have mental states that can be known and confirmed by acts of shared communication.

Young children are also aware of their own comprehension – 'I know that I know'. By pointing to the teddy bear, the baby is establishing her own mental state *as well as* prompting confirmation both of the accuracy of that mental state and that her mother also has a mental state which is both independent of the child's and yet comprehensible because it appears to share that understanding. The baby has signalled her own mental state and her mother's response confirms that it is recognisable and of interest to other people. Within such communicative transactions the child is establishing herself as an active and competent member of the social world. As the child increases her understanding of other people, so they increase their understanding of the child.

What matters in everyday communication is the point of the message rather than the message itself. In other words, we need to know *why* the speaker conveys *this* thought (rather than another), and as speakers we need to be understood in the way we *want* to be understood . . . We constantly pay attention to aspects of utterances that have to do not with their content, but with the intention of the speaker . . . In fact, in ordinary conversations bare messages (where only content matters) are so rare that they tend to be interpreted in terms of some ulterior communicative purpose *even* if none is there. (Frith 1989: 132–3)

## The emotions and social development

We have shown that (i) our personal experience of emotional states helps us to recognise the complex and often highly charged relationship that exists between how we feel and what we say and do; and (ii) that if we are to understand why other people might be saying and doing the things they say and do, again we need to recognise that there is a relationship between their mental state and their behaviour. But there is a third component to this equation. The *meaning* of many emotions is specific to particular cultures and certain social environments. We have to learn what our emotions mean within the social context in which we find ourselves. In turn, this will also help us to *interpret* other people's emotional states within their cultural context. However, the corollary of this thesis is that we might mis-interpret or fail to understand people and their emotions who lie outside our own cultural and social experience. This has implications for social workers who will regularly find that they are working with clients who are of a different age, race, gender or social background to themselves.

When preschool children are observed in their home setting, what impresses observers is their constant interest in other people – what they might be thinking, feeling, meaning. From a very early age, children not only react to other people's emotions, they also seem to provoke them into displaying emotional states. Infants are both interested in and alert to other people's moods and feelings.

By the age of two or three, children are beginning to develop social understanding. They realise that other people have a point of view and that these are worth knowing about. The ability of the human mind to conceive its own mental states and those of others is extremely important. It appears that young children are much more interested in psychological causality than physical causality (Hood and Bloom 1979). The exasperating habit of young children repeatedly asking the question 'why?' is as much to do with discovering other people's emotional states as it is to do with hearing a factual answer. By constantly quizzing people such as mothers, children provoke reactions and so they are able to explore how accurate and useful are the postulates they hold about other people's moods, feelings and beliefs.

As toddlers, children will wonder and speculate about why people laugh or cry, shout or show fear. It seems, according to psychologists such as Harris, that children first become aware of their own mental states before they begin to fully understand those of other people. Children talk of their own desires, beliefs and emotions before they comment on those of other people. Children learn about the meaning of their own psychological states by relating to other people.

Having developed some understanding of their own psychological states, they are then able to interpret the behaviour of other people by projecting their own mental states on to other people (Harris 1989: 57). The psychological world of other people is constructed out of the child's own psychological experiences. From about two years on, children talk about their own feelings and those of others; they enquire about and debate why people behave the way they do (Dunn 1993: 12; Brown and Dunn 1991; Dunn and Brown 1992). According to Harris (1991: 302), children understand others by analogy with their own mental states rather than deduction from a set of theoretical postulates. Children begin to recognise themselves and others as ' "things which think", as things which *believe, doubt, wonder, imagine* and *pretend*' (Olson *et al.* 1988: 1).

The sharing of feelings and experiences with another is a standard aspect of intimacy and is based on the deep curiosity and interest that we all have in other people's feelings and intentions. Here is an example given by Dunn (1993: 22) from her Cambridge studies of children at home with their family. The little boy is only 28 months old but he is vigorously concerned and interested in his mother's feelings. She is telling the observer about how she had been frightened by discovering a dead mouse behind a chair. The boy interrupts:

    C:  What's that frighten you, Mum?
    M:  Nothing.
    C:  What's that frighten you?
    M:  Nothing.
    C:  What is it? . . . What's that down there, Mummy? That frighten you.

M:   Nothing!
C:   That not frighten you?
M:   No. Didn't frighten me.

The boy really wants to know what his mother is feeling and how this might relate to her behaviour. His persistent questionning and the exasperation it engenders will be familiar to all parents who have children of toddler age.

Children also appear to be able to influence their mother's emotional states as well as anticipate her reactions and feelings. Dunn's (1988) studies allowed her to witness the subtle and sophisticated nature of the relationships that even two- and three-year-olds could manage with the various members of their family.

Jay is 30 months old (Dunn 1988: 30). He has an older brother called Len. Len and their mother discover a mark on the wall and the following conversation takes place between Jay and his mother:

*Mother to Jay*:   Was it you?
*Jay*:             Huh?
*Mother*:          Was it you?
*Jay*:             No. I think Len done it.

In spite of Jay's denial it is clear that he had made the mark. However, what has to be appreciated is that Jay's denial indicates that he could anticipate his mother's reaction (he knows that making marks on the wall is not allowed; he understands that people in this family who make such marks are likely to be in for an unpleasant time). If Jay is identified as the one who made the mark, he knows that he will not enjoy his mother's response. Jay tries to influence her response by denying that he was responsible. At 30 months, he recognises himself as the author of actions for which he is responsible, knows that there are standards of behaviour which other people hold and expect to be kept, and understands that other people have emotional reactions when those standards are breached which may well bode ill for him.

In this little exchange we see that even at 30 months, children are capable of some remarkably complex behaviour. Jay knows that other people have minds and that they are knowable; he understands that states of mind affect what people say and do; he can reflect on both his own and other people's psychological states; and he can try to influence other people's states of mind knowing that this might alter their behaviour and any possible consequences for him. Cognitively and socially Jay is already a sophisticated operator.

## Emotional empathy and social understanding

Harris (1989: 2) argues that young children soon 'grasp that people's emotional reactions differ depending on the beliefs and desires they have about a situation'. While the return of a father home from work will produce feelings of fear and anxiety in the child who is bullied and beaten, it will provoke feelings of pleasure and excitement in the child who knows that this means a game in the garden before bathtime. The point of torch-light in the dark distance will bring joy to the man with a broken leg lying on a mountainside awaiting rescue but it will bring fear to the fugitive hiding in the woods from his enemies (Donaldson 1992: 13). The child begins to realise that *different people bring different mental states to ostensibly the same situation and therefore experience different feelings and emotions in that situation.* It is not just the external properties of the situation that have to be appreciated but also the internal states of mind that people bring to them.

We have a 'mentalistic' concept of emotion; a working model of other people which helps us predict what they might or might not think, feel and do in particular situations. Children 'who experience parent–child relationships characterized by much discussion of feelings, psychological causality, and self-disclosure are likely to be relatively sophisticated in their emotional understanding' (Dunn 1993: 115). They will be taking part in relationships which use a mentalistic concept of emotion to make sense of social experience.

Dunn and her colleagues (Dunn *et al.* 1991) observed considerable variation in the frequency with which families discuss emotion and its consequences. Some families hardly ever mention or discuss feelings while others constantly consider and reflect on their presence, importance and implications for the child and other people. The researchers found that there was a stable link between talking about emotion and understanding emotion which added to the child's general social competence.

So, if children can *imagine* what other people might be believing or wanting, they can also work out what their possible emotional reactions will be in a given situation. Imagination, make-believe and pretend-play are therefore functional. Pretend-play 'allows the child to entertain possible realities that other people entertain. It is a key that unlocks the minds of other people and allows the child temporarily to enter their plans, hopes and fears' (Harris 1989: 51–2).

Make-believe play becomes increasily common during a child's second year. Dolls become mothers and fathers; balls of wool become tigers or wild animals. These objects are endowed with mental states by the child and these imagined mental states inform what the objects say and do. *Co-operative* make-believe play, when children play and chat together, continues throughout childhood. The combination of co-operative play *and* make-believe is particularly potent in the development of social empathy, the understanding of other people's emotional states and the 'theory of other minds' in children. Children who do not play well together or who do not engage in much make-believe play, fail to develop deep levels of social understanding and this is reflected in their failure to develop a strong moral sense. They may experience no concern when other people are in a state of distress.

It also appears that very disturbed children rarely engage in pretend play. In contrast, securely attached children play a good deal and their mothers often participate in their games and imaginative ventures. The broad finding now emerging is that children who are able to engage in pretend play on their own, with their siblings and with their parents are better able to 'mentalise', to develop social empathy and to imagine how the world might look from another person's perspective (Harris 1994: 20).

This constant imaginative exploration of the relationship between psychological states and actions allows the child to develop an increasingly refined ability to understand the nature and practice of social life. The child can begin to make sense of other people. She can begin to understand what her own thoughts and feelings might mean in particular social contexts. All in all, she is learning to be a competent social being, able to relate to others as they relate to her.

**Empathy and morality**

Talking with parents about emotions allows children to begin to recognise, understand and make sense of their feelings. The involvement, interest and responses of parents help children to understand and manage their emotional experiences. Parents who do not listen to what their children have to say, who are not interested in their feelings, who fail to react or who respond in an undermining and 'disconfirming' way, do not help their children to make sense of or control their emotional states.

Some parents even impose a preferred meaning on their children's emotional experiences; in effect they seek to control their children's understanding of their own feelings. Such children find it difficult to handle strong feelings in themselves and other people. Their 'self-knowledge' and understanding of self is incomplete. They have not been helped to make sense of what is happening to them emotionally. They learn to cope by either avoiding situations and people that provoke strong feelings, or developing strategies which allow them to divert attention and interest away from their own feelings.

Of particular interest in this connection is Sroufe's (1989a: 89) report which shows that compared to securely attached children, the play of those with avoidant relationship histories (children who have experienced unresponsive, rejecting or indifferent parenting) lacks complexity, elaboration and any element of fantasy play concerning people. As we have seen, such play tends to saturate the lives of most preschool children. The feelings and fate of other people appear to be of little interest or concern to those with rejecting parents and avoidant attachment experiences. They lack social empathy. Their working models used to make sense of other people and their behaviour are weak and underdeveloped.

Interestingly, a number of studies appear to show that the play of secure children has fewer themes to do with conflict. If conflict is present, the children with secure relationships with their parents are more inclined to bring the played scene to a satisfactory and happy conclusion. Sroufe (1988: 20) gives the following example. When injury or illness entered the fantasy play of securely attached children, the eventual outcome of the play was positive and happy ('He broke his leg . . . Here comes the ambilens. They take him to the hospital. Zoom . . . The doctors have mended his leg and made it better').

However, in the case of avoidant and insecure children there was less likelihood of fantasy play involving people in the first place, and if there was talk of injury, there was less chance of a happy outcome. In other studies conducted by Fury (1984 cited in Sroufe 1989a), children with avoidant attachment experiences were said to show 'negative empathy'. For example, when a young friend of one girl complained of a stomach-ache, she smiled and poked her in the stomach. When the complaining friend cried in pain, saying 'That hurts', the little girl smiled and poked her again.

This lack of empathy is closely tied with the child's lack of a moral sense. The child appears to show little ability to imagine or understand what the other person might be experiencing when he or she is in pain or distress. This lack of social empathy and the moral sense that goes with it means that some children are capable of quite horrific behaviour. A lack of social empathy appears to be associated with an increased tendency to show aggression (Feshbach 1989: 353). Other children can be injured or in extreme cases even killed; money can be taken; property can damaged; all seemingly without remorse.

## Culture, meaning and emotion

It is not sufficient simply to recognise other people's emotional states, we also have to be able to *interpret* what these states might *mean* in that particular family, social or cultural setting. By the age of one year babies are able to attach meaning to a wide range of emotional expressions. 'Older children . . . gradually appreciate that people's emotional lives are not only regulated by the consequences of their actions, but also an awareness of the emotions that other people will express towards those actions and their consequences' (Harris 1989: 81). From birth, children are cultural creatures. Social and cultural expectations add an extra layer of nuance which the child has to grasp if he or she is to develop social understanding.

There is much debate amongst 'emotion theorists' about which emotions are universal and expressed in the same way irrespective of the culture, and which emotions are cultivated or suppressed in particular cultural settings (Harris 1994). Attachment theorists have attempted to combine these two perspectives. As children build internal mental working models in an attempt to make sense of the emotional and relationship environments in which they find themselves, so they form expectations of other people's mental states and their relationship style. The models help children cope with anxiety and allow them to predict the availability of attachment support likely to be received from their prime caregivers. Secure and insecure attachment patterns are, in effect, modelling the emotional character of the parent–child relationship. The early established working model is then 'projected outward by the child – it is used to guide emotional reactions toward persons outside the immediate family – even when those expecations have limited validity' (Harris 1994: 4).

Feelings of pride, shame and guilt are culturally sponsored emotions. Certain emotions are imbued with social meaning. The child has to learn to recognise and interpret these accurately if he or she is to behave appropriately and have *feelings* suitable to the occasion. We learn about the meaning of many of our actions by how other people react to them. If boisterous behaviour in children causes their elders to feel disgusted and outraged, the child will learn to feel shame and guilt whenever he or she acts raucously. It is the *emotional reactions of others* who have already learnt the social meaning of particular behaviours which induces certain *other emotional* states in the child. By the end of the first year:

> the infant understands three major components of human emotion. First, a person's emotional expression has a meaningful content and with implications for one's own current emotional state. Second, other people are, under normal circumstances, responsive to the emotional states of the self. Third, other people's emotions are typically directed at an intentional target, a person, location or object in the immdediate environment; hence, another person's emotion can have implication for one's own emotion with respect to that target. (Harris 1994: 8)

In order to be successful at social relationships the child must show understanding at two levels simultaneously. The mental state of the other must be known. And, the child must know how the other person will feel when he or she exhibits those behaviours in that particular social and cultural context. Children 'become increasingly alert to the fact that the emotional state of one person is influenced by the emotional state of another' (Harris 1989: 104).

The interpretation of social life and the production of social competence are endlessly complex and wonderfully fascinating. The more we understand the way we handle our own emotional and mental states, the more accurate will be our interpretation of other people's behaviours and emotions. And the more perceptive we are in such matters, the more sensitive and responsive we shall be in our relationships with others. Our cultural environment might encourage us to put a brave face on things when we suffer a disappointment. We might feel pleasure at the downfall of a pompous man, but we know it would be socially impolite to smile. The more accurately we understand others, the more socially able we become. The ease with which emotions are shared, discussed and communicated within family life; the opportunities for co-operation, sharing and pretend play; and the frequency of reciprocal, sensitive social interaction all help the child become a socially adept and effective individual (Harris 1994: 14).

All of which brings us back to the quality of social relationships we experience during childhood. Without relationships which are experienced as sound, consistent and responsive, the opportunities to develop both personal and social understanding are limited. The capacity to develop social empathy and moral sensibilities will be poor. Privations and deprivations in the quality of early social relationships can upset our ability to cope with people and situations in later life.

## Autism and the failure to develop social understanding

As well as environmental and experiential deficits, a child may suffer biological and genetic disadvantages which deny him or her the opportunity to develop personal and social understanding. The devastating consequences of not being able to read other people's mental states and develop social understanding is vividly demonstrated in the case of autism. Autism illustrates the absolute importance that social relationships play in social and psychological development. Current explanations of autism describe it as a learning disability due to abnormalities of brain development (Frith 1989: 186). A neurological failure in the brain's processing functions means that the child remains unaware of, indeed uninterested in other people's mental states. The autistic child suffers impairments in socialisation, imagination and communication (Wing and Gould 1979). These impairments have a profound impact on the child's development and social performance. From the beginning, researchers recognised that one of the main characteristics of autistic children was the difficulty they had in forming social relationships. Friendships, if formed at all, lack elements of sharing and reciprocity, and autistic adults rarely form love relationships.

It has been suggested that individuals with autism lack a 'theory of other minds' (Baron-Cohen *et al.* 1985); that they lack 'the ability to attribute independent mental states to self and others in order to predict actions' (Happe 1994: 216). Without the desire or ability to show constant interest in what other people might be thinking, feeling, believing, desiring and intending, social life would either not start or it would soon break down. And with the breakdown of social relationships, the need for language would diminish, the generation of meaning and the need for interpretation would cease, culture would atrophy, and all that is so characteristic of human beings and social life would decline.

The sociablity of humans is more than a nice thing to experience. It represents the ability of our genes to create brains which can develop and structure themselves *out of* experience and so *transcend* the limited possibilities of simple programmed responses. And as this possibility also leads to the rise of ideas and explanations about the way the world works which can be transmitted through culture, human beings can escape the immediate horizons of their own experience and plug into the vast pool of experience that is stored in the cultural pool. Our predisposition to relate to others, as well as be curious and sociable, absorbs us into a common sea of understanding and shared knowledge without which we would remain forever isolated. We would be denied access not only to the potential usefulness of co-operating with other people but also to the huge body of knowledge that is stored by human societies. It is vitally important that we internalise our culture's range of knowledge and social meaning. Cultural evolution has now outpaced biological evolution in human beings. And as cultural differences become greater than genetic differences, people may differ culturally more than they do genetically.

Autistic people often find that other people appear to be something of a puzzle; their behaviour seems unpredictable and therefore frightening. Misunderstandings easily occur and other people easily get cross and exasperated. For the autistic individual, it seems altogether easier to avoid engaging in social relationships – they do not seem to make much sense. Although autistic children experience emotions themselves, they show little interest in wishing to communicate their feelings to other people. Equally, they are not interested in the cognitive or emotional states of those around them. In fact it appears that autistic children are unaware that other people have mental states that inform their behaviour. Leslie (1987) also notes that autistic children do not engage in pretend-play. He argues that the failure to understand other people's mental states and the lack of make-believe play are closely linked phenomena in the case of autistic children.

## The Sally-Anne experiment

Frith (1989) describes a simple but elegant experiment that reveals the poor mentalising ability of autistic children, known as the 'Sally-Anne' experiment. The experiment demonstrates that autistic children fail to take into account other people's *beliefs* when trying to understand their behaviour.

The experiment was conducted on three groups of four- and five-year-old children: children with no learning disabilities, Down's syndrome children, and autistic children. All the children had mental ages above the age of three and could solve logical problems with a literal content equally well. In the experiment, two dolls named Sally and Anne are used. The following play is enacted:

> Sally has a basket and Anne has a box. Sally has a marble and she puts it into her basket. She then goes out. Anne takes out Sally's marble and puts it into her box while Sally is away. Now Sally come back and wants to play with her marble. At this point we ask the critical question: 'Where will Sally look for her marble?' (Frith 1989: 159)

The answer is, of course, 'in the basket!'. Because Sally was away while Anne moved the marble into the box, on her return Sally *believes* that the marble is still in the basket and so that is where she will look. We can predict her behaviour because we know what she believes. Most of the non-autistic children give the correct answer. The game seems funny to them and they giggle about 'naughty' Anne and what she did. But few of the autistic children give the correct answer. They predict that Sally will look in the box which is where the marble actually is. They fail to take into account what Sally *believes* to be the case.

Autistic children assess situations literally in terms of logical behaviour. They do not generate any 'mentalistic' understandings of what is going on in other people's heads. 'Pretend play' is largely absent. Hence, the fun and playfulness that characterise much of early childhood relationships, and which require some appreciation of what the other person is thinking as well as feeling, is absent from the life of the autistic child (Rutter and Rutter 1993: 139).

Certainly anything as complicated as deception, insincerity or sarcasm is totally lost on the autistic child. All behaviour is interpreted literally. In contrast, most of us relentlessly interpret other people's behaviour. We are 'compulsive mentalizers' and rarely take other people and their behaviour at face value! (Frith 1989: 166). And yet without this almost perverse facility, social life and social relationships become impossible.

## Conclusion: from self to social understanding

The intimate relationship between the formation of the self, the emergence of personality, the development of social understanding and the quality of social experience can be summarised in seven stages:

(1) If human beings are social beings, then the ways in which we become social is a topic of central concern for those interested in how people cope with social life. There is a seamless dynamic between biology and the experience of social relationships. The self forms within this dynamic. The dynamic also describes how we learn to understand ourselves as we learn to understand others, and how we learn to make sense of others as we gain a better sense and understanding of self. We have to develop within social relationships in order to become social beings.

(2) In order to function within relationships, the infant has to develop social understanding – the ability to make sense of other people's behaviour, actions, beliefs, feelings and intentions. We therefore have to have some idea what is going on in other people's minds. The idea that children develop a 'theory of other minds' has added further weight to the importance of the social nature of much of human psychology.

(3) If the self and people's personalities form within social relationships, then the *quality* of those relationships will affect the selves and personalities which form. Individual selves and personalities represent the particular ways in which individuals have learned to organise their experience and make sense of it. The circle is completed by observing that the quality of the relationships exper-

ienced will influence the kind of cognitive organisation achieved by an individual. The models used to represent relationships gradually become internalised. The process of internalisation witnesses the formation of the self, the individual's personality, and the characteristic ways in which he or she makes sense of and handles social relationships.

(4) The quality of relationships experienced also affects the quality of social understanding developed by children. In turn, the ability of children to cope with social relationships is used as a measure of their social development.

(5) Therefore, personality and social understanding are both the product of social relationships and defined in terms of the individual's ways of reacting to and coping with social relationships. We tend to assess people's personalities and judge them in terms of the way they present and handle themselves in social relationships. Rutter *et al.* (1990: 139) define personality disorder as 'persistently abnormal interpersonal relationships associated with definitely impaired social functioning'. We talk of people being shy or extrovert, neurotic or self-assured, confident or insecure, anxious or unrealistic, open or conscientious. For example, psychiatrists will often classify personality disorders in adult life in terms of particular traits or behaviours, such as anti-social behaviour (Rutter and Rutter 1993: 155).

(6) So: (i) the quality and experience of an individual's past social relationships affect the type of personality he or she develops; (ii) the quality and experience of an individual's past social relationships influences the ways in which he or she copes with and handles current social relationships; and (iii) an individual's ways of coping with and handling current social relationships largely determines the way we define his or her personality.

(7) Therefore if we are to understand an individual's current performance and competence in social relationships we need to consider the quality and experience of his or her past social relationships. Both past and present experiences of social relationships are, in effect, capable of telling us something about an individual's personality, her ability to organise experience, her skills in social empathy, and her sensitivity to moral issues.

# 4

# Attachment theory and social relationships

It is now time to introduce the work of John Bowlby. He brought to bear both a very original mind and an interdisciplinary perspective to the study of children and their emotional development. The intellectual flowering of his work was the basic formulation of what we have now learned to call 'attachment theory'. The theory has proved to be extremely fertile ground for researchers and practitioners alike. It has helped us to understand how and why children develop close relationships with their caregivers. It has also provided us with powerful frameworks for understanding what happens to the psychological development of children who do not experience satisfactory relationships and who suffer poor attachment experiences. This chapter introduces the concept of attachment and examines its significance in the child's experience of early relationships.

## Maternal deprivation

In the second chapter, we said that for the developing infant, social relationships are both the problem and the solution. If the child is to develop social competence, he or she needs to become fully engaged in good quality social relationships. The maturing child will be exposed to a range of significant relationships, each of which will be capable of influencing the developmental pathway followed by that child. Forming a close attachment to a caregiving figure is still regarded as perhaps the most important early social relationship, but others, described as 'beyond attachment', become increasingly

45

important, particularly as the child grows older. The child is part of a social network and if attachment relationships are weak with, say, the mother, it might be that the father, an older sister or a grandparent serves equally well as that child's selective attachment figure. Rutter (1991: 341) notes the growing recognition that developmentalists now give to the quality and character of social relationships in understanding the formation of the self and the structuring of personality:

> Attention has shifted from 'mother-love' as such to the growth of social relationships. However, within the latter topic, the concept of attachment has come to dominate both theory and empirical research. The basic idea is that children have a natural propensity to maintain proximity with a mother figure, that this leads to an attachment relationship and that the quality of this relationship in terms of security/insecurity serves the basis of later relationships.

Throughout the late 1930s and 1940s John Bowlby had been investigating and reflecting upon the nature and purpose of the close relationships we form with people throughout our lives, and particularly those we forge in childhood. 'The making and breaking of affectional bonds' as he was later to call his subject of enquiry loomed ever larger in his attempts to understand the psychological behaviour and development of human beings. A trained psychoanalyst, he became increasingly dissatisfied with the ability of psychoanalytical theory on its own to explain many of the psychological phenomenon with which he was working. His discovery of the work of ethologists in the early 1950s revolutionised his thinking about early child development and was eventually to lead to his formulation of 'attachment theory'.

In his work with people like James Robertson, Bowlby recognised and described the upset and pain that children experience when they are separated from their parents. The mixture of tears, protest and anger observed by the researchers was both impressive and, they thought, in need of explanation. Such effects were witnessed when children were temporarily separated from their parents, but they could also be observed in cases where the separation was both more profound and traumatic. It was in these latter cases that Bowlby saw some of the longer-term effects of 'maternal deprivation' – neurotic and delinquent behaviour in the children when they grew older, and possible mental illness in adults. He needed a theory to explain why the serious disruption of particular childhood relationships seemed to cause such havoc in the psychological wellbeing and social behaviour of the deprived individuals.

In his intitial formulations, Bowlby believed that the 'evidence is now such that it leaves no room for doubt . . . that the prolonged deprivation of a young child of maternal care may have grave and far reaching effects on his character and so on the whole of his future life' (Bowlby 1951: 46). Such conclusions were based on a review of a number of studies appearing at that time including Bowlby's own work on juvenile delinquency. The World Health Organisation wanted to assess the mental health consequences for 'children who are orphaned or separated from their families for other reasons and need care in foster homes, institutions or other types of group care' (Bowlby 1951: 7).

Bowlby submitted his review of the research evidence to the World Health Organisation in 1951 under the title *Maternal Care and Mental Health*. It appeared to him that children who had been deprived of their mothers, particularly those brought up in institutions, suffered in terms of their emotional, intellectual, verbal, social and even physical development. By the time they had reached adolescence, these children had problems in forming steady or stable social relationships. They tended to be rather shallow and promiscuous in their dealings with others. Delinquent behaviour and personality problems appeared to be the fate of those who had experienced long-term separations from their mothers or mother substitutes during the first few years of life. It seemed that the lack of a warm, intimate and continuous relationship with the mother during infancy, rather than middle or later childhood, was likely to lead to a person with a disturbed personality who might also suffer cognitive impairment, anxiety and depression (Rutter 1991: 332).

However, not only were these claims soon to be qualified by Bowlby himself, but others began to subject them to critical scrutiny. Rutter (1981) observed that 'maternal deprivation' in fact conflated and therefore confused two categories of disturbed infant relationship. Bowlby, in his controversial and groundbreaking 1951 report to the World Health Organisation, was writing about maternal *privation* (children who had *never* had maternal care and were raised in institutions) and not maternal *deprivation* (children who had had a relationship with their mother but who had then lost or been removed from her). While the child who has had no maternal care or who has not received constant care by a substitute caretaker almost invariably displays long-term psychological disturbance, the developmental consequences are more complex and difficult to predict in the case of maternal deprivation.

Looking back, it now seems that in the early 1950s the case was somewhat overstated. It was simply too sweeping to argue that babies needed full-time and exclusive mothering if they were to develop into psychologically healthy adults. Certainly short separations from mother (illness, holidays, work), although temporarily upsetting, had no long-term adverse consequences. Indeed, research began to show that it was remaining in prolonged disturbed relationships that was more likely to lead to impaired development rather than simply losing a relationship. For example, the discord and emotional conflict surrounding parental divorce was shown to be much more damaging to a child's psychological development than parental death. However, this is not to say that losing a parent, whether by death or separation, is not disturbing. It clearly does cause emotional upset and even damage. Many children suffer a double blow: a history of conflict between parents often preceded their separation.

Nevertheless, it does seem that there are risks for the child when relationships are not sustained on a regular and long-term basis. According to Rutter (1991: 341 and 361), 'it seems that the postulate that a lack of continuity in loving committed parent–child relationships is central has received substantial support', and that 'What has stood the test of time most of all has been the proposition that the qualities of parent–child relationships constitute a central aspect of parenting, that the development of social relationships occupies a crucial role in personality growth, and that abnormalities in relationships are important in many types of psychopathology.' What has been qualified is that the mother–child relationship is the only important relationship in a child's development.

In the earliest formulations, there was the strong implication that no-one else but the mother was sufficiently important or would do. Feminist critiques were particularly fierce throughout the 1970s and 1980s. They argued that what was important for the child was not exclusive and concentrated care by one woman but stable, regular and shared care by a reliable number of adults and older children. The mother is clearly a very important member of this social environment, but fathers, grandparents and older brothers and sisters might also play a regular and significant role in that child's experience of social relationships.

But whatever the weaknesses in Bowlby's early conclusions, his work has stimulated a vast amount of research and reflection on the psychological significance of the mother–child relationship in particular and social relationships in general. Our understanding of the nature and significance of early life relationships has grown immeasurably since Bowlby's pioneering studies. So, although a genetic component has been added to an expanded notion of social experience (of which the mother–child relationship is likely to be very important), Rutter (1991: 338) is still able to state, almost twenty years after his first exacting review of Bowlby's work, that 'the evidence is now sufficient to conclude with confidence that the seriously adverse experiences encompassed within the concept of "maternal deprivation" may indeed influence children's development.'

## The emergence of attachment theory

Bowlby himself continued to develop and refine his ideas right up until his death in 1990 at the age of 83, but perhaps his greatest achievement was to respond to some of the critics of the concept of maternal deprivation by vigorously developing the original theoretical perspective into what we now know as attachment theory.

Like many original thinkers, Bowlby recognised that there were fundamentally important issues and potentially deep insights lying behind the seemingly obvious answers to the somewhat fatuous questions being asked about childhood experiences and psychological development. Why should children be upset when they are separated from their mothers? Why do children who are loved and cared for in a consistent and stable manner nearly always grow up into well-adjusted adults? Why do children who have never had a constant mother-figure find social life and relationships so difficult? It is only when you to stop to think about these questions that you realise that it is not at all obvious how they should be answered other than to say something like 'of course a loved child will grow up into a socially competent adult and an unloved child will not'. This answer tells us nothing about how these psychological states work or might come about.

Psychoanalysis's 'drive theory' attempted to explain these phenomena in terms of the child's 'libido', the psychic energy that builds up and demands release and gratification and which is the direct mental counterpart of the physiological needs that cause tensions in our body. In the case of young babies, the need to feed brings the infant into a close and powerful relationship with, usually, the mother. The mother, or her breast, can discharge the baby's libido by feeding the child. Any delay or failure to reduce libido is experienced as anxiety. The ability to feed and thereby gratify her infant is the basis of the baby's love for her – the 'cupboard love' theory of relationships according to Bowlby.

Taking this line of thought a stage further allowed Freud to suggest that it was not the mere loss of the food supply that caused anxiety but the actual or possible loss of the food *supplier* – the mother and her breast as the objects to which the child and his or her love were relating. Any prolonged separation from the mother threatens gratification of physiological needs. There is therefore a build-up in libido and anxiety.

Within this theoretical outlook, any relationship or attachment with the mother that happens to develop is simply the result of the infant's physiological needs being met. Such needs are generally concerned with food or the infant's sexuality defined in the broad sense of finding satisfaction and pleasure in responding to the environment for purpose of growth and development. Psychoanalytic theory reduced attachment behaviour to a by-product of the traditional instincts.

Bowlby comprehensively rejected this analysis and saw attachment as a primary, biologically sponsored behaviour in its own right. The need to be close to a parent-figure, to seek comfort, love and attention from that person, is every bit as basic as the desire for food and warmth. In other words, there is a biological predisposition to relate with particular human beings irrespective of anything else. 'The young child's hunger for his mother's love and presence is as great as his hunger for food . . . Attachment is a "primary motivational system" with its own workings and interface with other motivational systems' (Bowlby 1973).

## The work of the ethologists

However, Bowlby's development of attachment theory was not just in response to his criticisms of psychoanalysis. In the 1950s he became more and interested in the work and ideas of ethologists – scientists who study animals and their behaviour both under laboratory conditions and in their natural habitat. There seemed every reason to consider aspects of human behaviour in exactly the same way that ethologists were studying animal behaviour. Human beings and their behaviour are as much a product of evolution as are monkeys, cats and their behaviour. The science of ethology stimulated new and interesting answers to the old questions about why and how human infants become attached to certain adults. In fact, 'The distinguishing characteristic of the theory of attachment that we have jointly developed,' write Ainsworth and Bowlby (1991: 333), 'is that it is an ethological approach to personality development.'

Lorenz was showing how newly hatched geese followed their mother and became anxious if they lost sight of her. Harlow was experimenting with monkeys, discovering that under laboratory conditions infant primates preferred to spend most of their day clinging to a surrogate monkey covered in soft, furry towelling even though 'she' did not provide any milk. The surrogate wire-mesh monkey that did provide milk was only visited when the baby was hungry. It seemed that there was a biological need to relate to a mother-figure whether or not she supplied food.

These observations appeared to demonstrate that attachment behaviour is not derived from other primary behaviours such as feeding. 'Geese demonstrate bonding without feeding; rhesus monkeys show feeding without bonding. Thus, argues Bowlby, we must postulate an attachment system unrelated to feeding, which, adopting a biological approach from which psychoanalysis had increasingly become divorced, makes sound evolutionary sense' (Holmes 1993: 64). Attachment, as a class of behaviours, is therefore conceived as distinct from feeding behaviour and sexual behaviour and remains highly significant throughout life (Bowlby 1991a: 305).

## Attachment behaviour

Attachment behaviour becomes activated when an individual experiences stress. Stress is felt when the individual (i) has pressing physical needs (hunger, pain, illness, fatigue); (ii) is subject to environmental threats (a frightening event or attack); or (iii) experiences a relationship problem (long-term separation from attachment figure or rejection by attachment figure) (Simpson and Rholes 1994: 185). Three basic characteristics are associated with attachment behaviour (Weiss 1991: 66):

1. *Proximity seeking*. The child will attempt to remain within protective range of his parents. The protective range is reduced in strange threatening situations.
2. *Secure base effect*. The presence of an attachment figure fosters security in the child. This results in inattention to attachment considerations and encourages confident exploration and play.
3. *Separation protest*. Threat to the continued accessibility of the attachment figure gives rise to protest and to active attempts to ward off the separation.

Many developmental psychologists believe that babies are biologically programmed to become psychologically *attached* to their parents or other significant caretakers. Many also believe that parents, too, are biologically predisposed to *bond* with their child although the instinctual drive here is much less predictable and is often modified by the parent's own attachment experience. Furthermore, women are more likely, through evolutionary pressures and necessity, to show a biological aptitude for bonding and forming close, co-operative relationships (Ainsworth 1991: 35).

Odent (1984) studied mothers who had been allowed to give birth to their babies under relatively 'natural' conditions. Under these natural conditions, most mothers immediately display maternal behaviour. Once the baby is born he or she is held to the breast. The mother is keen to attract the baby's attention as she expresses her feelings towards the infant. She constantly looks at, talks to, explores, touches and caresses her baby (also see Trevathan 1987) and to this extent she behaves exactly like other primates who have been studied with their babies in natural settings. Fahlberg (1991: 28) refers to this initial examination of the baby by the mother as part of the 'claiming' process.

Premature birth involving the mother's immediate separation from her baby interferes with the natural expression of maternal responsiveness (Klaus and Kennel 1982). There is some evidence that a mother's ability to bond quickly with her baby is upset if the infant is immediately removed, for whatever reason (for example, see Klaus and Kennel 1982; Robson and Kumar 1980; Peterson and Mehl 1978). And although most adoptive mothers show maternal behaviour from the start, they report that it takes several weeks for full motivation and responsiveness to become established with their baby (David and Appell 1961 cited in Rosenblatt 1991: 215).

Lack of attachment relationships means that children's physical and psychological needs are less likely to be met. Evolution has therefore contrived to ensure that the inclination to form attachment relationships, along with sexual behaviour, eating behaviour and exploratory behaviour, is built into our natural make-up. 'To leave their development solely to the caprices of individual learning,' exclaims Bowlby (1988: 5), 'would be the height of biological folly.' And although most researchers have concentrated on the mother–child relationship as the axis along which attachment behaviour might be observed and assessed, there is increasing recognition that babies possess a general biological predisposition to relate with other human beings and that a selective attachment might preferentially develop with, say, a father or grandparent if the mother is emotionally or physically unavailable (Nash and Hay 1993).

## A secure base

Attachment – along with the seeking of food, fear and wariness, sociability and the exploration of new experiences – is one of a number of genetically based behaviours designed to engage the infant with the social and physical world whilst at the same time ensuring his or her safety. Attachment behaviour is triggered not by internal physiological needs, but by external threats and dangers. Attachment's prime biological function is to ensure that the vulnerable infant seeks protection when it feels anxious. In evolutionary terms this makes perfect sense. When anxiety levels are low, the infant is free to let his or her attention wander elsewhere, and in the case of older babies, the child can physically leave the mother's immediate vicinity and *explore* the environment of other people and things. The relaxed child can concentrate on exploring and learning about how things look, work and react. In Ainsworth's terms, the mother to whom the child is attached provides a *secure base*: a place of safety, comfort and warmth when anxiety levels rise (Ainsworth and Wittig 1969).

The primary developmental task, therefore, during a child's first year of life is for his or her parents to provide a social environment which promotes feelings of security and trust. Fahlberg (1991: 69) sees parents meeting the child's dependency needs and, quoting Hymes, she advises: 'During the first year when a parent wonders "What should I do when . . .?" the guideline for deciding should be, "What will help my child learn to trust me?" '

Novelty is a source of stimulation for infants. Relaxed, confident children seek out new experiences. We are programmed to model and make sense of experience, so the more stimulation and experience children have, the more flexible and useful their models become. Biologically we are constitutionally inclined to organise experience in an adaptive fashion. And the more versatile and sensitive are our representational models of experience, the more interesting and less stressful people and things become.

The environment can be perceived as potentially interesting, approachable and worth exploring. Those who set about investigating the world and building up knowledge about it (people as well as things) will be better able to cope and ultimately more likely to survive than those who have more limited or incomplete models. So, learning about the world is as important as avoiding danger. Exploration, too, is an adaptive response. It helps children become competent, confident and independent human beings.

During their second year of life, toddlers are beginning to separate from their parents and develop a stronger concept of self. The words *me*, *mine* and *no* as well as *you* and *me* are prominent in the child's vocabulary. Fahlberg (1991: 74), again quoting Hymes, advises that 'When parents are faced with a "What should I do when . . .?" question about toddlers, the standard for deciding is "What will make my child feel more capable?" '

Of course, there is a tension between the need to feel safe and the need to explore, between protection and independence. Anxiety inhibits play and exploration but promotes attachment behaviour. In contrast, feeling secure increases confidence and the ability to investigate the social and physical environment. Securely attached babies are confident that when they are upset or experience stress and uncertainty, their parents will be 'available, responsive, and helpful'; they will be encouraging and supportive as well as sensitive and loving (Bowlby 1988: 124).

Exploration of the environment and learning are necessary if the child is to become socially and physically competent, but in situations of threat and danger there comes a point when feelings of adaptive anxiety and the display of attachment behaviour must override the wish to play. Attachment behaviour ensures that the child lives to learn another day. We might say that attachment behaviour and exploratory behaviour are mutually exclusive (Bowlby 1979: 132–3).

> During this period the child's behaviour is very much influenced by the presence or absence of the mother. When he knows she or a familiar mother-substitute is around he displays much more confidence. As long as he is sure she is nearby, so that he can periodically check her whereabouts, he can explore and increase his skills and independence. At first the toddler cannot determine what is influencing his mother's movements towards or away from him; but later he acquires some idea of her motives and his own. 'Once that is so,' Bowlby says, 'the groundwork is laid to develop a much more complex relationship with each other, one that I term a partnership'. (Mattinson and Sinclair 1979: 48)

In general, young children appear to play and talk more when their mothers are present. Securely attached children who know that there is a secure base to which to return if things get difficult approach new situations with greater confidence. For example, a toddler can leave her mother sitting on a park bench while she plays anywhere up to eighty metres away (Anderson 1972). From time to time the child will return to tell her mother something or receive some physical contact before she runs off again.

The insecurely attached child finds it more difficult to relax, play and explore. If this child runs into difficulties, she is less certain that there is a safe, welcoming, sympathetic and secure base to which to return. She spends more of her energies on keeping a wary eye on what is happening and not on learning about the world of things, people and relationships.

So, if the human infant is to survive physically and become socially competent, it is necessary for him or her to be in close contact with and have access to others who are able to provide both protection as well as useful social experiences. An infant's caretakers must offer the developing child a combination of safety and stimulation. One without the other is not sufficient. If the child receives physical nourishment and protection but does not experience consistent and warm dealings with other people who also offer conversation, interest and understanding, then the child grows physically but not socially, emotionally or linguistically. He or she will not be able to cope adequately with the everyday demands of social life.

To this extent, attachment is a biological mechanism which helps ensure that the infant survives into adulthood so that he or she can, in turn, have children and so perpetuate the species. When a child is threatened, experiences uncertainty, is tired or feels upset, the level of anxiety rises, particularly if the child is some distance from his or her parents. Anxiety activates attachment behaviour and the infant seeks his or her attachment figure for safety and comfort. Rutter and Rutter (1993: 114) note that even when a child is punished or maltreated by a parent, there is still the inclination to cling to and show attachment towards that person if there is no-one else available.

### Loss and separation anxiety

Anxiety is at root an adaptive evolutionary response. It must also be emphasised that attachment is *not* the same as dependency. Indeed, the more securely attached a child feels the greater confidence and autonomy he or she displays throughout childhood. When we are feeling anxious or distressed, we tend to make particular demands on those relationships which are important to us. Although the frequency and intensity of attachment behaviour usually decreases with age, it stills plays a part throughout the life cycle. It is particularly likely to appear when we feel distressed, afraid or ill.

Throughout his writings, Bowlby (1969; 1973; 1980) was keen to emphasise the importance of loss and separation in understanding people's pain, anger and depression. Whereas loss and separation increase feelings of vulnerability and fear, grief requires expression and acknowledgement. Whenever a love relationship breaks down or is lost, we experience separation anxiety and grief (Bowlby 1973). The way other people react to those who have experienced a loss is important to the success of the grieving process. Any significant disruption in a meaningful relationship is experienced as a loss. We see it in its simplest and perhaps most direct form in young children who are separated from their prime caregiver.

In his studies with James Robertson, Bowlby observed the effects of temporary separation on young children who were admitted to hospital or residential nursery. The research was carried out in the days when hospitalised children did not see their parents and were looked after by a rota of nurses.

The researchers recognised three phases in the child's reactions to the separation: (i) protest, (ii) withdrawal, and (iii) detachment. Immediate separation from the parents resulted in unconsolable crying. There would be a general restlessness with regression to more babyish behaviours, including loss of bladder control. This was followed by a phase of apathy and listlessness with the young child showing no interest in anything or anybody. The final stage, after a few days or sometimes weeks, saw some settling down, recovery and a return to play but relationships remained shallow and uncommitted. Upon reunion with their parents, the children exhibited a mixture of extreme clinging, crying, anger and even temporary rejection in which the parent would be ignored. If the period in hospital was not too long, these effects were not prolonged and the child would return to normal levels of behaviour.

This separation and loss sequence was seen to be the direct corollary of attachment behaviour. The loss of an attachment figure represents a double blow. Having lost the mother or caregiver, the child feels insecure. Feeling insecure normally activates attachment behaviour and a return to the attachment figure, but she, of course, is not available. This is a particularly distressing experience. The combination of separation from the key attachment figure *and* a lack of personalised caregiving during the separation produce the greatest upset (Rutter and Rutter 1993: 127).

If it is also remembered that the young child's personality and emerging sense of self form within relationships, it will be appreciated that any disruption to that relationship is not simply just a loss but a threat to the integrity of the self. Fraiberg describes the child's personality as essentially an *interpersonality*: 'Therefore, when that bond is broken, the very structure of the personality is endangered' (quoted in Fahlberg 1991: 143). This has major implications for children placed with new caregivers, including adopters or foster parents. They need to understand that they are dealing with a young personality that was still in the process of forming within the now disrupted attachment relationship.

Peter had lived happily with his maternal grandmother for three years. His mother then married, resumed her care of Peter and had another baby son. Relationships between Peter, his mother and stepfather deteriorated and by the time he was nearly five he became violent, particularly towards his half-brother, and difficult to handle. In his foster home his behaviour proved to be very demanding. He ripped up his clothes and destroyed his toys. He continually defied his foster parents, doing the opposite of whatever they asked. He would do dangerous things such as stand on a very high wall and attempt to walk along it. He refused to eat at meal times but would then raid the fridge and devour whatever he could find. 'He's a very angry little boy,' observed his experienced foster mother, 'which isn't surprising. By the end of the day we're both exhausted but we're getting there.'

It was soon recognised that experiences of loss and disruption are present throughout the life cycle (Parkes 1986). 'Grief,' says Fahlberg (1991: 141) 'is the process through which one passes in order to recover from a loss.' Whenever we lose someone or something very important to us, we suffer some form of separation anxiety and find ourselves obliged to travel along the following sequence of normal grief reactions associated with loss:

1.  Numbness, shock and disbelief;
2.  Yearning, searching, pain, tension and misery;
3.  Anger and resentment, and in some cases guilt;
4.  Disorganisation, despair, depression and withdrawal;
5.  Adjustment, reorganisation and, if all goes well, resolution.

The research also shows that our past experiences of loss along with the quality of our current relationships can have a significant impact on how well we grieve and eventually adjust to our loss. The example of women who have given up babies for adoption illustrates many of the strong reactions people experience when faced with a significant loss (Howe *et al.* 1992). The majority of women report considerable problems in adjusting to the adoption of their baby. Twenty or thirty years later they still describe feelings of pain and anger. The child's birth date or having another baby could easily trigger all the old feelings of hurt and despair.

Depression affected many of the mothers. Their grief remained unresolved. Only if they could talk openly about the experience and have their pain acknowledged and accepted were they able to complete the grieving process. However, most of the mothers experienced a 'conspiracy of silence' – to have a baby as an unmarried mother and give it away for adoption was something about which other people (parents, professionals and friends) found it difficult to talk. The following examples illustrate some of the feelings the mothers experienced as they tried to adjust to the loss of their adopted baby. All the quotes are taken from Howe, Sawbridge and Hinings (1992) unless otherwise stated:

1. *Shock and immediate feelings of loss:*

> 'I handed over the child, I've blacked out exactly what happened'; 'I was in a terrible state, I couldn't work properly, it's a wonder they kept me on. I couldn't concentrate at all'; 'The pain of it! I couldn't sleep at night at all . . . for weeks and weeks I would cry and cry and cry . . . Nothing could ever hurt that much again.'

2. *Yearning, searching and misery:*

> 'I found myself looking at babies in the street wondering if they were my daughter all the time'; 'I couldn't watch TV because the commercials would show bouncing happy babies you didn't know when. I couldn't open a magazine without babies peering at me . . . I'd start following a baby around the city shopping and think that's my baby . . . Then I'd see another and follow that one. All the time I was close to breakdown.' (Inglis 1984: 99)

3. *Anger, and feelings of both hopelessness and helplessness:*

> 'But after a while instead of crying I seemed to be screaming all the time. I was so mad, angry, you know that this happened to me, that other people had decided that my baby was going to be adopted'; 'I remember this hatred thing for her adoptive mother . . . She was really nice, but I used to think "That barren bitch has got my baby".'

4. *Guilt:*

> 'I mean I was seventeen, but you start thinking whether perhaps you should have tried harder. I couldn't afford a flat, there were all kinds of obstacles. I just wouldn't have been able to cope, but you do wonder whether you might just have managed. And you're left with a heck of a lot of guilt'; 'I still have so much guilt; I gave away my own baby. I know I was very young and there were so many very good reasons but it seems about the worst thing you can do.'

5. *Depression, despair and unresolved grief:*

> 'She's now twelve and there's hardly a day goes by without me thinking of her. I can get so depressed'; 'I still feel as if a part of me is missing. I feel incomplete.'

Similar feelings are reported by all those suffer loss. Widows, abandoned lovers and parents of children who have died describe the shock, the pain, the anguish and the despair that afflicts the bereaved. Bereavement, seen as an irreversible separation experience, is now a very fully documented phenomenon. Understanding the bereavement process has thrown considerable light on a vast range of loss experiences (Parkes 1986). Any significant loss activates feelings of anxiety which in turn have their origins in attachment behaviour and our need to seek out safe environments and caring responses. But when it is the attachment relationship itself which is under threat (or has been lost), the anxiety is peculiarly heightened and very difficult to handle because the secure base itself is no longer available.

## Attachment experience and the quality of social relationships

Feelings of anxiety inevitably become entangled with other dimensions of the relationships we have with other people. It is our awareness of emotional states that propels us into relationships with others. Even in our earliest relationships, we have to recognise not only our own thoughts and feelings but also those of the person to whom we are attached. If the attachment is to provide a safe haven, it is important that the infant learns to read the psychological condition of the other as accurately as possible. But here we meet one of those binds that so often characterises the development of the human personality and its formation within social relationships.

In order for children (i) to be able to hold their feelings and not be overwhelmed by them, and (ii) to develop cognitive structures which enable them to understand and handle their own experience, they need good quality relationships. Such relationships should provide structures which are consistent, effective and good at organising experience. If, within parental relationships, children can learn to monitor, regulate and make sense of the thoughts and feelings of both the self and others, they are then laying down mental structures which will be sufficiently well organised and coherent to help them cope with the increasing demands of social life.

If, on the other hand, attachment relationships do not supply structures which allow the child either to cope with present emotional demands or to be able to handle future social experiences, something of a vicious circle sets in. When children feel anxious and distressed, attachment behaviour increases. Children who experience unreliable and disorganised attachment relationships do not learn how to cope with anxiety and distress, nor do they learn how to make very good sense of social relationships. Those who do not learn to make very good sense of social relationships are more likely to experience feelings of anxiety and distress. And so the circle is complete and the cycle continues on its downwards spiral.

The recognition that children have to handle social relationships *beyond attachment* takes us into the world of other people and new social relationships – with brothers and sisters, grandparents and teachers, family and friends. It is no surprise to note, for example, that in relaxed situations young children prefer the novelty and stimulus of playing with peers to sitting by their parents. And different cultural groups *expect* different things of their young child's development. For example, mothers in Polynesian societies are readily available, responsive and indulgent with their infants at least up to the age of two, after which children are expected to move out into a wider social world. In some East African agricultural societies, children are looked after by older siblings or young aunts from around the age of twelve months. They help socialise the infant and help him or her become socially competent (reported in Leiderman 1989: 167). Dunn (1993: 46) describes various pieces of research, including her own, in which there is clear evidence that siblings can become attached to one another. They show all the responses towards their older brother or sister that other securely attached infants normally show towards their mother. There is delight and happiness when a sister returns. An elder brother can act as a secure base from which to explore. There is sadness when the older children in the family are away.

## Responses of the baby

Human beings are born with the capacity to relate. Attachment develops as a consequence of parental responsiveness to the infant's innate tendency to seek proximity and be in relationship (Rutter 1980: 275). By the end of their first year, most children have developed a strong attachment, usually to one or both of their parents. If they are separated from them for short periods of time, they become temporarily distressed.

According to Stern (1987), a baby begins to experience a sense of emergent self from birth. The baby is programmed to interact with and be interested in other human beings. Even at ten weeks of age, a baby will not only prefer her mother's face but will be sensitive to any expression of emotion by the mother. Babies show happiness and interest when their mothers smile. They display upset, anger or a frozen startled look when she is angry.

As the human infant matures, he or she becomes more and more accomplished at making perceptual discriminations. There is a growing preference for things which are visually complex and interesting, things which move rather than remain still, and objects which have depth and interest. After the age of three months there is a distinct preference for the human face over all other kinds of objects. For sound, too, there is an increasing preference for the human voice and speech. The baby will respond by babbling in a 'conversational' way. By three months, a baby will be able to differentiate her mother from other people. The ability to discriminate in favour of a particular person is clearly important if attachment behaviour is to be targeted accurately at the person most likely to provide security and comfort. Between two and six months 'infants sense that they and mother are quite separate physically, are different agents, have different affective experiences, and have separate histories' (Stern 1987: 27).

Studies by Fouts and Atlas (1979) observed that while infants found their mother's face rewarding, at six months the faces of strangers were experienced as neutral and by nine months they were seen as negative. By nine months, therefore, substitutions in caregiving are more difficult to negotiate. Emde (1989: 42–3) refers to these transformations in the first year as 'the awakening of sociability' which occurs around two to three months and 'the onset of focussed attachment' which appears at about seven to nine months. 'These shifts,' he continues, 'inaugurate new levels of organization in the infant's social world of experience in terms of what is demanded, what is rewarding, what is expectable, and what is reciprocated.'

These steps in the maturation process witness the baby's increasing ability not only to recognise her mother or attachment figure but also to begin to 'make sense' of her; to develop a 'working model' of her so that her actions, feelings and intentions can be read and anticipated. This marks the beginnings of social understanding, so important if the child is to become socially competent. Such understandings between mother and child result in phased, co-ordinated and mutually satisfying interactions.

## Responses of the mother

Bowlby (1988: 4) believed that parents also have a strong biological predisposition to interact with their offspring. Elements of parenting and mothering are pre-programmed. Strong feelings are aroused in parents in matters which concern their children. However, the quality and effectiveness of the parent's own nurturing instincts can be modified by their own developmental experiences. The way parents were reared themselves affects the way they respond to their own children. The stresses of parenthood may be particularly difficult to handle for those who received poor quality parenting themselves. This is another example of how genes and experience can interact in a complex dynamic, making any clear division between nature and nurture impossible to sustain.

'Maternal sensitivity' is defined by Ainsworth (1973) as the mother's ability and willingness to see and interpret her baby's behaviour and emotional states from the infant's point of view and respond appropriately. Responsive mothers will soon recognise and react to their baby's social signals. Smiles and babblings as well as crying will attract the interest and attention of the parents. The sensitive parent begins to regulate her behaviour so that it co-ordinates and meshes with that of her child. Her movements are slower; the voice is softened and pitched at a higher note. When the mother's responses begin to phase exactly with those of the baby, a kind of dialogue takes place giving both partners considerable pleasure. Cuddling, talking and paying attention all help to soothe an infant's distress. All of these things help build a strong relationship between parent and baby. By three months, babies smile more often to their mothers than to strangers.

## The quality of interaction between parent and child

Studies of mothers and babies make it clear that their relationship is very much a two-way affair. Babies, like their mothers, display individual and temperamental characteristics which influence the evolving dynamics of the relationship. Babies are *active* partners in the relationship and not simply passive recipients of new experiences. From around seven or eight months, babies recognise that other people have minds and subjective experiences. These other people are also authors of their own actions. This realisation opens up both a wider sense of self and the notion that there is a domain of intersubjectivity in which people can relate (Stern 1987: 27).

Mothers and babies are alert to what each other is doing and each adapts their behaviour accordingly. There is 'behavioural synchrony' in which 'infants and parents mesh their behaviours in delicately timed mutual interchanges during social interaction' (Emde 1989: 39). There is reciprocal interest in the other's thoughts and feelings. This is the basis of forming a good relationship. The effect of this mutual interaction 'is to bring the child and the mother-figure close together and to maintain them there, hence the inclusive term "attachment behaviour"' (Bowlby 1991b: 304).

When the two parties are interested in and aware of the other's mental condition and when they are prepared to acknowledge and respect that condition, we have the makings of an open, effective and accurate relationship. An appreciation of the other person's point of view and state of mind encourages empathy and reciprocity, co-operation and regard. Mutual understanding promotes good communication between mother and child. The child not only feels secure and valued when she is understood, she experiences the kind of stability and consistency that allows her to develop a coherent sense of self and sound working models of other people. All of this helps promote social understanding and further increases the child's sense of wellbeing, security and efficacy.

Early observers of children and their development assumed that it was the close proximity between mother and child, brought about by the need for physical care and the child's prime concern with food, that led to attachment and bonding. But the evidence does not support this. Neither physical care nor the amount of time spent with the child will, in themselves, bring about attachment (Ainsworth 1973; Bowlby 1969).

What is of critical importance is the *quality of interaction*. If an attachment relationship is to form, the caregiver must be regularly available over time on a reliable basis. These caregiving relationships display warmth, responsiveness and consistency. Parents who show *interest* in their child, who can read her signals accurately and with *sensitivity*, who are *alert* and *aware* of what is going on in the relationship, and who offer *comfort* and *consistent responses* at times of distress will become that child's attachment figure. In such relationships, interaction and dialogue are *reciprocal*. Parents talk *with* their children; they are interested in what they do; they value and enjoy their progress and achievements. There is play and fun, stimulation and excitement, security and satisfaction, recognition and validation, dialogue and harmony. So, for example, if a baby shows spontaneous interest in a toy, a sensitive mother will look in the same direction as her infant to acknowledge and share the object of interest. She may start to talk about the toy and in such fashion enter into dialogue. Such responses and the relationship within which they occur are a source of stimulus and satisfaction for the baby. 'Human infants,' notes Bowlby (1988: 9), 'are preprogrammed to develop in a socially co-operative way; whether they do so or not turns in high degree on how they are treated.' Bretherton (1991: 27) defines attachment theory in its wider sense, seeing it as 'a theory of interpersonal relationships'.

Dunn, and many other developmental psychologists, extend the significance of early life relationships beyond a single, simple *secure* attachment to one parent-figure. Although security is an immensely important feature of young children's relationship experiences there are other elements which have major consequences for their *social* development. Mothers and children may communicate about feelings. According to Sroufe (1989b: 118), communication is a logical outgrowth of attachment because it is based upon two people sharing a focus of attention in which understanding and meaning are also shared. They may share humour (a key feature of adult intimate relationships, Dunn reminds us). They may appreciate mutual self-disclosure about thoughts and feelings. And children may exert control in the relationship every bit as much as parents. 'All of these features are considered important in adult relationships; might they not also be important in the relationships between young children and their parents?', wonders Dunn (1993: 21).

The quality of interaction also extends to language development. It is not the busyness and noisiness of the language environment which in itself is stimulating and conducive to the acquisition of strong verbal and language skills. Indeed, young children in large, noisy families in which the children enjoy comparatively less interaction with their parents, are often behind in their language development compared with children in smaller families. Rather, it is the quality of verbal interaction between a parent and child that affects language ability. 'The need is, not for noise and bombardment of talk directed *at* children,' write Rutter and Rutter (1993: 223), 'but rather for responsive, reciprocal interactions and communications *with* them.'

As the relationship develops, both baby and mother continue to adapt their responses to one another. Richards describes the growth of intersubjectivity as an evolving sequence of mutual understanding:

> One of the first things that is required in social communication is for you to be sure that your partner is actually attending to you and is involved in communication with you. Are you listening? Do you see what I see? Do you see what I mean? Clearly this degree of intersubjectivity is not present in the newborn and will take many months to develop. But within weeks of birth one can observe its beginnings. There are long sequences of interaction where the first fumbling links of intersubjectivity are made. The infant looks at the caretaker's face. The caretaker looks back into the eyes of the infant. A smile moves on the infant's face. The adult responds with a vocal greeting and a smile. There is mutual social acknowledgement. The 'meaning' of this exchange does not simply depend on the action patterns employed by the two participants. Each must fit his sequence of actions with that of the other; if this is not done, the exchange may well become meaningless. An important means of knowing that a message is intended for you is that it follows an alternating sequence with yours. (Richards 1974: 92)

A strong, mutually enjoyable and rewarding relationship provides a set of important experiences for the child. It is within such relationships that our sense of self and personality form. Our ability to understand others and become socially competent is a direct product of the demands made in such early interactions. When the quality of interaction is poor, the ability to understand others and become socially competent can be severely impaired (Bretherton 1985 cited in Belsky and Nezworski 1988b).

## Temperamental differences and the character of relationships

Attachment theory emphasises the qualities that parents bring to the interaction and links these to the child's subsequent personality development. But it is consistent with the full-blown interactional nature of our thesis that the baby also brings a range of temperamental, cognitive and social characteristics to the relationship. Chess and Thomas (1990: 205) identify three temperamental constellations:

1. *Difficult temperaments* made up of a combination of withdrawal, intensity of mood expression, slow adaptability to change, and negative mood.
2. *Easy temperaments* comprised of a combination of ability to approach new situations, quick adaptability, low or moderate intensity of mood expressions, and predominately positive mood.
3. *Slow-to-warm-up temperaments* comprised of a combination of a tendency to withdraw from new situations, slow adaptability, and mild intensity of mood expression.

A 'difficult' baby will produce a different quality relationship with her mother compared with the relationship generated by a responsive, contented baby with the same parent. Children with difficult temperaments appear to provoke more negative responses from their parents (Rutter 1978; Lee and Bates 1985). Mothers react differently to different qualities in babies as babies react differently to different qualities in mothers. For example, a number of studies have found that there is a signficant genetic component in parental warmth and supportiveness (Plomin and Bergeman 1991). This partly explains why siblings experience different kinds of relationship with their parents; inherent differences produce different interactional dynamics.

The interaction between, say, a naturally warm, responsive mother and a tetchy, fractious baby will develop along rather different lines from the kind of relationship generated between an energetic, methodical mother and a shy, quiet baby (see, for example, Hinde 1982; Kagan 1989). Bowlby (1991b: 311) also believes that temperamental characteristics can be modified under social environmental influences. He writes about studies which describe how difficult babies can become happy easy toddlers with sensitive mothering, and how placid newborns can be turned into anxious, moody and awkward toddlers with insensitive or rejecting parenting.

Kagan (1989) and his colleagues have argued strongly that there is a biological basis to shyness, irritability, withdrawal and sociability. Recent research also claims to have found genes for such things as shyness and irritability that continue to explain individual differences in childhood and through into adulthood (Daniels and Plomin 1985: 121; Fox 1994). And in his very thorough and detailed twin and adoption studies, Plomin (1986) has established that neuroticism (negative affectivity) and extroversion (positive affectivity) are among the most heritable individual traits.

**The growth of social competence**

Ainsworth (1973) was one of the first to show that there was a link between the responsiveness of the caregiver and the child's later social development. She demonstrated that babies whose mothers responded with sensitivity, promptness and accuracy to their signals cried less at home, were more confident explorers of physical and social situations and generally behaved well compared with more insecurely attached babies. Securely attached infants show greater independence in early childhood. By the time they are one year old, babies who have enjoyed secure attachments appear as active, confident and effective participants in their relationships with familiar figures.

McHale, Crouter and their colleagues (cited in Dunn 1993: 21–2) assessed the degree of reciprocity and mutuality between parents and their school-aged children. The measures included such things as how much time the parents and children spent together and what they were doing (playing, working etc.). The studies revealed that children who saw themselves as competent and had a sense of self-worth were likely to have relationships with their parents which were heavily characterised by feelings of mutual warmth and involvement. Indeed, the ability and preparedness of parents to sustain warmth, interest and involvement with their children, at whatever age, seems to correlate highly with well-adjusted personalities who are easily able to cope with the normal demands of everyday social life.

Sroufe's (1989a: 86–7) review of the research literature shows how the securely attached, well-integrated child grows in social competence. By the time they are two to three years old, securely attached children are more enthusiastic, likeable, and confident problem-solvers compared with children diagnosed as insecurely attached. They are able to stick to tasks and pursue goals with tenacity and purpose. There is good evidence that children who enjoy success in accomplishing tasks establish more positive self-concepts. Securely attached children are more sociable with adults; more competent with peers. By the age of five, on blind testing, teachers begin to rate securely attached children as more independent and resourceful than their insecure counterparts. In the classroom, securely attached children are less prone to want physical contact or seek attention through negative behaviour, although they do greet teachers and use them more appropriately as a resource. In general, secure children perceive other people to be more available, potentially helpful and useful.

## Self-worth and self-esteem

Experiencing the self as potent and loved is closely linked with experiencing the self as *worthy*. Securely attached children cope better with difficulty and frustration; they sustain problem-solving strategies for longer periods than children judged to be insecure. Compared with anxiously attached children, securely attached children appear to have higher self-esteem and lower levels of anxiety. They play more frequently in a friendly and positive manner with peers. They are more prone to initiate play and interaction. They are higher ranked socially, have more friends, and are capable of deeper relationships and social empathy. For example, Park and Waters (1989) studied four-year-olds who had a 'best friend'. If both were securely attached to their mothers, their relationship was likely to be more harmonious, responsive and less controlling than friendships involving insecurely attached children. The securely attached friends would resolve conflicts by peaceful negotiation and would share toys fairly and equally.

## Conclusion

Thus, it appears that the characteristics of early relationships become paradigmatic for the character and conduct of later social relationships with peers and adults. 'From a history of empathic responsiveness,' continues Sroufe (1989a: 89), 'securely attached children have internalized the capacity for empathy and the disposition to be empathic. What is characteristic of their early relationship has become part of the core self.'

# 5

# The organisation of experience

Children's ability to make sense of other people depends on how well they are able to mentally model social experience. In this chapter we see how the properties of children's external relationships with others assists in the development of these inner working models. The models help children to understand how others view them, how they might view others, and how the relationship between self and others might best be interpreted. Once the inner working models become established, they are increasingly likely to define social experience rather than be defined by social experience.

## Inner working models

'To the extent that experience becomes more organized, problems in adaptation will diminish. To the extent that experience becomes chaotic, problems in adaptation will increase' (Sameroff 1989: 21). The developmental approach identifies the social factors and the key relationships which influence the child's ability to organise experience. The more the child is able to organise experience, the higher will be his or her level of adaptive functioning.

Perhaps the most important bit of the environment which the young infant has to model and aim to understand is her mother (or prime caretaker) and the relationship she has with her. The child has to 'read' this person and the relationship she has with her so that her behaviour can be recognised, anticipated, relied upon. The mother needs to feel predictable, responsive and be capable of being influenced.

The baby's behaviour and relationship with her mother becomes increasingly goal-directed. The child will point to things in which she is interested or wants; she will raise her arms when she wishes to be picked up from the floor; she will demand attention. All of these behaviours indicate that the baby is beginning to develop ideas about how to make sense of this other person, what to expect from her, and how to influence her behaviour. It also shows that the baby recognises her own needs and internal states and knows what to do about them.

In effect, the infant is modelling her own behaviour, her mother's behaviour and actions, and the relationship that exists between them. This is an extraordinarily impressive thing to be able to do and it means that the infant is well on her way to being able to cope with the world both physically and socially.

Bowlby (1973) also recognised the importance for the child of these 'internal working models' during the early stages of development. 'The function of these models is to simulate happenings in the real world, thereby enabling the individual to plan behaviour with all the advantages of insight and foresight' (Bowlby 1991b: 307). This notion of an inner working model of attachment relationships indicates that the infant's early attachment experiences eventually become transformed into *inner representations*. These internal mental models of relationships influence *expectations* about new relationships and how we might behave within them. The child's internal working model, said Bowlby, should give him a 'notion of who his attachment figures are, where they may be found, and how they may be expected to respond' (Bowlby 1973: 203).

The self is the inner organisation of attitudes, feelings and expectations. It is the product of earlier social relationships. In due course the inner working models come to organise behaviour in all significant relationships. Although new experiences can alter the organisation of the self, the current organisation of the self is just as likely to organise new experiences. To a degree, all new relationships are created and re-created in the light of previous relationship experiences – for good or ill. New information becomes organised by and assimilated into existing internal models, and although the models may be revised in the light of subsequent relationships, with time, they become somewhat more resistant and inflexible, preferring to organise experience rather than be organised by it.

## Internalisation of external relationships

According to Winnicott, the mother or the prime caretaker initially should be able to 'hold' the child's relatively disorganised experiences so that they do not overwhelm him or her. The responsive mother knows when to feed her three-week-old baby; she does not seek to play with an infant who is wanting to sleep. In effect, the attachment figure and the relationship which she has with the baby act as a framework in which the baby can first feel emotionally secure then ontologically potent. She begins to structure and organise her own experience using the psychological scaffolding and experiential trelliswork initially provided by her mother.

Over time, the qualities of the child's dyadic relationship with her prime caretaker become internalised and they begin to define elements of the child's own personality. It is from their initial relationships with their primary caregivers (who might be biological parents, adoptive parents, or foster parents) that children develop inner working models or 'internal representations' of:

1.  the self,
2.  other people, and
3.  the nature of the relationship between them.

It is by being in relationship with other people that the self both forms and recognises itself. The self, formed in its relationship with others, then seeks to make sense of other people based on its understanding of its own self. It is in this sense that the patterns of attachment and the quality of social interactions experienced by the child also become a property of that child.

The way other people view, define and treat the child are features of the relationship which the child has to model if he or she is to try and make sense of what is going on. But it is also the case that these views, definitions and responses build up the child's cognitive structures and understandings of her self. The child's internal working models seek to represent the relationship but the models also begin to establish the child's psychological self. Hence, the quality of the relationships which have to be understood also influence the character of the infant's psychological self (personality) which forms in those relationships.

The more coherent and consistent are the qualities of the attachment relationship, the more accurate and therefore useful will be the child's 'working model'. If the infant is 'modelling' a relationship which is regular, consistent and responsive, the model itself will reflect those qualities. And if the models and their associated cognitive structures represent beginnings of a sense of self, selves which form within such coherent and integrated relationships will themselves become coherent and well integrated.

> Certainly, it is obvious from young children's talk and play that they are seeking actively to make sense of experience, and in so doing, they derive concepts and schemes of various kinds. Their awareness increases markedly at about the age of eighteen to twenty-four months . . . There is every reason to suppose that from the second year on, experiences are internalized in some way and incorporated into organizing self-concepts. It is also evident that, with increasing age, these concepts grow in complexity, abstractness and ability to include ambivalent and conflicting feelings. (Rutter and Rutter 1993: 102)

Within reliable relationships, the infant can build up a central, subjective experience of self as something which is solid, permanent and above all *potent*. Working models built up within secure attachments give the infant confidence in his or her ability to make sense of the world. *Experience is organised* so that it is meaningful and manageable, intelligible and accountable, ordered and usable.

In cases where parents do not offer the child an accurate understanding of the social world and relationship experiences (for example, when the parent is hostile, inconsistent or rejecting), the child does not have opportunities to learn how to model the self. There is insufficient sensitivity and mutuality in the relationship for this to take place. The child is unable to use the other person's experience to help her to interpret and make sense of the self, other people and social relationships.

Early inconsistencies in the attachment relationship may generate models in which the mother is expected to be unpredictable, and the child experiences the self as lacking efficacy and value. *It is hard to generate inner working models if other people and social experience are inconsistent.* Models generated in such inconsistent environments, by definition, are not very good at predicting other people's behaviour or the consequences of one's behaviour. These external inconsistencies and contradictions become internalised. The psychological result can be feelings of confusion, anger and despair often expressed as difficult behaviour.

Similarly, early parental insensitivity may encourage the infant to construct inner working models of the social environment as 'essentially hostile and unresponsive and that of the self as inadequate or unworthy of help and comfort. These preconscious models of self and world would necessarily engender chronic anxiety as they are used to anticipate, order, and assimilate future experience, especially in times of stress, novelty and crisis' (Nezworski, Tolan and Belsky 1988: 356). The models generated to handle inconsistent social experiences are likely to be fragmented and incoherent:

> In contrast to the 'integration of information relevant to attachment' seen in secure children and adults . . . is the incoherence and lack of integration of, or lack of access to, information seen in those who are insecure with respect to attachment. Pressed to describe and evaluate their attachment experiences and relations, insecure individuals frequently present a jumble of contradictory thoughts, feelings, and intentions which can only loosely be described as a 'model'. (Main 1991: 132)

Infants who are in a relationship with an attachment figure whose responses are unpredictable, insensitive and conflicting find it difficult to develop an 'organized overview' of that figure. The only way to represent the attachment figure is by developing 'multiple models' of that person, each model working for only one aspect of the attachment figure's behaviour profile (Main 1991: 137). But if the infant has to learn about her self in relationship with others, relationships which require multiple models produce fragmented, inconsistent and confusing understandings of self. The infant feels herself to be in a variety of seemingly arbitrary relationship experiences with the other person. Certainly, it seems that the child herself feels that she has little ability to affect the content or outcome of such a relationship. Social experiences of this kind disconfirm any notion that the self is lovable or potent. The quality of the relationships in which the self forms therefore influences the quality and coherence of the self which forms. For example: 'If my attachment figure rejects me, I must be unlovable and therefore a bad person'.

**The quality of communication**

The quality of communication offers us another way of under-standing the development of personality. If a child's inner representational models of self, others and relationships depends on the fullness and accuracy of communication between herself and her parent, more effective and flexible representational models will arise in those relationships where communication is appropriate and sensitive. Secure attachments are associated with free-flowing conversation; feelings are expressed and fully acknowledged. Insecure attachments are characterised by restricted and disjointed communication; some signals are read while others are ignored or misinterpreted; there is less talk about feelings; and there is less conversation and dialogue.

The fuller and more open and direct the conversation, the more opportunities each participant has to recognise and understand the other's experience and point of view. Freedom of communication, say between a mother and her child, allows the child constantly to revise and refine his or her internal working models of the self, the other, and their relationship. This allows the child to establish incre-asingly more accurate and effective understandings of other people and social relationships.

The insecurely attached child does not experience conversations which are fully direct, mutually attuned and harmonious. Even by the age of one or two, insecure children are either not able or they are unwilling to risk the expression of certain emotional states: 'It is not difficult to see what a very serious breakdown of communication between child and mother this represents. Not only that but, because a child's self-model is profoundly influenced by how the mother sees and treats him, whatever she fails to recognize in him he is likely to fail to recognize in himself' (Bowlby 1988: 132)

Main (1991: 138) cites work by Cain and Fast as well as Bowlby. These researchers studied children all of whom had lost a parent by suicide and whose surviving parents had told lies about the manner of the death even when the children had witnessed the event. A mother was said to have drowned when in fact she had slit her wrists; a father had hanged himself but his daughter was told that he died in a car crash. The psychiatric problems suffered by many of the children, which included feelings of unreality, were provoked by parents disturbing the child's experience and perception of reality.

Children under three, says Main (1991: 138), are quite likely to develop 'multiple models in response to parental misconstructions, denials, and deceptions regarding events the child directly witnesses'.

## Conclusion

Gradually, the infant begins to play a more active role in both the relationship and the organisation of experience. The self emerges as that locus of being which makes sense of and controls experience. The emergence of an autonomous inner organisation therefore represents the beginnings of the formation of self. The child will slowly begin to realise that she is someone who is either effective or ineffective, potent or impotent in regulating experience, emotional states, and the content of close relationships. Which side of these personality divides a particular child will fall depends on the kind of relationship she has with her prime caregivers.

# 6

# Ainsworth's attachment classification system

The existence of secure and insecure types of attachment received early recognition by attachment theorists. However, it was not until the work of Ainsworth that the various patterns of attachment experience were fully explored, identified and made available for testing. This chapter describes five basic types of attachment behaviour. Cultural variations are also recognised in the distribution of the different types of attachment patterns. We conclude with a discussion about the anxieties children and adults experience when they fear that a close and important relationship might be lost. The way we manage and react to such losses forms the basis of the various psychological defence mechanisms we all use to try and cope with the anxieties and pains associated with difficult and stressful situations.

**Five types of attachment experience**

Bowlby recognised that although attachments are biologically desirable, their strength and quality vary a great deal. Some children show little or no sign of attachment behaviour. In these relatively rare cases a clear genetic cause might explain the failure. Autism, as we have seen, is a biological condition which results in abnormalities in brain development. Autistic children find it difficult to form or understand social relationships. However, the majority of cases in which attachment behaviour is weak or disordered appear to be the result of relationship difficulties between the child and his or her parents or caregivers.

It was Mary Ainsworth, an early colleague of Bowlby's, who was the first to explore thoroughly the various types and qualities of attachment relationship. She designed an experimental situation which tested the level of 'security' experienced by children in their relationships with their parents. The 'Strange Situation' procedure evaluates the representational models which children have of their relationship with attachment figures (Ainsworth *et al.* 1978).

The test takes place under laboratory-like conditions and may be repeated up to eight times. Children are exposed to various degrees of *stress* which include a number of two-or-three-minute separations from their parents. They are then reunited. The child under test is left in a 'strange', unfamiliar room, sometimes with strangers. The behaviour of the children is observed before and during separation and then again upon reunion.

Essentially, the Ainsworth Attachment Classification System is a scheme for classifying relationships (Ainsworth *et al.* 1978). It originally arose out of Ainsworth's work in Uganda where she studied mothers' levels of sensitivity to their babies (Ainsworth 1967). Adapted to the American laboratory context, the test situation examines how infants adjust their behaviour in stressful situations. Particular note is made of (i) how much the infant plays and explores when the mother or caregiver is either present or absent, and (ii) how the child reacts to the mother or caregiver when she is present, departs and, most important, returns.

The test works best with children aged between twelve and eighteen months. In the original experiments, analyses of home observations revealed that those infants who had shown insecure attachments during the laboratory test also appeared not to have particularly good relationships with their mothers when seen in the home setting. This evidence appeared to validate the laboratory findings and gave the researchers confidence in their results.

The early experiments revealed three types of attachment: secure; insecure–avoidant; and insecure–ambivalent. More recent work (see Main in 1991) has added a fourth type known as disorganised attachment. There are also extreme cases in which children have failed to form any kind of attachment relationship. These have been called disorders of nonattachment. In total, then, we might recognise five types of attachment experience:

1.  *Secure attachments* (known as type B) in which children show some distress at separation. On reunion, they greet their parent positively, seek some comfort, contact or friendly acknowl-

edgement but soon return to contented play. Secure babies show high levels of eye-contact, vocalisation and mutuality when relating with their parents. There is a clear preference for the mother or caregiver over strangers. The parent's care is consistently responsive. The mother or caregiver is alert and sensitive to the infants signals and communications. The child is confident that the caregiver will be available and helpful in adverse or frightening situations.

2. *Insecure and Avoidant attachments* (known as type A) in which children show few apparent signs of distress at separation. When the parent returns, these children ignore or *avoid* her. They do not seek out physical contact. They are watchful of the parent and remain generally wary. Their play is inhibited. Such children show little discrimination regarding with whom they interact. They demonstrate no particular preference for either parents or strangers. The parent is indifferent and insensitive to or rejecting of the child's signals and needs.

3. *Insecure and Ambivalent or Resistant attachments* (known as type C) in which children are highly distressed at separation and are very difficult to calm down upon reunion. They seek contact but do not settle when they receive it. When reunited, they resist attempts to pacify them and continue to cry, fuss, squirm and thrash about. However, they will run back to the parent if he or she walks away. 'Ambivalent' children both demand parental attention and angrily resist it at the same time. Such ambivalent behaviour – displays of need and anger, dependence and resistance – is the key characteristic of this type of insecurity. When the mother reappears, ambivalent children are reluctant to return to play. They can be nervous of novel situations and people. The parent's care is inconsistent and insensitive, though not hostile and rejecting.

4. *Insecure and Disorganised attachments* (known as type A/C or type D). Children in this category show elements of both avoidant and ambivalent kinds of attachment behaviour. Upon reunion with the parent they show confusion and disorganisation. They appear to lack a defensive strategy to protect them against feelings of anxiety. Sometimes these children will just 'freeze' throughout the separation and reunion. On other occasions, they may make mechanical contact but behave throughout the reunion without much show of feeling or emotion. So

although the children tolerate being held, they tend to gaze away. In the child's eyes, their parents are experienced as either frightening or frightened and therefore not available as a source of safety or comfort. This compounds the child's anxiety. The infant is left with an irresolvable conflict: to approach the attachment figure who is also the cause of the anxiety (Main 1991: 140).

5. *Nonattachments.* This term is reserved for children who have had no opportunity to form affectional bonds with other people. This is most likely to be observed in children who have been raised in institutions from early infancy. These children typically experience 'many, anonymous serial caregivers' (Lieberman and Pawl 1988: 331). It is also possible, though less likely, that infants whose caregivers are extremely emotionally unavailable and unresponsive may fail to form attachment relationships. This may happen, for instance, if the mother suffers a serious mental illness or has a heavy substance addiction. Nonattached children show a number of profound developmental impairments. They have problems with social relationships. Their social dealings with other people are based on need. There is little preference for or interest in one human being over another. People appear to be interchangeable so long as basic needs are met. Little distress is expressed at the departure of a caregiver. Nonattached children experience difficulties in controlling their impulses and feelings of aggression. There is some evidence that their cognitive development is impaired, although this is probably more to do with being reared in a grossly understimulating environment.

The children in the test are classified according to how their behaviour is organised with respect to the caregiver. Sroufe (1989b: 115) continues his review of the procedure by noting that the relationship witnessed betweeen infant and caregiver reveals the character of previous relationship patterns established between them. Generalising beyond the test situation, Fahlberg (1991: 31) notes that observing children when they are tired, frightened or feeling unwell is a useful way of learning about their attachment patterns.

Securely attached children seek out their primary caregivers who in turn usually know the best way to give comfort and care. Securely attached children know, through previous experience, that their caregiver will be available and accessible in times of upset and will provide a relationship in which the distressed emotional state will be contained and regulated. It is the structure and charactersitics of this relationship that help to form the child's mental structures and personality. The 'inner working models' that children develop within relationships which offer emotional availability and sensitivity allow the children to see themselves as lovable and other people as responsive and trustworthy. This promotes a strong sense of self-worth, esteem and potency. The mothers of securely attached babies are inclined to hold and cuddle their infants as a regular part of their caretaking behaviour. Upon return after a brief absence, they acknowledge their baby with smiles and conversation. Their voice quality is often 'tender-warm' and they respond to infant vocalisations more often than insensitive mothers (Grossmann and Grossmann 1991: 97).

Broadly, 'mothers who are insensitive to their children's signals, perhaps because they are preoccupied and worried about other things, who ignore their children, or interfere with their activities in an arbitrary way, or simply reject them, are likely to have children who are unhappy or anxious or difficult' (Bowlby 1988: 48).

Children who *anxiously avoid* contact have experienced a history of rebuffs or indifference when they approach the caregiver for emotional support and regulation. The child's balance betweeen needing autonomy and wanting dependence is upset. These children have no confidence that when they need love and care they will receive it. In fact, they come to expect rejection. If the rejection or loss of the attachment figure is severe, children lose all trust in the adult world. These children see the parent as essentially unavailable. In interaction with their infants, parents use more controlling than co-operative tactics. Psychologically, avoidantly attached infants try to cope with distress by turning inwards, or at least not outwards to the parent (Steele and Steele 1994: 96). They generate inner working models which represent others as emotionally unavailable, untrustworthy and rejecting and the self as unlovable and of low value. 'Such individuals attempt to live their lives without the love and support of others' (Bowlby 1991b: 308).

Insecure patterns of attachment represent strategies developed by the child to cope with parental insensitivity. Avoidant children therefore attempt to become independent and emotionally autonomous, withholding affection, and in effect try to 'parent themselves' (Fahlberg 1991: 144). If the felt need for love and comfort only seems to bring rejection and pain, maybe it is better to do without;

better not to trust other people; safer not to form close relationships; less painful to switch off.

*Ambivalent* and *anxiously attached* children have experienced inconsistent or chaotic care. The parent is not hostile or rejecting but rather inconsistent, insensitive and lacking in accurate empathy. The child is uncertain whether the caregiver will be available or responsive when the child needs her. This causes the infant to experience separation anxiety, the effect of which is to make him or her more clingy and nervous about play and exploration of the world. There is a proneness to whine as attempts are made to keep the parent in sight and close by. The child intensifies and sustains attachment behaviour as he or she attempts to attract the caregiver's interest and maintain his or her presence. The intensification of attachment behaviour is mingled with anger and resentment at the uncertainty that seems to be inherent in the relationship. Since the anxious, ambivalent child cannot rely on the mother's or caregiver's availability, the child remains watchful for any indications that she might not be available. Distress is therefore shown at the slightest hint or threat of separation.

So, whereas avoidant infants fear what they want (proximity), ambivalent infants fear that they will not get what they want (also proximity) (Simpson and Rholes 1994: 183). In the case of ambivalent children, 'this pattern is promoted by a parent being available and helpful on some occasions but not on others and, clinical evidence shows, by separations and, later, especially by threats of abandonment used as a means of control' (Bowlby 1991: 308). The nine-month-old child's wish to be close to her mother may be mistaken for a secure relationship. While the securely attached child may view a strange situation as an opportunity for exploration and so not worry too much about her mother, the anxiously attached child may feel distress and demand to be close to the parent.

Mothers of ambivalently attached children are not only inconsistent in their responses, they are also insensitive. While at one moment they may ignore the child's effort to gain their interest and attention, at another the mothers may may intrude inappropriately and thoughtlessly into whatever their child is doing or feeling. The child's emotional boundaries do not feel to be under his or her control. Responses come when they are not wanted and fail to arrive when needed. In interactional terms, the caregivers of ambivalently attached children generate confusion rather than co-operation. The inner working models developed by ambivalent children have to represent and make sense of caregivers who are inconsistently responsive and erratically sensitive. The children are uncertain about their self-worth and the availability of others. It has to be assumed that caregivers are unpredictable and that the self has little control over the emotional events of their world. The self-image which forms is one in which individuals experience themselves as ineffective in obtaining the love and interest of others. This is interpreted as meaning that they are probably unworthy of such love; there is something unloveable about them. The result is low self-esteem, low self-confidence and relationships racked by self-doubt, uncertainty and ambivalence.

Fahlberg (1991: 144–5) makes out a good case for social workers being extra alert to the needs of children who have been separated from their parents or who have had poor attachment experiences. For both avoidant and ambivalent children, one of the main issues is the child's lack of trust in others. The ambivalently attached child is saying 'I can't count on you wanting to stay close so I will have to keep my eye on you', while the avoidantly attached child is saying 'I can't count on you being close when I need you, so I will have to count on myself.' Developmentally, these experiences are in danger of disposing ambivalent children to behave like 'victims' and avoidant children to behave as 'victimizers' (Fahlberg 1991: 145).

*Nonattached* children are liable to suffer the most damaging developmental experience. This is the reason why child-care workers strive to provide all children with permanent selective attachment figures. In terms of attachment, someone is generally better than no-one. As Fahlberg (1991: 24) says:

> Although interrupted relationships are traumatic – and should be avoided whenever it is possible to meet the child's needs without a move – the long-term effects of a child without attachments for significant periods of his life are even more detrimental. Once a child has experienced a healthy attachment, it is more likely that with help, he can either extend this attachment to someone else or form additional attachments if necessary.

## Cultural differences

The Ainsworth Strange Situation classification has proved extremely helpful in studying the relationship between the quality of early life experiences and the pattern of later personality developments. In typical North American and British non-clinical samples, about 60 per cent of infant-mother relationships are categorised as secure attachments, about 25 per cent insecure-avoidant attachments, 10 per cent insecure ambivalent attachments and around 5 per cent disorganised attachments (Leiderman 1989: 174–5). In clinical samples, the numbers of secure attachments can fall dramatically.

However, the proportions of children in each category are found to vary as you move between classes and across cultures. For example, a slightly higher proportion of German children are placed in the insecure–avoidant category (Grossman *et al.* 1988) while Japanese and Israeli children have a marginally higher chance of being classified as showing insecure–ambivalent attachments (Miyake *et al.* 1985, cited in Leiderman 1989). Dunn (1993: 32) interprets such findings, pointing out, for example, that most Japanese babies have little experience of being separated from their mothers and therefore separations are extremely stressful. Kagan (1989) argues that cultural differences in styles of parenting are more than likely to account for these cross-cultural patterns. German parents, in contrast to American, promote and value independence and self-control in their children. As a result many German children show less concern when they are separated from their parents. They may well feel secure and loved but they have learned not to show upset and continue to trust the behaviour of their parents.

Stevenson-Hinde (1991: 322–3) adds another layer to the possible interpretations that parents might give to their child's behaviour. For example her studies showed that in American children, mothers tended to value shyness in girls but not so much in boys, particularly as they grew older. Whereas shy boys were a source of worry and even condemnation, shy girls were viewed favourably by their mothers who talked with pleasure about their daughters still preferring to be at home with them.

## Development of attachment throughout childhood

Attachment behaviour continues to develop and evolves rapidly over the first few years of life. During this time, attachment to a primary figure is increasingly mediated by the child's growing use of language. At the same time, the development of social empathy means that the young child is able to relate to others with increasing subtlety and sophistication (Crittenden and Ainsworth 1989: 436). Clear-cut attachment is usually achieved by about six months when the baby can begin to move and crawl: the 'active' phase. The infant is therefore able to take the initiative in keeping close and seeking contact with the attachment figure.

By the age of three, the child begins a more sophisticated phase. Bowlby (1969) sees the child begin to develop a 'goal-corrected partnership' with his or her mother. This is made possible by the child's improving language skills and the development of social understanding – the ability to see the world from the other person's point of view. 'As the child becomes more able to understand that the mother has motivations, feelings, and plans of her own, and as he or she becomes better able to communicate motivations, feelings and plans to her, they, as partners, become able to negotiate differences in plans and often reach mutual agreement about them' (Crittenden and Ainsworth 1989: 436).

With the development of language, inner working models and social empathy, the child can begin to understand that relationships continue to exist even when the other is absent. As trust and understanding are established, the child can tolerate longer and longer separations. However, this growth in security is upset if the parent himself or herself is unable to show social empathy and finds it difficult to communicate feelings and motivations. This frustrates the child's need to build coherent models of the self and others. Trust and mutual understanding fail to develop in such social relationships.

By adolescence, secure children can cope with long separations from their attachment figures. Letters and phone calls are often quite sufficient to sustain the relationship. Adolescence is also the time when people are beginning to form new attachments outside the family and so there is a gradual shift in both the style and direction of attachment behaviour. Children are on the receiving end of love and care. By adolescence, people are learning to *give* love and care as well as receive it. Reciprocity in adolescent relationships becomes more 'symmetrical' and less 'complementary' (Hazan and Shaver 1987).

### Separation and the origins of anxiety

A developmental task required of all children in the formation of personality is the need to regulate feelings of ambivalence; to learn to understand and control the need for others and the anger felt when that need is not met or the other is not present. Paraphrasing Bowlby (1979: 6): Children who follow a favourable course will grow up not only aware of the existence within themselves of contradictory impulses but able to direct them and control them. The anxiety and guilt which they engender will be bearable. Children whose progress is less favourable find themselves beset by impulses over which they feel they have inadequate or even no control. As a result, they will suffer acute anxiety regarding the safety of the people they love. They will be afraid, too, of the retribution which they believe will fall on their own heads.

Threats by parents to abandon a young child or to commit suicide are particularly terrifying experiences for the infant. The level of separation anxiety is raised massively. Feelings of extreme anger as well as upset are also provoked in those threatened with abandonment, whatever their age: children under threat of losing their parents, adolescents in danger of being abandoned by family or friends, adults rejected by lovers or partners. And as well as anger, children and adults may be made to feel guilty when parents or partners suggest that if they do fall ill or die, it will be their fault.

Mattinson and Sinclair's (1979) excellent and highly illustrated study of social work practice with disturbed families in a busy but typical social services department describes a large number of families in which children are regularly threatened with abandonment. Of seventeen cases considered in detail, seven mothers 'had at some stage abandoned their children, six others had accused themselves or been accused by others of neglecting them, and two others had felt so unable to manage that they had asked for their children to be received into care' (Mattinson and Sinclair 1979: 33). Indeed, the practice of seeking and precipitating separations was not restricted to the mother–child relationship. It was a wider feature of family life:

> In thirteen of the seventeen cases, one or other spouse had at one time left home. In fourteen of them there clearly was, or had been, an issue over whether the children should be received into care. In eleven cases, children had actually been removed. In two more cases the department was actually or potentially involved in separating the family. (Mattinson and Sinclair 1979: 35)

Not surprisingly, these families were highly demanding of the social workers' time, skills and emotional energies. Similar disturbed and disruptive experiences were identified in the research carried out by Pitcairn *et al.* (1993: 76). They looked at 43 child abuse cases and noted the following background characteristics about the parents:

> Most mothers (75%) grew up in nuclear families, with a slightly lower figure for fathers (67%); 8 per cent with step-parents; 4 per cent (8% for fathers) in public care. Separation from their parents at some point in childhood was not uncommon, occurring in 57 per cent of the mothers and 25 per cent of the fathers, and a further 25 per cent of the parents were split up from their siblings. Thirty-three per cent of mothers and 25 per cent of fathers spent part of their childhood in care, usually a children's home. Marital breakdown and parental illness were given as the two most common reasons for family break up, with no parent reporting abuse as a precipitant factor.

More generally, Bowlby (1988: 80) recognises three types of relationship which produce anger when the relationship is under threat: relationships with a sexual partner; relationships with parents; and relationships with offspring. Thus, when significant relationships are in danger of breaking down or being lost, we experience that highly charged mixture of anxiety and anger that so often leads to uncontrollable behaviour, including violence. 'This anger, the function of which is to dissuade the attachment figure from carrying out the threat, can easily become dysfunctional' (Bowlby 1988: 30).

The inconsistent and disorganised character of *insecure–ambivalent* relationships generates a social environment which frustrates the child's ability to form well-integrated mental structures and a personality able to cope with stress and difficulty. The child develops a strategy of emphasised dependence to a mother who is unpredictable (Egeland and Farber 1984).

The *insecure–disorganised* infant (type D) acts as though both the environment *and* the attachment figure are threatening and are to be feared. Normally, an infant seeks out his or her attachment figure when the level of fear or anxiety rises. But if the attachment figure is the source of fear or anxiety, the infant experiences a dilemma. He or she is drawn to the source of the anxiety and at the same time attempts to move away from it. This would be the experience of an infant who suffers physical abuse. It is also the experience of the child whose parent is herself frightened. The frightened mother no longer offers the infant the prospect of a secure base or a safe haven.

'Indeed,' write Ainsworth and Eichberg (1991: 162), 'most of the anomolous behavioral markers of disorganization/disorientation are compatible with these explanations.' When faced with a frightening or a frightened parent, children 'freeze' and their behaviour is inhibited in the presence of the attachment figure. In clinical populations in which children have been maltreated, the number of disorganised attachments can rise to upwards of 50 per cent (Lyons-Ruth *et al.* 1990; Carlson *et al.* 1989).

## Defensive strategies and adaptive responses

In general, it appears that both parental and child characteristics influence the type of attachment formed. Insecure attachments tend to develop 'when parents are depressed or exhibit personality difficulties, when the marital relationship is strained, when there are external stresses, and when there is a lack of social support' (Rutter 1991: 358).

It has to be emphasised that children's behaviour in relationships which are defined as *maladaptive* is only viewed as such as far as future social competence is concerned. *The behaviour of insecurely attached children is an adaptive response within the context of the relationship in which they find themselves.* The behaviour adopted is a defensive strategy developed by the child in order to cope with feelings of anxiety, uncertainty and fear. 'Each child,' writes Sroufe (1983: 76 cited in Sroufe 1988), 'is making a particular and unique adaptation to his or her world.' Attachment behaviour is designed to bring proximity and security. When this goal is blocked or unforthcoming, the child has to develop psychological strategies that either attempt to ward off the anxiety or try to seek new ways of securing the attachment figure.

In secure attachments, the inevitable emotional conflicts that any child is bound to experience between needing the other and feeling angry when needs are not met is normally contained and handled within the parent–child relationship. Strong and potentially unmanageable feelings can threaten the child's psychological equilibrium. It takes time for the infant to learn to cope with conflicting feelings and handle frustration.

However, if the parent–child relationship is poor and inconsistent, conflicts are not always contained or resolved within that relationship. The child is then subjected to the full stress of the tension and can only cope with it by *excluding, distorting, redefining* or *avoiding* the experiences that cause the emotional trauma. These are examples of *defence mechanisms* and they serve to modify reality. And although they are a reasonable response to unreasonable events, nevertheless they impair and confuse long-term efforts to cope with the social world.

Ambivalent and avoidant insecure attachment patterns simply represent children's efforts to cope with the adverse social environments in which they find themselves. They are, in effect, adaptations which allow them to survive and function, albeit at a psychological price, within disturbed social environments. The various types of insecure attachment patterns just happen to be the best adaptations possible under the circumstances, though they may *not* serve the individual well in coping with future social relationships (Sroufe 1988: 25). Apparently 'maladaptive' behaviours therefore make sense when seen in the context of poor quality relationships and adverse social environments. They can be considered to be 'psychobiologically appropriate' to the particular social situation in which the child finds himself or herself:

> insecurely attached infants have established relationships that must be considered adapted to the circumstances of their rearing, even if they prove problematical as they move into the world beyond the family. Thus, insecure relationships are considered to be functional in that they serve to protect the child against anxiety, which arises in the face of a caregiver who may be less than optimally available. When seen in this light, avoidance, for example, serves as a strategy for avoiding anger that may evoke negative responses from the caregiver. (Belsky and Nezworski 1988b: 8)

Sachel's mother was a very self-centred woman who used to belittle her daughter at every opportunity, saying she was ugly, stupid and fit-for-nothing. Sachel could only cope with this hostile onslaught by 'switching-off', as she put it. Whenever she felt angry or upset with anyone, she simply went quiet, said nothing, shut down her feelings and stared impassively at the person who was either annoying or upsetting her. People called her a 'cold fish' and said that she was 'as-hard-as-nails'.

Bates and Bayles (1988: 257) cite Horney who suggested that feelings of profound anxiety arise when the individual senses 'being alone and helpless in a hostile world'. Such feelings are most likely to arise in a child if he or she receives inadequate, indifferent or hostile care. These core anxieties might be *defensively* resolved by one of three basic strategies:

(i) moving *towards* people (compliance) generally associated with secure attachments (type B);
(ii) moving *against* people (aggression) often associated with anxious–resistant and ambivalent attachments (type C); and
(iii) moving *away* from people (withdrawal) often associated with anxious–avoidant attachment (type A). (Bates and Bayles 1988: 257)

So, for example, *avoidance* as a form of attachment behaviour can be seen as a defensive strategy in response to the experience of parental rejection. Infantile attachment behaviour which fails to trigger comforting and supportive behaviour by the parent causes the child to experience increased feelings of anxiety and anger. Anxiety normally activates attachment behaviour. But in this case it appears that the attachment behaviour annoys the parent who may either attack or rebuff the child. Expressions of anxiety and upset normally bring about parental concern and care. However, in the case of avoidant patterns of attachment, the expression of anxiety and upset by the child seems to threaten and to damage the attachment relationship. The child appears not to be able to win. She is pulled in two ways at once and experiences a psychological dilemma.

One way for the child in this situation to avoid conflict with the parent is to cut herself off from her own feelings and emotions. If the child learns to switch off, thereby precluding the need to have any emotional engagement with the attachment figure, rejection and the associated feelings of pain, anxiety and anger can be kept at bay. Emotional self-containment therefore means that attachment behaviour – ironically the cause of the increased anxiety and anger – can be avoided. The child does not communicate her distress and instead contains and controls her feelings as part of the avoidant strategy (Cassidy and Kobak 1988: 304). Bowlby (1973) calls this 'compulsive self-reliance'. The price that the individual pays is that he or she finds it difficult to make and sustain close relationships. It is not easy to trust other people. Intimacy is threatening and increases feelings of anxiety.

In the six-year-old, for example, avoidance is seen in the child's attempts to keep *physically close but emotionally distant* from a parent. The child may play with an object in an intense and very absorbed fashion. The young girl or boy may be courteous but cool. People, including parents, are treated in a neutral fashion with feelings of affection and anger kept well hidden (Cassidy and Kobak 1988: 301).

Children who exhibit *disorganised* patterns of attachment (type D) have often been maltreated or severely deprived. They show confusion and disorganisation in their attachment behaviour. Unlike other children they appear to *lack* any defensive strategy in the face of anxiety. They freeze or simply appear confused, showing a mixture of avoidance and resistance. It is as if the relationship with the caregiver is the cause of so much anxiety that the young child has no organised psychological strategy that is able to cope with the threat. There is neither avoidance nor dependence, withdrawal nor aggression, only stark immobilisation. This is the most psychologically damaging of the defensive reactions practised by the child trying to deal with conflict and feelings of extreme anxiety.

Many of these findings hark back to Hinde's work with rhesus monkeys. He found that infant monkeys who showed the most distress *following* separation were those who exhibited the most tense and disturbed relationship with their mothers *before* separation (Hinde and Spencer-Booth 1970, cited in Dunn 1991). The children who cope least well with experiences of separation, stress and change are those who are already experiencing unsettled and disturbed parent–child relationships. Insecurely attached children, it appears, will often react badly to a change of school, a house move, parental divorce and even a switch of routine.

Helen, aged nine, was the middle child of a family of five. Life at home was disorganised. The noise and chaos seemed constant and every few months Helen's mother would give up and sink into a deep lethargy. In an attempt to give the mother a break and the children a treat, the social worker arranged for Helen to spend a week with an aunt who lived in a small town by the sea. At first Helen was excited and planned all the things that she might do at the seaside. But as the time approached for Helen to visit her aunt, she became increasingly moody. She would complain that she did not feel well and became tearful at the slightest upset – a lost pencil, a mark on her dress, a brother teasing her. On the day the social worker came to collect her, Helen cried and behaved in a frantic, panic-stricken fashion and simply refused to go.

The defence mechanisms, used by all of us at some time or another, have their origins in these early attempts to cope with anxiety, abandonment, loss, conflict and emotional pain. In essence, the defences we use involve either (i) keeping painful information out of consciousness (for example, *denial* and *avoidance* mechanisms) or (ii) redefining or trying to control painful experiences (for example, *projecting* one's anger on to others and blaming them).

The child's feelings of fear and anger when threatened with the loss of an attachment figure are very difficult for the young mind to handle. Defence mechanisms help the child cope with these powerful and frightening feelings. If the attachment figure is the cause of the child's anxiety, the infant will simultaneously experience yearning for and anger with the caregiver, a desire to be close and a wish to be rid of the cause of the pain.

One way of coping with these conflicting feelings is simply to try and *avoid* the conflict. Parents who cannot visit their sick children in hospital or social workers who make excuses not to see difficult clients are practising avoidance. But as well as physically leaving the relationship it is also possible to be emotionally absent from the relationship. This can be achieved by becoming emotionally detached from the other person. This defensive strategy attempts to *deny* that the relationship has any emotional significance or meaning. Feelings of love, fear or anger are first blocked and then denied. Individuals cope by cutting themselves off from their own potentially strong feelings: 'I feel very angry but I won't let it bother me'; 'I could be hurt by what she's saying but I will not let it affect me.' Other people may find the strategy exasperating; the more the emotional stakes rise, the more detached and unconcerned the person becomes. This, of course, simply fuels the other person's emotional state. Bowlby (1988: 34 and 71) calls the *repression* of strong and conflicting feelings 'defensive exclusion'.

Another method of coping with emotional conflict is to *split* the contradictory feelings so that only one is acknowledged and used to guide behaviour. Children and adults may say they hate the other even as they continue to demand their attention and concern. Or they may claim that they love them and need them while they appear to be intent on hurting and punishing them.

The inability to contain and cope with the simultaneous arousal of need and anger is typical of all insecure, anxious attachments. Whereas the avoidant child cuts off and denies any feeling of emotional interest in the other, the ambivalent child is more likely to struggle with the conflict and eventually resolve it by the defence of splitting: other people are either all good or all bad. In the long term this is an unsatisfactory strategy because the repressed feelings of either love or anger constantly confuse and distort the surface quality of relationships. Interpersonal dealings proceed in a somewhat turbulent, volatile fashion with need and dependency alternating in heightened manner with hostility and anger. The case of Mrs Talbot, who had physically abused her nine-month-old son, Steven, illustrates the use of splitting and the *projection* of her 'bad', hostile and angry feelings on to other people:

Mrs Talbot had a difficult childhood with a mother who was rather self-absorbed and inclined to be dismissive of her daughter. As a young mother, Mrs Talbot acted most of the time in a cool, unconcerned manner but periodically she would rage about the unfairness and hostility of other people. She would blame her mother, the demands of her baby son, the social worker and the hospital that treated Steven's head injury and accuse them all of 'getting at' her. There were strong suspicions that Mrs Talbot had deliberately inflicted Steven's injuries. In her calmer periods, Mrs Talbot resigned herself to being looked after and directed by her mother and social worker. She would stop smoking and eat packets of sweets. But this dependent phase rarely lasted long. She would soon resent the control, the restrictions, the all-too-familiar feelings of devaluation and most particularly her mother concentrating on Steven and not herself. At such moments she would leave, with her baby, and try to cope on her own again. She would then deal with her son in a calm, almost unconcerned way for a while before her simmering anger and resentment of his dependency on her would surface once again and she would do him some physical harm.

When social workers are made to feel that they are either 'suckers' or 'bastards', providers or deprivers, soft or hard, by their clients, they should be alert to the presence of splitting as a major defence mechanism, particularly by those who have had ambivalent attachment experiences. Splitting arouses conflictual feelings in social workers too. According to Mattinson and Sinclair (1979: 141), the wish to help and the fear of being overwhelmed are simultaneously aroused. The end result can be that the social worker feels impotent and then angry before finally rejecting the client whose demands seem to expose the worker's inability to satisfy and succeed.

Mattinson (1975) examines how social workers can easily become caught up in their clients' defensive manoeuvres. Very often, the social worker will act out and reflect a client's defences in supervision. She will behave towards her supervisor in the same way that the client behaves towards her or her partner or her children. To this extent, the social worker's own behaviour can indicate what is happening in other people's relationships.

In the 'reflection process' Mattinson developed 'the idea that *the responses of workers which are out of character with their normal behaviour and which are defensive in quality give an important indication of the strength and type of disturbance to which they have been subjected*' (Mattinson and Sinclair 1979: 56; emphasis in original). Good supervison and thoughtful practitioners can learn a lot about their clients as they examine and analyse the nature and origin of their own feelings. The alert supervisor will recognise what is happening in the supervision process and so help the social worker understand what might be going on in the case.

## Conclusion

The quality of children's relationship experiences with their caregivers determines which type of attachment behaviour they will display at times of anxiety. The way we learn to handle the anxieties that most close relationships generate from time to time gives us an insight into the nature and purpose of the defence mechanisms we all find ourselves employing in stressful situations. For children who are insecurely attached to their caregivers, such defensive strategies make sense: they are an adaptive response to situations in which anxieties are running high.

# 7

# Disturbed social relationships

In this chapter we look at how the experiences of past relationships influence the way an individual copes with and handles current relationships. The links between past and present experiences becomes particularly important when we try to understand the nature and character of disturbed social relationships. Relationships remain important for people throughout the human life cycle. If social workers are to make sense of people's behaviour in situations of high anxiety and stress, attachment theory and a developmental perspective provide a range of powerful ideas which are practically useful as well as intellectually satisfying.

**Past and present relationship experiences**

The quality of the immediate social environment in which infants find themselves affects their social development and ability to cope with people and situations. Adversity in childhood can have a long-term impact on an individual's personality, social competence and ability to cope with and sustain intimate relationships.

> Insecurity becomes more probable with parents who are stressed and unsupported, who are irritable and critical with the children, who have a strained marital relationship and when there is poor 'mesh' between the parent and the infant. This 'mesh' will, of course, be influenced by the child's characteristics as they impinge on and are perceived by the parents, as well as by the parents' own personal qualities. In that connection, the child's own temperamental qualities are likely to be influential. (Rutter and Rutter 1993: 119–20)

Attachment theory offers a particularly useful conceptual framework in which to explore the relationship between *past* and *present* experiences. The quality of both past and present social environments have to be understood if current behaviour and experience is to make sense. Acute stress triggers attachment behaviour. The security which the attachment figure ideally brings, helps to relieve feelings of anxiety and gives people both the structure and the emotional support to learn to deal with the difficulty.

However, individual differences in attachment styles influence the way people cope or fail to cope with stressful events. Positive childhood experiences help people cope with upsets and difficulties. Disturbed relationships in the past increase the individual's vulnerability to current stresses. Long-term, chronic stress undermines attachment behaviour, both in children and adults (Simpson and Rholes 1994). Parents who suffer financial hardship, low quality housing, poor marital relationships and a problem neighbourhood may well experience chronic stress and anxiety. Their ability to be emotionally available for and responsive to their children will be severely taxed. On average, mothers of anxiously and avoidantly attached toddlers have experienced more stressful life events than mothers of securely attached children (Vaughn *et al.* 1979).

Part of attachment theory's power and great appeal is its insistence on linking both *social* and *psychological* perspectives in trying to understand personality and development. The social environment and the individual's psychological interior are intimately and integrally linked. The individual's psychological experience and social context define a unique developmental pathway. If the qualities of children's social relationships are weak, disturbed or disordered, they will adversely affect social development. The consequence of disturbances and deficiencies in early social relationships is the upsetting of children's ability to organise and model social experience, form a core concept of self, cope with anxiety, develop social understanding, make sense of other people, and cope with social relationships. Developmentally, the pathway in these cases is likely to spiral downwards. If the quality of relationships and social experience is poor, then the child fails to develop fully coherent and useful internal representational models. Her ability to make effective sense of other people and social life is thereby impaired.

The model which people use to represent self and others helps them *construe* what is happening and sets up *expectations*. If the relationship experiences which help people form such models are poor, constructions and expectations of other people and social situations will be inaccurate and incomplete. When other people and social situations do not make sense or feel problematic and unpredictable, anxiety levels rise and defensive reactions come into play.

For children who find it difficult to organise and regulate emotional experience, the relationships of which they most need to make sense and experience as caring and available are those they have with their prime caregivers. But these are the very people who have failed to provide them with secure and good quality social relationships in the first place. These are the relationships which are both the cause of the children's social incompetence and the source of their current social difficulties.

In his studies, Bowlby kept returning to three themes in his attempts to understand disturbed and upset behaviour (Holmes 1993: 87): (i) the loss of a close relationship and the disruption of affectional bonds; (ii) the failure of the attachment figure to provide a reliable and secure base as well as help the child contain feelings of anger in reponse to loss; and (iii) the development of defensive strategies, particularly emotional withdrawal, to cope with the pain of loss and the associated feelings of anxiety. The combined effect of these experiences all too often leads to difficult behaviour and disturbed relationships.

Developmentally, children might find themselves in a variety of adverse social environments. The most extreme disadvantaged upbringing occurs when children find themselves in a social environment which prevents them even forming a selective attachment. They are unable to experience a continuous good quality relationship. For instance, infants raised in large institutional nurseries may fail to form any kind of selective attachments. Relationships may be available but they are too fleeting and erratic for children to be able to form regular and reliably available attachments. Children in such environments do not experience any individualised continuity of care and no-one shows them any deep, prolonged personal interest.

Less severe, but still capable of upsetting psychological development is the situation in which children do find themselves selectively attached to someone but that person is unable to provide a good quality social relationship. There is a selective attachment figure but she is not reliably available or predictably consistent in the care and responses which she gives.

Three different types of adverse experience may bring about any one or more of these disadvantages, all of which pose a distinct psychiatric risk in either childhood or adult life (Rutter *et al.* 1990: 151):

1. changing and inconsistent patterns of personal care-giving as mothers and fathers move in and out of the child's early life. These relationship patterns are likely to jeopardise the formation of secure parent–child attachments;
2. family discord associated with quarrelling, hostility and blame directed at the child; and
3. a harmonious, physically caring but loveless upbringing in an' institutional setting that lacks continuity in personal care for each child.

In each of these adverse environments, the child is *denied* two key experiences which a relationship might normally be expected to provide. (i) A good relationship will help a child regulate his or her emotions and feelings. In the first instance, it is the structural properties of the relationship itself which will hold and manage the child's emotions. But in time, the child will internalise the properties of the relationship and so she will be increasingly able to contain and handle strong emotions herself. (ii) A good relationship also offers the child a harmonious and synchronous exchange of responses, feelings and understandings.

Therefore, relationships between caregiver and infant, mother and child can become disturbed when any one or more of the following features are identified:

1. Lack of consistent and continuous love and care.
2. Insensitive reactions or unresponsiveness to the child's mental and physical states.
3. The caregiver either overstimulates or understimulates her child. Emotions and affect are either overregulated or underregulated.
4. Lack of synchrony and harmony between caregivers and child. The mother or father is either not in-tune with or not interested in the child's responses and contributions.
5. Lack of reciprocity and mutuality in the parent–child relationship. The child fails to receive confirmation of what he or she understands to be going on in social situations.

The importance of the caregiver's emotional availability has been stressed thoughout these pages. When emotional availability is present, each partner in the relationship can exchange a range of emotions. There is 'clarity of emotional signalling' (Emde 1989: 47). The relationship generates interest and pleasure rather than distress. However, social development is unlikely to be on track if emotional availability is compromised. When the range of emotions that the relationship can display and contain is restricted; when emotional signalling is confused, ignored or misread; and when there is a predominance of disengagement, distress, or avoidance in interaction; then development is impaired (Emde 1989). The child withdraws from the emotional content of the relationship, and therefore fails to recognise, understand and regulate his or her emotions in the context of a lively, sensitive, well-tuned, two-way interaction.

## The child's influence on the social environment

There is a good deal of debate about the extent to which early life experiences fundamentally affect and determine social development throughout the rest of childhood. It may be that because the neurological and psychological structures form while the very young brain is still in its highly responsive and sensitive state, it is particularly difficult for subsequent experiences to have as great an impact on development as earlier ones. If the early life experiences are of good quality, the child will have psychological structures which are capable of coping with and integrating new social experiences. And to the extent that the child is able to handle social relationships in a competent manner, other people are likely to respond to the child positively and constructively. In other words, a socially competent child will create a benign and responsive social environment.

In contrast, if early life experiences are disturbed, the child will develop psychological structures which are less capable of coping with new social experiences, particularly those which are demanding and difficult ones. To the extent that the child fails to cope with social relationships, other people are likely find that child difficult or unrewarding and so will respond negatively. In other words, a socially incompetent child will create an adverse social environment for which she lacks the psychological resources to cope. As Rutter

(1991) says, many people experience a chain of connected experiences between a disrupted childhood, a poor marriage and difficult relationships with their own children. It seems that for many people 'one bad (or good) experience makes another one more likely'.

Another variation on the theme of self-perpetuating environments sees socially competent children in all likelihood remaining in the same social relationships that helped them become competent in the first place. These relationships continue to strengthen and develop the children's social understanding. In like manner, socially incompetent children are also likely to remain in the same family, neighbourhood and matrix of social relationships throughout their childhoods. However, their social environment inhibits and continues to inhibit the development of social understanding. It is not simply that the early deficiences have a long-term, irremedial impact on the children's social performance. The children continue to experience difficult and disturbed relationships and social situations. There is no remedial environment in which improvements in social understanding might take place.

It is therefore difficult to say whether, for example, children who were insecurely attached as infants are socially incompetent at the age of ten because of the long-term consequences of disturbed early relationships, or whether they are socially incompetent because of the continuing poor quality of their *current* social relationships. Most children who suffer discordant and disturbed relationships in early life continue to live with the same people who generated psychologically hazardous environments in the first place. It is difficult to disentangle the long-term effects of early life relationships from the effects of contemporary adverse social experiences.

Furthermore, the poor quality relationships experienced by delinquent children could also be because behaviourally disordered children create abnormal environments. This argument forms part of the thesis that temperamentally difficult children affect parents and their behaviour every bit as much as disturbed parents influence the behaviour of their children (see Rutter 1991: 336 for a review of this research). For example, in a study of mentally ill parents, it was found that children with adverse temperamental characteristics were particularly likely to be the target of parental criticism and hostility (Rutter 1991: 353). People shape their environments, for good or ill, every bit as much as they are shaped by them. This adds yet another layer to the nature–nurture dynamic.

**Attachment and relationship disturbances across the life cycle**

Children form attachment relationships with parents while adults form attachment relationships with agemates. 'With a shift from parents to peers as partners, the quality of attachment relationships also shifts. With parents, children typically have dependent, asexual attachments; with peers, adults typically have reciprocal, sexual bonds' (Perlman and Bartholomew 1994: 8)

The evidence is suggestive, even compelling, that disturbances in the quality of early relationships continue to have adverse affect on relationships throughout life. Mothers and fathers who were insecure or neglected as infants may experience problems coping with the stresses and strains of bringing up their own children. Men and women may find it difficult to establish and sustain relationships with other people, especially relationships involving intimacy and sex. Adults rejected as children by their parents may hold hostile attitudes towards people in authority even though this may be self-defeating. For others, stressful situations may all too easily provoke feelings of anxiety, despair and depression.

For example, Rutter's (1988) study of women who had experienced institutional care looked at their experiences in adult life. When they became mothers of two-year-old children, 40 per cent of them (compared with only 11 per cent of a control group of mothers from the same neighbourhood but who had grown up in families) experienced relationship difficulties with their toddler. Although a variety of adverse factors had affected the lives of these women, the best predictor of relationship difficulties with their own children was whether they had experienced serious breakdowns in their relationships with their own parents before they were four years old.

The investigations by Caspi and Elder (1988) examined relationship patterns across four generations. The study first looked at the families of children born in Berkeley, California in 1928 and followed them over subsequent generations. They paid particular attention to the children who grew up in families in which relationships between parents and children were hostile and unaffectionate. These children themselves developed a variety of personal instabilities. As adults, they were likely to experience tensions in their relationships with their marriage partners. They experienced discipline difficulties and conflict with their own children who, in turn, were likely to have behavioural problems. And when this third generation eventually became parents, they were seen as bad-tempered and temperamentally explosive by their own, fourth-generation children.

Caspi and Elder argue that problem behaviours lead to problem relationships, which then create adverse social environments in which the new generation's psychological development has to take place:

> Unstable personalities undermine supportive relationships with others, and weak ties are conducive to the expression of unstable tendencies. In reality, the primary flow of influence *within* a generation moves from problem behaviour to problem relationships . . . tense, explosive adults tend to create marital stress and discord. The latter has relatively little influence on problem behaviour within a narrowly defined time period, but we know its effect is stronger when lagged over a number of years and becomes especially noteworthy when viewed across the generations. (Caspi and Elder 1988: 236)

Much of the research carried out in the field of relationship and attachment theory looks at the impact of childhood experiences throughout the life cycle. It is concerned with how adults cope with the social and *interpersonal* demands that are part of living and working with other people. The strategies that people employ can be more or less successful in dealing with the ordinary as well as extraordinary stresses of everyday social life. There is a general interest in understanding and assessing how different personalities, each with his or her particular history of relationships, cope with the full range of social and emotional needs throughout the life span.

> an urge to keep proximity or accessibility to someone seen as stronger or wiser, and who if responsive is deeply loved, comes to be recognised as an integral part of human nature and having a vital role to play in life. Not only does its effective operation bring with it a strong feeling of security and contentment, but its temporary or long-term frustration causes acute or chronic anxiety and discontent. When seen in this light, the urge to keep proximity is to be respected, valued, and nurtured as making for potential strength, instead of being looked down upon, as so often hitherto, as a sign of inherent weakness. This radical shift in valuation, with its far-reaching influence on how we perceive and treat other people, especially whose attachment needs have been and still are unmet, is, I believe, the single most important consequence of the change of conceptual framework. (Bowlby 1991a: 293)

Some of our strongest feelings arise around the making and breaking of attachment relationships (Bowlby 1979: 130). Falling in love, being rejected, and grieving over the loss of someone to whom we were close all produce intense and difficult emotions. Prospects of intimacy or threats of loss can make us feel happy or sad, valued or hurt.

We are now in a position to examine more systematically the developmental continuities between good and, more particularly, poor quality social experiences in early childhood and the levels of social competence achieved in later life. These continuities will be discussed under the following six chapter headings:

1. Relationships with parents and family.
2. Relationships with peers.
3. Relationships with self.
4. Relationships with society.
5. Relationships with partners.
6. Relationships with children.

# 8

# Relationships with parents and family

Children can be on the receiving end of parenting skills which range from good to bad. There is a variety of caregiving environments and family contexts in which children can find themselves. This chapter outlines the full spectrum of attachment experiences, from children who are denied the opportunity to develop close relationships with a caregiver to children who enjoy a close and secure relationship with one or more selected caregivers. Most children remain with the same people in the same social setting throughout most of their childhoods. We consider the developmental implications of living in the same social and psychological environment for the first fifteen years or so of life. If the relationships in that environment are disturbed, which is the case when parents quarrel and fight excessively, this can have an adverse effect on the children's development. We also consider the kinds of relationship children experience when one or both of their parents suffer a mental health problem.

Attachment theory, as well as being a specific example of a more general theory of relationships and psychological development, is also a theory that involves an understanding of the emotions. In its developmental guise, the theory is interested in the *psychological strategies* which children use to understand their social environment and adapt to it. Radke-Yarrow *et al.* (1988: 52) describes how parents and children relate to each other along many dimensions, including those of love, authority and dependence; and how the two generations interact in a variety of ways, including those of care, control, instruction and companionship. The core themes of security, trust and closeness run throughout all parent–child relations. The quality and character of the relationships and interactions in which children find themselves will play a large part in determining their personality, level of social competence and developmental pathway through life.

**Nonattachments**

The most developmentally adverse social environments for children are those in which there are no opportunities to form attachment relationships. In these environments, children show impaired ability to form close, meaningful and intimate personal relationships. Children reared in institutions from a very young age, for example, are most likely to suffer disorders of *nonattachment*. Their relationship with other people is based merely on the satisfaction of needs. Little upset is experienced when one caregiver goes and another takes their place. The children's ability to control aggressive impulses and feelings of frustration are very limited. When they are in their early school years they are prone to throw temper tantrums. They do not enjoy good peer relations and are somewhat quarrelsome. As a consequence they are often unpopular with their agemates. They also have strikingly low levels of concentration. Many of these characteristics continue into adolescence and beyond.

Cadoret *et al.* (1990) reported that adopted children who suffered social disruption during their first year or two of life *before* joining stable adoptive homes were at an increased risk of poorer mental health, such as depression, in adulthood. Having been removed from their birth mothers, these children typically would be looked after by a number of different caretakers over a considerable period of time before finally being placed with their adoptive parents. These findings help confirm the general belief that upsets in early relationships lead to future psychological disturbance as well as difficulties in conducting and sustaining social relationships.

**Sensitive and insensitive parents**

Next we can consider children who do have opportunities to develop attachment relationships. However, for any one child, the quality of social experience may range from good to bad, secure to insecure. The studies by Grossmann and Grossmann (1991: 98–9) reveal how young children, aged 12 months and 18 months, respond to different styles of parenting. They observed that when distressed, securely attached children turned to their parents for support. 'Emotional communication' was direct and to the mother or the father. This behaviour invariably resulted in help and comfort. In contrast, insecure children with avoidant patterns of attachment communicated less emotion in the direction of their parents. This lack of communication was particularly pronounced in situations in which the children were upset and distressed. Indeed, the more distressed the children became, the less they communicated with their parents. The infants were left to handle difficulties on their own. As they got older, they began to keep feelings to themselves. Bitter and painful experience had taught them that when they revealed and attempted to communicate their feelings, the result was hurt and rejection. The lack of parental responsiveness meant that the infant's distress was not relieved and there was less 'togetherness' in sorting out the problem.

The Grossmanns also observed parents and young infants playing. Other studies have revealed that secure children play longer on their own and with greater concentration than insecure children (Suess *et al.* 1989, cited in Main 1991). The Grossmans also observed that if securely attached children were absorbed in a piece of play, the parent tended to watch but not interfere. However, if the child became bored or lost interest, the parent became involved, suggesting toys to play with or things to do.

The reverse pattern was observed with insecure and anxious children with avoidant attachment patterns of behaviour. If parents themselves had not enjoyed secure attachment they tended to respond inappropriately and insensitively to their children's mood. In these cases, if the infant was happily playing, the parent joined in and interfered, tending to upset the child and what he or she was doing. But if the infant was distressed or uncertain what to do, the parent failed to recognise the child's psychological state and respond appropriately. Toys were not offered and ideas were not presented. By the age of one year, infants in secure attachment relationships:

> experienced more support for their independent activity, communicated more openly with their parents, especially when distressed, and were more sympathetic with a new adult play partner's changing emotions. Before the emergence of spoken language the infants had learned different functions of social–emotional communication within a relationship, whether it serves as means to elicit support and comfort from the attachment figure, or whether communications of distress are discouraged or ignored by the parent. (Grossmann and Grossmann 1991: 99–100)

The researchers (1991: 100) conclude that the quality of a parent's interactions with his or her young child can be resolved into three *ideal* factors: '(1) the cheerful, supportive parent, (2) the explaining, teaching parent, and (3) the patient, accepting parent'. These factors are independent of each other. Parents who seriously depart from any of these ideals are likely to compromise the quality of the child's attachment experience.

## The 'frozen' child

For one group of children, their attachment figure maintains a consistently negative and hostile social relationship. This generates high levels of anxiety which can overwhelm the children's defences leaving them simply 'frozen'. Hopkins (1991: 192–5) gives the example of a three-year-old child experiencing an insecure–avoidant attachment with his mother. Paddy, who did not have learning difficulties, had no speech and was not toilet trained. He was indiscriminate in his interest in adults. No upset was shown when he experienced short separations from his parents, nor did he greet them with any warmth or interest on their return. He appeared to show no awareness of danger and would often wander off and get lost unless the doors were locked. 'When he injured himself, even severely, he appeared to feel no pain. He regularly ate dirt and rubbish, and even occasionally his own faeces. He rejected being cuddled and was a constant thumb-sucker' (Hopkins 1991: 192). He showed no real evidence of play as such. Other children crying did upset him. When he met strangers he could smile and he could make eye contact though there were times when his eyes glazed over.

Hopkins describes Paddy's mother as an anxious woman and chronically depressed. She had attempted suicide in her teens. 'She suffered from severe eczema and explained that although she loved Paddy she had always avoided touching and cuddling him for fear that his germs would infect her skin' (Hopkins 1991: 193). She lost confidence as a mother when Paddy was one month old. A paediatrician mistakenly wondered whether her baby might have Down's Syndrome. She stopped breastfeeding and handed over much of his care to a series of temporary au-pairs. Her husband was not very supportive and the marriage was unstable.

In therapy Paddy would close his eyes tight shut when he was particularly pleased with something. Hopkins mentions the work of Main and Weston (1982) who explain that one way an avoidant child might cope with a mother's rejection is by turning his back on her, closing his eyes or becoming absorbed in fiddling with some object. Using such mechanisms, the child can remain near his mother but not face directly the aversive qualities of her rejecting behaviour. 'Paddy avoided eye contact at moments when he most wanted physical contact and so feared both . . . rejection and the expression of his own hostility' (Hopkins 1991: 193).

In the presence of their parents, abused toddlers show either a 'frozen watchfulness' or a heightened sense of alertness to their parents' moods and behaviour. Tense 'freezing' appears to be a frequent response used by children in reaction to strong expressions of anger. In terms of a preventive strategy, it is in the child's interests to anticipate the needs of a parent. One way of trying to placate an unsettled and potentially violent parent is for the child to 'lie low' and try to attend quietly to his or her needs. This wary, but subdued behaviour makes psychological sense.

## Continuities in patterns of attachment

Research suggests that children classified as secure or insecure at age one, continued to exhibit similar attachment behaviour when they had reached the age of six (Main and Cassidy 1988). After one hour's separation from their mothers, the six-year-olds who had been classified as secure when they were babies greeted mothers warmly and shared experiences about what had taken place during her absence. Those who exhibited avoidant attachments either ignored their mothers or greeted them coolly. Children originally classified as insecure and ambivalent continued to behave with a mixture of anxious responsiveness, hostility and immature behaviour upon reunion. The Grossmanns (1991: 102) also found that 87 per cent of those classified as securely, avoidantly or ambivalently attached at age one were similarly classified when they reached the age of six. It appears, then, that there is a general continuity of attachment experience across childhood for most children.

Further work by the Grossmans with the six-year-old children from Bielefeld looked at their reactions to imaginary situations in which a child became separated from his or her parents (Grossmann and Grossmann 1991: 103). The children were shown various pictures depicting the imaginary situations. Securely attached children, although relaxed during the interview, nevertheless sympathised with the child's probable feelings of anxiety. However, they also suggested positive ways in which the child might cope with the separation including asking for support from other people. Children with an avoidant attachment history seemed more strained and tense when the pictures were shown. Feelings of anxiety and vulnerablity were denied by some children, while others felt pessimistic, and a few even doubted whether the parents in the picture story would ever return.

> As Bowlby suggested in 1979, a child who is certain of his parent's acceptance and support is able not only to tolerate his ambiguous feelings toward his parents but also to be confident that he can control them without having to deny them. This we saw in the reactions of the securely attached 6-year-old children from the Bielefeld sample. They were not afraid to admit negative effects as a consequence of an imagined parental leave-taking, because they could imagine a positive, constructive solution. (Grossmann and Grossmann 1991: 103–4)

These same patterns were still detectable in 10-year-old children. Children with an early secure attachment could admit negative feelings and generally saw the world of other people and relationships as a source of help, support and comfort. Children with a history of avoidant patterns of attachment saw themselves having to work out difficulties on their own. They did not see other people as potentially helpful or supportive.

**Forming fresh attachments to new caregivers**

Children who are placed for adoption or with foster parents are expected to relate to these caregivers as securely attached children. However, children's previous attachment experiences will initially affect the way they relate to new caregivers. Children with avoidant attachment experiences will have learned to mistrust closeness and intimacy. Having become emotionally closed and self-reliant, they will be very slow to trust their new parents or place any long-term hopes in this fresh relationship. There is no wish to be rejected and hurt yet again, so the child makes no initial commitment to the relationship. They behave as if they do not care; they test out their new parents by behaving in difficult ways. And if this results in anger and rejection, then they feel that their wariness, suspicions and unwillingness to trust these new parents were entirely justified for they have been let down once again. These difficulties and a general detachment can feel very unrewarding to the new parents. The adoptive parents have little choice but to be very patient and persist with consistent love and care.

Matthew, now aged 14, was adopted when he was 9. After a very disturbed and neglected early childhood he was first placed in a children's home before he was finally adopted. Matthew remembers some grim events before he joined Mary, his adoptive mother. In a television (BBC 1994) interview he recalled:

> I saw it one time when there was this man. He was drunk and he started stamping on my natural mum's face . . . stamping and I could see all this blood and I was only young and so I kind of felt really helpless and I didn't know what to do. So I just sat there, stood there and I think I was crying. I think I was just so helpless, really . . . I used to spend a lot of time on the streets because my mum would leave me and things. I was wandering round the streets day and night. Sometimes I slept at my friend's house. Sometimes I slept at my mum's house. Sometimes I slept in sheds. But it didn't seem as if I really had a mum because she was never there.

Matthew has not been an easy boy since his adoption. He's been on the fringe of trouble at school and in the community. His friends are also on the edge of delinquency. In his own words, he thinks Mary, his adoptive mother, 'must be very patient to have me and Peter [his adopted brother]. I'm surprised she's not had a nervous breakdown by now.' But Mary is an experienced and very successful adopter of older, difficult children. She fully understands the impact which his very disturbed background has had on bringing about his 'avoidant' personality. The only way to cope with such horrific childhood experiences seems to have been for Matthew to cut down his emotions and their availability to himself and others. Mary says that:

> Matthew is independent; stubborn. He won't allow himself to be influenced by other people. Matthew, really, had had to take decisions for himself and his younger sister Sarah and so he started to think for himself, do things for himself and started to go his own way. He doesn't really want to be parented. He's a warm child, a very loving child, but he doesn't have that give in him that allows you to come close. He likes to build a firm fence around himself that's fairly impregnable. And I'm having to try really hard to try and make my relationship with Matthew really work.

Children who have experienced ambivalent attachments have experienced inconsistent and unpredictable parenting in which love and attention have been unreliable and intermittent. These children approach new relationships with some hope but also considerable ambivalence. This shows itself in exasperating mixtures of over-compliance, irritablity, emotional rejections and tearful reconciliations. There is a superficiality to the child's behaviour and emotional responses. These behaviours are designed to ingratiate and gain attention. The child is not yet secure or relaxed with the idea that love can be unconditional and that he or she can be valued simply for what he or she simply is.

Adele's mother committed suicide when she was three years old, and after a year in which Adele was passed around from one unwilling relative to another, she was eventually adopted by Mrs Marett. For the first few months she trailed after her adoptive mother wherever she went and would not let her out of her sight. Adele kept making her little presents. Her anxiety to please was almost desperate. Whenever Mrs Marett mentioned anything about Adele's past or family, the little girl blocked her ears, stamped her feet and threw things across the room. Her appetite was insatiable. For a long time, Adele had the habit of chewing her clothes and unpicking her dresses. She coped badly when she started school and was poor at making friends as well as keeping them.

Children who have never enjoyed any kind of attachment are the most developmentally damaged. On first encounter with new parents they will have a surface charm. They will relate happily but without discrimination. The new parents will engender no feelings of permanence or continuity. The social world is a place of temporary relationships in which the opportunity to get to know, understand and model the self, others and one's relationship with them has been severely limited. Mutuality is missing; impulses are rife; and emotional reciprocity is limited. Nonattached children have limited experience and poorly structured representational models on which to build intimate relationships. Their experience has been one of contingent relationships which have lacked both depth and security. They have a lot to learn about relationships and will present new parents with behavioural challenges and emotional confusions that will require considerable understanding and long-term love.

**Conflict and disharmony between parents**

We also need to remind ourselves of Dunn's (1993: 10–11) injunction that children respond not only to those who relate directly to them, but are equally sensitive to the emotional inter-actions that take place between other people. Confidence, security and constructiveness develop in children whose parents relate to each other in a reasonably harmonious and co-operative fashion. Uncertainty, aggression and a lack of concentration tend to develop in children whose parents quarrel and fight on a regular basis. In general, the expression of anger between people is one of the most disturbing and difficult experiences which children have to handle. It can produce some of the most problematic social behaviour.

Overt conflict between parents in the form of shouting, swearing, threatening to walk out and throwing things at each other is likely to cause children both emotional and behavioural problems. The impact on children is most often seen in the form of 'externalised' problems such as aggression and social misconduct. Cohen *et al.* also found that as overt conflict between parents increased, children appeared to experience less parental care and control and higher levels of parental aggression directed towards them. Aggressive behaviour also appears in children whose parents attempt to control them by using 'power-assertive punishment techniques'. These include screaming at the child, threats, hitting, isolating, and taking away privileges (Cohen *et al.* 1990: 247).

On the positive side, parents who are open, sensitive and responsive in their dealings with one another increase the level of emotional understanding in their children. This has a knock-on effect and allows children to improve their social competence, especially with peers (Dunn 1993: 108). Moreover, there is considerable research evidence to support the idea that if relationships are good between a child's parents, they are good between the parents and the child (for example, Belsky 1984, cited in Dunn 1993: 76).

In contrast, poor marital relationships appear to lead to poor child outcome (Gable *et al.*, reported in Dunn 1993: 76). For example, children whose parents are in the process of separating or divorcing often suffer some psychological disturbance. However, these disturbances frequently *precede* the divorce, suggesting that it is not simply a reaction to the loss of parent. More likely, the disturbances appear to be the product of unhappy homes where there is much chronic discord, disturbance and tension in intimate family relationships. As Rutter and Rutter (1993: 134) point out, psychologically disturbed children are as common in discordant non-divorced families as in those where one parent has left. The most common kind of disturbances tend to be in the child's conduct – aggression, poor impulse control, non-compliance and disturbed peer relationships (Rutter and Rutter 1993: 134). When exposed to discord, boys tend to externalise their feelings and react with aggression and awkwardness while girls tend to internalise their feelings and experience distress (Cummings *et al.* 1985).

However, while boys and younger children seem to benefit from their mother's remarriage, girls, particularly adolescent girls, seem to cope less well (Hetherington 1988; Hetherington 1989). It is speculated that prior to the remarriage, girls possibly develop a close relationship with their mother which, upon remarriage, then has to be shared with the step-father: 'From the girls' point of view they had not gained a father; rather they had lost a mother!' (Rutter and Rutter 1993: 135).

## Children of depressed parents

Further evidence that it is the disturbed quality of parent–child relationships which leads to an increased psychiatric risk for the child is to be found in cases where mothers suffer poor mental health. It is the discord and disruption that appears in the families with a mentally ill parent that upsets the child's development (Rutter and Quinton 1984b; Quinton *et al.* 1990). Radke-Yarrow (1989) in her studies of children of depressed parents found that a number of three-year-olds of manic-depressive mothers appeared as cheerful, confident, uninhibited, and engaging children. When she observed the children again at age five, they were withdrawn, anxious and distressed. It has also been observed that children of mothers who are very depressed often begin to exhibit conduct disorders as they grow older (Fendrich *et al.* 1990).

## Conclusion

In general, children of depressed parents appear to be two to five times more likely to develop behaviour problems than children of normal parents (Cummings and Davies 1994: 73). Various explanations have been considered to account for this increased risk. It may be that the depressed mother's emotional unavailability and psychological insensitivity produce an insecure pattern of attachment. If the child learns to *avoid* intimacy, this serves as an adaptive function by limiting the child's involvement in a relationship which he or she finds stressful and difficult. It might also be the case that parental depression increases family discord and it is this raised level of conflict within the home which is disturbing the child's emotional development (Cummings and Davies 1994: 100).

In general, we might observe that the early childhood experiences most likely to lead to poor social functioning in adult life involve disruptions and upsets in upbringing and rearing experiences. Children who, before the age of two, suffer short-term admissions into foster care, persistent parental discord, separation from one or both parents, or admission into long-term institutional care have a high risk of showing poor social functioning as adults.

# 9

# Relationships with peers

The quality of children's relationships with their caregivers correlates closely with the type of relationships they have with their peers. The more disturbed the parent–child relationship, the less successful is that child likely to be with social relationships in general. In this chapter we explore this phenomenon and follow it through into adulthood. We also recognise that the quality of a child's relationships with his or her peers is a good predictor of that child's social competence in adult life.

## The growing importance of peer relationships during childhood

Throughout childhood there is a gradual shift in the amount of time and interest expended away from parents towards peers and friends. Even by the age of three, children are seeking out and playing with their agemates, often in quite complex and involved ways. Whereas attachment relationships with parents provide comfort and security, *affiliative* relationships with peers furnish children with stimulation and pleasure (Hazan and Zeifman 1994: 156). As children enter the later stages of childhood and begin adolescence, friends, rather than parents, also begin to provide increasing amounts of emotional support and confiding relationships.

Psychologists have long recognised the importance and value of peer relationships in the development of social competence. Play with friends demands co-operation and negotiation; it triggers conflict as well as mutuality. When playing with peers, children have to take increasing account of other people's feelings, intentions and points of view. Children who are poor at social understanding are soon regarded as socially incompetent. Many will become isolated and excluded from the very experiences they need in order to develop both a well-integrated sense of self and sound social understanding. Developmentally, therefore, children who are socially withdrawn, excessively shy or socially isolated and rejected might be seen to be 'at risk', according to Rubin and Lollis (1988: 221).

## Attachment experiences and play with peers

In her review of several studies which examined possible links between the quality of parent–child relationships and the quality of a child's relationships with his or her friends, Dunn (1993: 95–7) points out that the correlations are not always simple or straightforward; that it is not always the case that 'all-good-things-go-together' and in many instances there are no connections across relationships. Indeed, it can be argued that some young children might even compensate for poor relationships with their parents by developing richer, more emotionally satisfying relationships with friends. But one or two interesting associations do appear in the research. For example, in her study of five-year-olds, Dunn (1993: 97) noticed that 'children who had enjoyed a high degree of involvement with their mothers were more likely to use compromise and negotiation in their arguments with friends'.

In a study of seven year olds by Stocker and Mantz-Simmons (reported in Dunn 1993: 97), children who reported high levels of maternal warmth also said that they enjoyed good companionship and little conflict with their friends compared to children who did not report such high levels of maternal warmth. This study also reminds us that we must not conflate a child's separate relationship experiences with each of her parents. For instance, if fathers relate to their children in a controlling or uninvolved way, the children are less likely to be co-operative with their friends than children whose fathers are more involved or less controlling. This pattern is not true for mother–child relationships.

Sroufe and his colleagues have made a number of studies of how young children with histories of secure and insecure attachment experiences played with each other and how they were viewed by teachers. Securely attached children initiate relationships with their peers in a positive and responsive manner. They expect playing and dealing with other people to be a positive experience. They are higher ranked socially and they have more friends than their insecure peers (LaFreniere and Sroufe 1985). These same children show greater empathy, sense of fairness and reciprocity. Grossmann and Grossmann (1991: 101) also report that securely attached five-year-olds played with greater concentration and resolved conflicts with their peers more effectively than their avoidant counterparts. More specifically, children who showed secure attachments with their fathers initiated more play activities with other children.

In the case of children with avoidant attachment experiences, the findings suggest that they either show greater hostility and unprovoked aggression with their peers or become detached and emotionally distant. When avoidant children play with anxiously attached children, the latter are likely to be exploited and become locked in the role of victim. They can be taunted. The relationship, at least in the case of avoidant boys, sponsors immature and impulsive behaviour. Children with secure attachment histories were not observed to be either exploitative or victimised (Fury 1984, cited in Sroufe 1989a).

If two children in a peer relationship both have histories of avoidant attachments, there is likely to be little 'give and take'; there are few compromises and so the relationship never really becomes mutually satisfying. In the case of boys, very unhealthy relationships develop. There is much tension, conflict and provocation (Fury 1984, cited in Sroufe 1989a).

Abused toddlers find it harder to make and sustain peer relationships. They also tend to be significantly more aggressive with other children as well as caregivers (Main and George 1985). The research in this field also reveals that the type of aggression shown by children who themselves have been abused can be particularly hostile. The unjustified harassment of other children with the sole intent of causing distress was repeatedly observed in a nursery setting. Many of the 'victims' retaliated, with the effect that hostilies rapidly escalated.

## Peer rejection

By middle childhood, children who regularly exhibit hostile aggression are likely to experience social rejection. Children who are occasionally aggressive but who do not experience repeated social rejection seek to end the aggressive episode on a positive note with the intention of restoring some kind of harmony in relationships. In contrast, socially rejected and aggressive children increase their levels of aggression in an attempt to get their own way. They belittle their victims and show little regard or concern for the feelings of the other child. Although this aggressive strategy is immediately success- ful in terms of the child getting what he or she wants, the aggressive child experiences increasing social rejection, which is likely to lead to more aggression, and so on (Coie *et al.* cited in Rutter and Rutter 1993: 171). Children who persist in being hostile with their agemates find themselves suffering increased social isolation.

Aggressive children seem to lack sensitivity to social cues. They are relatively inept in their social interaction with others, eliciting negative responses from peers when they attempt to make interac- tional overtures. The inability to read social cues also seems to be a characteristic of unpopular children. They often read a hostile or negative intent when it is not present. This misreading causes them to react aggressively to situations which never warranted such hostile reactions in the first place. Such misperceptions and inap- propriate responses compound their unpopularity.

Dexter had a violent father who behaved brutally towards his son. Throughout his schooldays, Dexter repeatedly became confused in social situations and often reacted aggressively. On one occasion, aged twelve, he was playing football in the school playground when the ball he had kicked struck a girl. She told him to watch where he was kicking the ball. His friends laughed and said that Dexter fancied her. Suddenly he lost his temper, viciously punching and kicking the girl who ended up in hospital with a cut face and a broken rib.

## Early attachment experiences and the older child's peer relationships

Grossmann and Grossmann's (1991: 105) studies of 10-year-old children and their relationship experiences with their parents and peers confirm the general pattern. Those who had enjoyed secure attachments when younger usually had one or two good, close friends who were viewed as trustworthy and reliable. These children possessed a certain confidence in themselves and their friends. In contrast, 10-year-olds who had experienced insecure attachment relationships in early life 'either had no good friends or reported very many friends without being able to name one. They more often reported problems like being exploited, ridiculed, or excluded from group activities by their peers' (Grossmann and Grossmann 1991: 105)

In some intriguing studies by Kobak and Sceery (1989 cited in Cassidy and Kobak 1988), 53 first-year college students were interviewed. The students were asked to rate themselves and other students along various adjustment parameters. Peers who rated other students already identified by the researchers as avoidant individuals (with 'dismissing' attitudes about their own childhood attachment experiences), saw them as less ego-resilient, more anxious, and more hostile than students identified as secure.

> However, on self-report measures, the avoidant individuals reported no more self-related distress than did secure individuals. This finding was interpreted as representing a cognitive bias among avoidant individuals toward minimizing the acknowledgement of distress or difficulty in adjustment. Avoidant individuals also reported receiving much less social support from their families than did secure individuals . . . There was a general tendency towards 'compulsive self-reliance' based on a deactivation of attachment thoughts and feelings. (Cassidy and Kobak 1988: 309).

The adaptive strategies and inner working models developed by insecure children in order to cope with the anxieties experienced in their relationships with their parents are transferred to their relationships with peers. Insecure children's failure to feel either valued or potent within their primary attachment relationships leaves them inept and socially unskilled when dealing with their agemates.

*Ambivalent children* are inclined to demand too much of their friends. In their anxious need for closeness, attention and intimacy they can be overbearing and ingratiating. Some may seek an exclusive friendship with a popular child who simply is not prepared to limit his or her range of close relationships. Children with a history of ambivalent attachment experiences find that their anxieties make them over-sensitive to the normal ups and downs of relationships. Although they want to be liked, they cannot trust the other or take the friendship for granted. They constantly demand confirmation of the other's regard. They readily perceive rejection and disfavour when no such reactions initially exist. The emotional tides of any relationship make it difficult for them to keep their bearings and so they are inclined to become moody. As friends, they can be very wearing. Their demanding and clinging, cloying and moody behaviour can easily exhaust the interest and good-will of more relaxed, secure children.

Alex's mother suffered violent mood swings. When things were good, she involved Alex in all the fun she was keen to enjoy. But there were also long periods when she felt very low and suicidal, sitting around the house, forgetting to feed Alex or put him to bed. When he was a baby, his nappy would not be changed and he would cry with hunger until a neighbour or a friend or a grandparent would appear and look after him temporarily. By the time he reached school age, Alex was a very disruptive boy in class. He constantly showed off and got into trouble. He would always do whatever other children dared him to do – draw a rude picture on the board, carve his initials on the desk, let down the tyre on a teacher's car – and again, he would find himself in trouble and complain that he was always being unfairly picked on. In play and games, he would always push things one step too far and annoy the other children. When they refused to let him join in, he would go home and sulk, saying that nobody liked him. When he was in this mood he would destroy toys, and once he tried to cut off all his hair 'because he didn't care'.

Children with a history of *avoidant attachment* experiences are even less adept at understanding the demands of peer relationships. They have little experience of the give-and-take and the mutuality of satisfying relationships. Whatever is to be extracted from a relationship has to be demanded or taken by force if necessary. There is that lurking, often aching need for intimacy and recognition but the children have no skills in acquiring such experiences. Aggression only brings rejection and social isolation. For hostile children the world *is* a hostile place. The only way to cope with the repeated hurt of rejection is to develop emotional neutrality and an aggressive independence. And for those with a high threshold of emotional arousal (whether temperamentally inherited or experientially acquired), it means that not only does it take a lot of excitement and stimulation to produce an emotional response but it also explains why their feelings of anxiety and concern remain low in situations where others might experience acute distress. The same mechanism also explains why the more severely disturbed avoidant individual is sometimes capable of quite violent acts of behaviour. It takes more extreme emotional experiences to produce even moderate levels of emotional arousal.

George was five. His smartly dressed mother said she 'couldn't stand him'. She didn't know or understand why, but almost from the day of his birth she said she felt hostile to him. This was not the case with George's two-year-old, pretty, doll-like sister, Danielle, whom she adored. Over the last six months George's behaviour had 'become impossible'. He had stopped talking. He never smiled and, in the words of the social worker, 'behaved like a little automaton, a robot'. He had tried to kill the budgerigar. The 'last straw' was when his mother found him standing close by the electric fire deliberately allowing his legs to burn rather badly, 'and he never made a sound'. Mr Hart, George's father, said he could not understand what was going on and so he spent most days and evenings working in his successful car-body repair business: 'I'm best off out of all this.' George went to live with foster parents.

Feeney *et al.* (1993) assessed attachment styles in adolescents' relationships with the opposite sex; 193 unmarried undergraduates were questioned. Avoidant individuals reported fewer and less intense love experiences than the other groups. They were most likely to say that they had never been in love. They seemed to avoid intimacy, preferring shallow, casual relationships. Students who were assessed as anxious–ambivalent reported frequent but less enduring love relationships. They were the group least likely to have had any interaction with strangers; the fear of rejection means that new relationships are seen as risky and potentially hurtful. Those who were rated as secure tended to have more satisfying and more loving relationships.

## Coping with social relationships

The studies by Hodges and Tizard (Tizard and Hodges 1978; Hodges and Tizard 1989a; Hodges and Tizard 1989b) are particularly informative about the short, medium and long-term impacts of early life social experiences. The authors studied a sample of children who spent much of their preschool years living in a residential nursery. Although physical care at the residential nursery was good, staff turnover was high: 'By the age of 2, an average of 24 different caregivers had looked after them for at least a week; by 4, the average was 50' (Hodges and Tizard 1989a: 53). While at nursery, at age two the children were clingy and diffuse in their attachment behaviour allowing anyone familiar to pick them up. By the time they were four years old, the children had become attention seeking and indiscriminately friendly with the staff who said that the children appeared 'not to care deeply about anyone'. In essence they showed no selective attachment behaviour.

During their third and fourth year, some of the children were adopted (mainly into socially advantaged, well-functioning families), some returned to their biological parents (who were mostly socially disadvantaged and ran discordant and troubled families), while the remainder continued to live in the institution. The institutional and ex-institutional children were also compared with a matched sample of similar aged children from comparable social backgrounds.

At age 16, no long-term effects of early institutionalisation in itself were found on the children's IQ levels. However IQ was affected by the quality of family life into which the children were placed, the positive effects being more pronounced the younger the child at the age of placement. The adopted children (going mainly to middle class homes) achieved higher IQ scores than the children who returned to their biological families (mainly poor, working class) who in turn scored better than the few children who had remained in residential care throughout their lives.

By the time they were eight years old, the adopted children had developed good relationships with their adoptive parents. However, like their peers who had remained in the institution or who had returned to their biological families, they were still inclined to show some social and attentional problems, particularly at school. These behaviours included restlessness, distractability and poor peer relations. These difficulties had lessened by the age of 16, though teachers still noted the presence of at least some of the problems in around 35–50 per cent of the ex-institutional children. When the adopted and 'restored to families' children were compared in adolescence, the adopted children showed slightly greater levels of anxiety and hostility towards adults, though in no sense could they be described as maladjusted. The restored adolescents showed more 'antisocial' types of behaviour and apathy.

When the children were studied at age 16 with reference to their social and family relationships (Hodges and Tizard 1989b), in general the adopted children were functioning much better than their counterparts who had returned to live with their biological parents. Good quality and secure attachments were reported in most of the children who had been adopted in spite of their very poor attachment experiences prior to placement. The biological families to which the other children returned continued to display many disorganised and disturbed relationships as well as having to cope with many social and material adversities. Only about half the biological parents felt that their restored children were strongly attached to them at age 16. The children of this 'restored' group were much more likely to exhibit high levels of behavioural disturbance and many had been in trouble with the police. Nevertheless, both the adopted and restored children shared a number of behaviours which were not present to the same extent in the comparison group of children who had never experienced insitutional care and had remained with their families since birth.

The difficult behaviours shown by all the ex-institutional children, whether adopted or 'restored', included: (i) being more adult-orientated in their relationships; (ii) more likely to have difficulties in peer relationships; (iii) less likely to have a special friend; (iv) less likely to turn to peers for emotional support when anxious; and (v) less likely to be selective in choosing friends. Of the ex-institutional children, whether adopted or restored, 50 per cent showed at least four out of five of these characteristics compared with only 4 per cent of the comparison group.

The adopted 16-year-old children were more likely to have problems in forming deep and selective relationships with their peers rather than displaying any significant psychiatric disorders. They tended to be slightly more anxious and fearful in demanding situations. Although the study has not yet extended beyond the age of 16, it is recognised that poor peer relationships in childhood are a strong predictor of later social difficulties (for example, see Parker and Asher 1987). The research by Hodges and Tizard suggests that the lack of a close, continuous and personalised parent–child relationship during the first few years of life does produce some long-term developmental impairments. The researchers conclude by saying:

the study gives evidence that children who in their first years of life are deprived of close and lasting attachments to adults can make such attachments later. But these do not arise automatically if the child is placed in a family. They depend rather on the adults concerned and how much they nurture such attachments. Yet despite these attachments, certain differences and difficulties in social relationships are found over 12 years after the child has joined a family. These are not related to the kind of family, and appear to have their origins in the children's early experience in institutional care. Since they affect relationship with peers, as well as with adults outside the family, they may have implications for the future adult relationships of these 16-year-olds. (Hodges and Tizard 1989b: 96–7)

## The views of teachers

Teachers develop different types of relationships with securely attached and insecurely attached children. Sroufe (1989a: 92) observed that teachers, who did not know how the children had been assessed by the researchers, expected children who had been assessed as experiencing secure attachments to be well behaved, follow rules, and generally be easy to manage.

> In contrast, children with histories of avoidance were shown more discipline and control, lower expectations for compliance, less warmth, and, at times, even anger. Children with histories of anxious resistant attachment were also controlled more. Yet they were often shown more nurturance and tolerance; that is, teachers, perceiving their emotional immaturity, made more allowances for them, accepting minor infractions of classroom rules and indulging their dependency needs. (Sroufe 1989a: 92)

If the teacher became angry at all, it was most likely to be with those who had a history of avoidant attachment experiences. The anxiously attached children also show more emotional dependence on their teachers along with lower levels of curiosity, lower self-esteem and self-confidence, and less enthusiasm and persistence in problem solving. Overall, 'in terms of the developmental issues of exploration, mastery, autonomy, initiative, and peer competence, anxious attachments fail to serve the child's development' (Sroufe 1989b: 117). Anxiously attached children experience much distress and misery as they attempt to develop and sustain relationships with others.

**Relationship with others**

Children who either lacked secure attachments or suffered disturbed early relationships continue to experience relationship difficulties through into adult life. We have already learned that children reared in institutions from an early age often show indiscriminate friendliness towards adults and peers. They also lack social inhibition. In adulthood, women who had been raised in group foster homes often found making and sustaining social relationships difficult (Quinton and Rutter 1988). This adversely affected their ability to make close friendships, manage sexual love relationships and become competent parents. The evidence is increasingly strong that failure to make close, selective and secure attachments in infancy plays a significant part in people's ability to develop close relationships in adult life.

In their review of the research literature, Rutter and Rutter (1993: 159) point out that children's ability to be empathetic and responsive to other people is influenced by the way the children themselves have been treated. The children of parents who talk about and consider with them what other children might be thinking and feeling, tend to show more comforting behaviour to others. Children who have been physically abused are inclined to react aggressively to other people's distress and upset. If children witness family conflict but are not abused themselves, they show distress and concern if they see other people being angry. 'It is clearly *not* true,' assert Rutter and Rutter (1993: 159), 'that it does not matter if parents quarrel in front of young children. Interestingly, children are sensitive to whether or not conflicts are resolved; this is more so with young school-age children than preschoolers.'

**Adult peer relationships**

*Secure adults* tend to see themselves as reasonably confident and socially competent. Self-evaluations are positive. They also regard other people as generally well-intentioned, acceptable and trustworthy (Hazan and Shaver 1987; Collins and Read 1990). Secure adults desire intimate relationships with others. They seek a balance within the relationship between closeness and autonomy (Collins and Read 1990: 65). Secure adults are good at acknowledging their own distress and are happy to seek support from other people, particularly those with whom they are in close relationship.

In contrast to adults who display secure personalities are those who exhibit anxious, ambivalent and avoidant personalities. 'One of the most robust findings in the adult attachment literature,' record Simpson and Rholes (1994: 200), 'is that avoidant and anxious/ ambivalent persons tend to be involved in less satisfying relationships.'

*Anxious, ambivalent people* are inclined to be more cautious and wary in their social relationships. Other people are thought to be complex and difficult to read. Anxious people are also more fatalistic and feel that they have little ability to control where life takes them. Anxious, ambivalent adults desire close relationships but they cannot enirely trust the other person. They constantly seek approval and reassurance; they also fear and attempt to avoid rejection. They are therefore alert and extra-sensitive to any signs of disapproval by others. Thus, close relationships with other people are sought but they provoke feelings of uncertainty – 'I want to be loved but maybe I will be ignored, abandoned and hurt'. This uncertainty produces feelings of ambivalence and so the attachment figure is often resented even as he or she is desired.

It is also the case that ambivalent people tend to expect the worst; they are quick to perceive negatives and slow to acknowledge positives in their relationships with others. This approach, of course, becomes self-fulfilling. The clinging, possessive, jealous individual often drives partners away, which seems to confirm the mental model's expectations that other people are unreliable and rejecting. These pressures often see them quickly entering into relationships of fierce intimacy in which personal autonomy is, in the short term at least, willingly and easily sacrificed. Under stress, anxious and ambivalent adults find their emotional state becomes very heightened. In desperate attempts to ensure that partners or other people notice, respond and take control, their levels of distress, anxiety and anger rise rapidly. For example, being left alone by a partner may produce feelings of intense anger, anxiety and frustration. Ambivalent and anxious people respond more to the emotional factors in a situation than the cognitive elements.

*Avoidant adults*, according to the findings of Collins and Read (1990), are much more likely to hold negative beliefs about human nature. They are suspicious of other people's motives and often see them as untrustworthy and not dependable. Although avoidant adults have strong views of their self-worth and assertiveness, they are less sure of themselves in social relationships and on the whole do not see themselves as interpersonally orientated. In social relationships they attempt to maintain an emotional distance and a lack of commitment. Avoidant personalities find it difficult to deal with distress in interpersonal behaviour. Intimacy is feared and emotional independence valued. This strategy is effective insofar as it helps people avoid rejection. 'Avoidant adults,' report Collins and Read (1990: 65), 'may also place greater weight on non-attachment related goals, such as achievement in school or in a career' (also see Hazan and Shaver 1990). There is a general preference for tackling social situations cognitively rather than emotionally. Experiences are 'intellectualised' and feelings tend to be explained.

Both these defences are a form of control, a way of keeping potentially overwhelming emotions at bay. Avoidant adults tend to manage stress by cutting themselves off from their own emotional reactions. They neither seek nor trust emotional support. They are fearful of feelings, sensing that they represent weakness and help-lessness. There is also great sensitivity to signs of intrusion or control by others.

Mrs Allen visited her local social work department with her two daughters, aged four and six. The girls were quiet and unresponsive. Their mother told the social worker that she wanted the girls to be fostered as she could no longer cope with home life: 'I'm cracking up; I've got to get out.' She then placed a sealed envelope in front of the social worker and promptly left the office. A short letter inside the envelope explained that life with her husband was impossible. Mrs Allen said that he was a weird, frightening man who controlled the girls as well as herself 'in a cool, kind of quiet way although there are times when he loses his temper and becomes totally mad'. He had very firm and narrow views about family life and she believed the future for their daughters was bleak under his care. It was no use her trying to escape with the children because he would always find them. She added that on no account should the social workers return the girls to their father. Although he was a very plausible man, he was also dangerous and on past occasions he had subjected the girls to severe physical punishment when they did not behave as he wished. The girls were placed with foster parents.

Two days later Mr Allen, an unemployed school teacher, visited the office. He was neatly dressed, extremely articulate and spoke in precise tones. He said that he could not allow his daughters to be raised by the local authority because he had been in foster homes and children's homes on a number of occasions himself as a child. His wife, explained Mr Allen, was an emotionally unstable woman who, no doubt, had told the social workers that he was not a very nice person. She was not to be believed. He had delayed getting in touch with the social work department because he had spent the last two days studying the 1989 Children Act in order to understand his position and his rights. Now that he was fully conversant with the legislation, he felt able to proceed on an equal footing with the social workers who 'would not be able to catch him out on any legal technicality'. Later that week the social worker dealing with the case learned that Mr Allen had only recently moved to the town and that the family had been known to the social work department in the city where they had been living previously. The health visitor in that city had expressed worries that the girls appeared 'constantly switched off and never laughed, never played'. Not once in these early proceedings did Mr Allen ask about the welfare of his daughters or the whereabouts of his wife. He conducted all his dealings with the social worker in a very formal manner and without any concern, anger or emotion.

Collins and Read (1990: 74), after reviewing their own studies, conclude that adults with different attachment styles explain and interpret the *same event* in very different ways. People's relationship histories generate different inner working models and social expectations. The models guide, and to some extent, provoke certain types of interpersonal behaviour and social relationships which then become characteristic of secure, ambivalent and avoidant attachment styles through childhood into adulthood. We are prone to create and re-create our social environment. Our working models are apt to become self-fulfilling.

## Conclusion

In general, research into peer relationships shows that particular environments, experiences and behaviours are often maintained throughout an individual's childhood. Disturbances in the quality of early relationships is strongly associated with difficulties in conducting and sustaining social relationships in later childhood, adolescence and adulthood.

# 10

# Relationships with self

Social development not only affects the way we relate to other people, it also influences the way we feel about ourselves. We now examine such feelings about self as they occur in childhood, adolescence and adulthood. It seems that many personal states and emotional conditions can only be understood in terms of our own relationship history. Low self-esteem, low self-confidence and depression often have their roots in disturbed early childhood relationships.

### Self-worth and self-esteem in children

Sroufe (1989a) describes a number of studies which report on the level of children's self-esteem. Whereas securely attached children persisted longer with problems and handled setbacks reasonably well (they continued to 'expect well'), insecurely attached children showed frustration and anxiety and easily gave up in demanding situations. The securely attached children showed resilience, they were cheerful and popular, co-operative and resourceful.

Children who had a history of anxious resistant (ambivalent) attachments were unduly attention seeking. They tended to be tense and impulsive, becoming either easily frustrated or passive and helpless. Children with histories of avoidant attachment experiences displayed feelings of low self-worth, isolation, and angry rejection. 'Teachers' ratings in the preschool placed them low on emotional health/self-worth and confidence' with the suggestion that such children were more likely to see themselves as bad and unworthy (Sroufe 1989a: 87–8). Teachers describe these children as emotionally insulated, anti-social and attention seeking.

Sroufe (1983 cited in Sroufe 1989a) gives a nice example of two children dancing to music in a preschool setting. As new children arrived, one boy asked another child to dance. The child said no and the little boy withdrew to a corner and sulked. A small girl also asked a new entrant to dance and she, too, was rejected. But she skipped on and asked another child who agreed to join her in the dance. The girl had a history of secure attachment experiences. She did not feel personally 'rejected' and her successful second try confirmed that she was a 'worthy' individual and that people would respond to her. In contrast, the little boy experienced intense rejection. He cut himself off from any further opportunities 'to disconfirm his model of himself as unworthy. He had a history of avoidant attachment' (Sroufe 1989a: 88).

## Adolescence

Erikson (1959) believed that industry and responsibility begin to characterise the behaviour and outlook of adolescents. Vaillant and Vaillant (1981) measured the presence of these behaviours in a large number of teenagers. They looked at school performance and out-of-school activities; they examined work habits and job commitments. The adolescents were prospectively followed through into adulthood. High scores on the relevant measures were shown to be associated with cohesive, supportive and positive family relationships and be good at predicting the maintenance of warm relationships and work success in adulthood. Research into adolescence repeatedly recognises a strong association between stable, harmonious family life with fair and consistent discipline and 'psychologically integrated, productive, dependable, self-assertive, considerate and non-impulsive' teenagers who carry these characteristics through into adult life (Belsky and Pensky 1988: 205).

One of the main developmental tasks of adolescence is to complete the final phase of psychological separation from the family and emerge with an independent identity. Fahlberg (1991: 108) sees the adolescent trying to answer four questions about himself or herself: '(1) Who am I? (2) Where do I belong? (3) What can I do, or be? and (4) What do I believe in?'

The separation process and the young person's role and sense of self will run more or less smoothly depending on the individual's relationship history. At the same time adolescents separate emotionally from their families, they are reinvesting in peer relationships. Disengagement from parents and the family is necessary if independent and robust identity formation is to be achieved. And with this separation is the personal and social requirement that the individual shifts from external controls to internal controls of their social conduct. All of these developmental tasks, of course, are confused and compounded by the young person's emerging sexuality. Throughout childhood there is a gradual shift in attachment behaviour away from parents to peers, and eventually, in adulthood, to intimate sexual partnerships. The 'secure base' moves out of the home and into peer friendships.

Looking somewhat paradoxical at first sight, the more secure the child's attachment history, the easier it is for him or her to separate and achieve an independent, well-integrated personality. If security leads to coherent personality structures and if they in turn promote social competence and confidence, adolescents with secure attachment histories have a deeply founded and well-integrated personality which is able to handle the demands of separation and independence and relationships beyond the family. Adolescents who have experienced insecure and anxious attachment histories find both the separation and the requirement to meet their relationship needs outside the family more difficult and disturbing.

Children placed for adoption in their teens find themselves in a peculiar and developmentally contradictory position. They are expected to form a new attachment relationship with their adoptive parents at the very time they might normally expect to relax this relationship in favour of increased independence and separation. The adoption of older children poses particular problems of integration and separation for both parents and children. These issues represent extra developmental 'tasks' for adopted children and their parents (Brodzinsky 1987; Howe 1992).

## Social origins of depression

The work of Brown and Harris (1978; 1986; 1989) offers a highly detailed and thorough study into the relationship between poor parental care in childhood and the feelings of low self-esteem and the generation of a negative self-concept in adult women. Although they believe that these early life experiences themselves do not directly cause depression, Brown and Harris argue that they do make women psychologically vulnerable when faced with stress, upset and difficulty. When a vulnerable personality experiences a negative life event, the result can be depression. Furthermore, children of depressed mothers who are on the receiving end of their parents' negativity in turn can go on to develop low self-esteem and a negative self-concept (Hammen 1990 cited in Rutter and Rutter 1993).

In broad terms, there are two major influences on a mother's (or caregiver's) quality of parenting: (i) the type of parent–infant relationship she experienced herself as a child, and (ii) the amount, or lack of emotional support she currently receives from other adults with whom she is in close relation.

Brown and Harris's first study (1978) was carried out on a population of London women living in Camberwell. They looked at the psychosocial factors that appeared to play a part in the onset of depression. The researchers identified particular severe experiences of loss as 'provoking agents'. If these interacted with other background 'vulnerability factors', the chances of a woman becoming depressed increased. In other words, a vulnerable woman has a higher risk of becoming depressed if she has an enhanced susceptibility to life stressors.

Four vulnerability factors were indentified as particularly important: (i) current absence of a confiding and supporting relationship with a partner; (ii) loss of mother before the age of eleven by death or long-term separation; (iii) three or more children aged under 15 years living at home; and (iv) no job outside the home. The first two factors are of particular interest to attachment theorists. For example, depression was more prevalent in women who had lost their mother before the age of eleven and who subsequently failed to form a close, caring and supportive relationship with another interested adult. *Lack of care* in childhood and indifference after the loss of a mother increased the likelihood of depression. Indeed, lack of care proved to be the childhood adversity which was most related to depression in adulthood. Harris (1993: 97) explains this, saying:

> Since the regard of others is often a source of one's own self-regard, those exposed to deficient care in childhood are likely to place a lower estimate on their own worth and will thus prove more vulnerable to depression in the face of provoking agents in adulthood.

The second two factors involve women's roles. If women received positive experiences in a role outside the home, this might balance some of the negative experiences suffered in the home. A sense of hopelessness is said to characterise the depressive experience (Harris and Bifulco 1991: 235). The poorer the self-image, the greater the feeling of hopelessness. When self-reliance disappears and you feel that the world is not under your control, depression is more likely. 'We see an important link,' said Brown *et al.* (1986: 259), 'between mastery of problems and self-esteem, but any factor contributing to low mastery would be relevant.' Lack of care and loss of mother make children feel that no matter what they do or how they behave, they are unable to control events and what happens to them. This increases feelings of fatalism and hopelessness and leaves the individual prey to setback, stress and depression throughout the life cycle. Those who fail to find social support and intimacy in their adult relationships are particularly vulnerable.

Later studies elaborated and refined these initial findings. Pre-marital pregnancy was highly associated with later depression in women who had lost a mother and suffered a lack of care after the loss (Harris *et al.* 1987). If a woman also had an undependable partner in whom she could not confide and who provided no emotional support, this further increased her susceptibility to feelings of hopelessness and depression.

## Loss

Parkes (1985; 1986; Parkes and Weiss 1983) has made extensive studies of the grieving process. To some extent, the way people mourn is a product of their past relationship and loss experiences on the one hand and the quality of their current social relationships on the other. Two factors in particular affect the way a loss is experienced: 'the strength of the relationship that is being broken and the abruptness of the separation' (Fahlberg 1991: 142). This formula is true for children and adults. Sable (1989) looked at widows who had lost their husbands in the previous 1–3 years. She found that the women with the more secure early attachment histories coped better with their bereavement and experienced less distress or depression. Several types of grief reaction can be identified.

A sudden loss is experienced as an *unexpected grief* by most people and it normally precipitates them into a state of shock and disbelief.

People who characteristically use *avoidant-attachment style* behaviours and show 'compulsive self-reliance' in their relationships often display *delayed grief* reactions. The typical attempts to be emotionally self-reliant and wary about forming intimate relationships means that the loss of someone close, whether by death, departure or divorce, triggers the usual defence mechanisms of emotional shut-down and distancing. In the short term at least, the person suffering the loss may not cry or appear to be unduly upset. Those who fail to grieve remain vulnerable to future losses. Seemingly exaggerated grief reactions to a loss experience (say, rejection by one's lover) can sometimes be accounted for when it is realised that the individual never really acknowledged or adjusted to the earlier loss of a significant attachment relationship (say, the death of one's mother).

Mrs Rayal suddenly fell into a deep state of depression. She felt suicidal, extremely irritable with her two young sons and that her life 'was out of control'. She said that her husband's recent vasectomy had triggered her depression because it meant that she would not be able to have the daughter she had always wanted. In discussion, it was learned that Mrs Rayal's father was killed in a road traffic accident while she was abroad on holiday. She did not get on with her mother whom she described as 'cold and correct . . . She never once gave me a cuddle when I was a little girl, preferring instead my younger brother who, in her eyes, could do no wrong.' Within two months of her father dying, Mrs Rayal suffered a miscarriage of a baby girl. She soldiered on, 'never having enough time to grieve, though a vague feeling of guilt wouldn't go away'.

If the attachment style is one of *ambivalence* in which the other person is needed but proves to be emotionally inconsistent, erratic and unpredictable, the feelings of anxiety engendered result in a turbulent, highly ambivalent conflict-ridden relationship in which there are equal measures of desperate clinging and resentful anger. If the other person is lost, the bereaved partner experiences both guilt and self-blame (because anger and hostility had been a constant feature of the relationship) and acute pain (because there is now no-one emotionally available).

In cases of *chronic grief*, individuals cannot seem to escape their feelings of despair and depression. It may be that their relationship with the lost other was in fact characterised by deep feelings of ambivalence. People who have been in a highly dependent relationship with their parents or their spouse may experience chronic grief. The simmering resentment that may have lurked beneath the surface of the relationship is still difficult to acknowledge and so the true range of feelings associated with the grief fail to receive proper expression and therefore remain unresolved.

Out of such observations, Parkes (1991: 288) formulates a general pattern of grief reactions in adults and links each type to early parenting experiences:

1. Anxious and conflicted parents predispose their children to become insecure and very anxious after bereavement.
2. Absent or rejecting parents predispose their children to depression after bereavement in adult life.
3. Negative parental influences interfere with the development of trust in self and/or others. Low 'self-trust' predisposes to 'excessive grief' after bereavement and leaves the person unusually vulnerable to the death of a parent. Low 'other-trust' predisposes to a tendency to avoid others and to minimize grieving after bereavement.
4. Conflicts between parents in childhood increase the risk of marital conflicts when the children marry, and render them vulnerable to 'conflicted grief' when their parents die.

By way of an example, Parkes (1991: 285–7) describes the case of 41-year-old Florence whose elderly parents both died within the space of eight months. Florence was experiencing severe grief, she had lost confidence, was sleeping badly and was feeling extremely anxious and tense. She was finding it difficult to talk about her feelings although her parents were constantly on her mind. It was felt to be unusual for a daughter to be reacting so badly to the death of two parents who were in their eighties. What factors contributed to her disturbed grieving reaction?

The patient was the seventh of eight children and seems to have had an ambivalent attachment to her mother. 'Neither parent had been been able to show affection or to hug or cuddle her, yet they did seem to care about her and she described them both as over-protective and inclined to worry excessively about her health and safety' (Parkes 1991: 285). It appeared that Florence's mother was insecure. She was prone to worry and she was inconsistent in her care, although according to Florence she constantly interfered in her life. Florence felt closer to her father whom she described as a placid man, although he was unhappy in his relationship with his wife. He left home when Florence was aged eight, but she retained regular contact with her father.

Florence was an insecure and anxious child who lacked confidence and was something of a loner. 'She sees herself as having been a helpless, timid, and passive child who was easily upset by separation from her parents. People regarded her as delicate and fragile yet she was always looking after others' (Parkes 1991: 286). At school she under-achieved.

When she was 25 she married a publican and had three children. She was very close, even dependent on her husband and was intolerant of any separation from him. In spite of its apparent success, the marriage confirmed Florence's feelings of fragility and dependence. Her two sons were difficult: one was a 'tearaway' and the other was 'highly strung'.

Her brothers and sisters gave her father a surprise 80th birthday party. Shortly afterwards he died. Florence did not attend the party because there were tense feelings between her and some of her siblings. Her failure to see her father increased Florence's feelings of guilt. In the following months, some of her sisters accused her of not putting in her fair share of looking after their mother. Two months later her mother died and this marked the beginning of Florence's difficulties. Her long-established defences were breached and she could no longer cope. It was only when she could eventually recognise and acknowledge her feelings of deep ambivalence about her mother and her childhood that Florence could continue with the grieving process and work towards a full recovery.

Rutter and Rutter (1993: 131) identify four factors which complicate the grieving process and adversely affect behaviour. First, they note the consequences of losing someone with whom one had a dependent or ambivalent attachment relationship. Second, they mention the impact of the untimely death of someone to whom one was close. Third, they observe that if the loss occurs at the same time other upsets and stresses are being experienced (such as a job loss or abortion), disorganised behaviour increases even further. And fourth, the authors remind us that if someone has experienced earlier losses which have not been completely resolved (death of an abusive father, a mother who committed suicide, an aborted foetus), the new loss will be amplified and intensified by the old unresolved feelings.

It is the combination of the loss of a loved one *and* the lack of a current love relationship that is particularly potent in intensifying the feelings of pain and grief. The corollary seems to be if the more extreme feelings associated with grief are to be mitigated, the availability of social support and other intimate relationships are of considerable benefit to those suffering the loss (Rutter and Rutter 1993: 132).

## Compulsive self-reliance

Whereas the anxiously attached child may grow up and experience poor self-esteem and low self-confidence as well as exhibit a variety of neurotic behaviours including ambivalent dependent relationships, anorexia nervosa and depression, the future behaviour of the child who experienced an avoidant pattern of attachment is very different. Having experienced rejection and believing that nothing he or she could do ever affected the emotional availability of other people, the avoidant child learns to be compulsively self-reliant. If wanting close relationships only brings hurt and pain, it seems better to learn to do without them.

For these children, emotional investment and interest in other people is a risky venture. We might see the beginnings of such reactions in the 'stiff upper lip' of children sent away to boarding school at an early age. But such a defence is potentially fragile. It means that intimate relationships are avoided or it might mean that they are handled casually or even badly. However, there is still a deep underlying desire for love, security and support. Too much stress and the veneer of self-reliance is liable to crack.

> Many such persons have had experiences not unlike those of individuals who develop anxious attachment; but they have reacted to them differently by inhibiting attachment feeling and behaviour and disclaiming, perhaps even mocking, any desire for close relationships with anyone who might provide love and care. It requires no great insight to realize, however, that they are deeply distrustful of close relationships and terrified of allowing themselves to rely on anyone else, in some cases in order to avoid the pain of being rejected and in others to avoid being subjected to pressure to become someone's else's caretaker. (Bowlby 1979: 138)

**The long-term effects of sexual abuse**

Much evidence has now been gathered to show that the experience of being sexually abused in childhood also seems to be linked with problems in functioning during adulthood. The risk of psychiatric illness appears to be greater for those who were either physically or sexually abused as children. For example, Riekar and Carmen (1986: 362) found that 43 per cent of the psychiatric in-patients in a hospital had been subjected to either physical or sexual abuse during childhood. They also observed that that 'in an effort to reduce the inevitable feelings of helplessness and vulnerability, victims frequently tend to assume responsibility for the abuse, thereby restoring the illusion of control; alternatively, they may redefine and minimize the event, thereby protecting a view of the world as just and orderly' (Riekar and Carmen 1986: 362). The authors go on to describe the long-term effects of experiencing sexual abuse as a child: 'This is observed clinically in the form of low self-esteem, self-hatred, affective instability, poor control of aggressive impulses, and disturbed relationships with inability to trust and to behave in self-protective ways' (Riekar and Carmen 1986: 368)

Other researchers have confirmed this broad picture. The work of Finkelhor and his associates has been particularly important in exploring the relationship between sexual trauma in childhood and later psychological ill-health (Finkelhor *et al.* 1986). In reviewing the long-term effects on women who have been victimised as girls, Browne and Finkelhor (1986: 72) suggest that they are more likely to experience depression; exhibit self-destructive behaviour; have feelings of anxiety, loneliness, emptiness and poor self-esteem; abuse drugs and alcohol; and form relationships with men who may well subject them to further sexual and physical violence.

Adult victims often find it difficult to trust other people and sexual behaviour is either inhibited or exaggerated. There is an all-pervading feeling of powerlessness and an absence of control over one's own body and fate. As girls, their body space was repeatedly invaded and nothing they did seemed to stop it. A disturbing mixture of shame, guilt, confusion, fear and badness continually distorted their psychological development. However, a minority do pull through and appear not to suffer too much psychological disturbance. They exhibit a resilience that appears to see them through into adulthood (see Chapter 14).

Even so, the figures cited in many studies paint a grim picture of upset and long-term dysfunctioning in women who have suffered the trauma of childhood sexual abuse. The proportion of such women in clinical samples is particularly high. In one study, 82 per cent of women who were diagnosed as suffering 'multiple disorder syndrome' had been sexually abused (Coons and Milstein 1986). Briere (1984 cited in Smith 1991) reported that 43 per cent of the 153 women who visited a community health counselling centre had been subjected to some form of sexual abuse as girls. And of the sexually abused women, 31 per cent (compared with 19 per cent of non-abused clients) had shown a desire to hurt and injure themselves.

Smith (1991) in his interviews with women who had been sexually abused as girls, asked them to reflect on how they felt the experience had affected their lives. Sheila said that sexual relationships were very difficult for her and that sexual feelings felt destructive and dangerous. Mary said how the abuse 'buggers you up altogether. I mean you feel dirty; I can't ever remember feeling clean, right from when I was a child; I thought no boy is going to want to marry me or know me. You've lost all your value in your own eyes – you're a thing; you stop being a person' (Smith 1991: 76). Janet lost trust in everyone: 'It made me go very much into myself,' she said.

Many women said that they simply could not remember large periods of their childhood. It was a time they had blocked from memory. Mary, who was sexually abused by her mother, says 'I can remember my life until I was 7, and then from 7 'til 10 I cannot remember a thing' (Smith 1991: 83). Their life-stories, and therefore their full understanding of self, remains incomplete so long as these gaps continue to exist in their lives. Counselling and work with sexually abused women often attempt to help them remember these traumatic times. They are encouraged to re-tell their story in such a way that they no longer blame themselves but instead learn to blame their abusers and to feel the anger and sadness that is appropriate to the experience. We cannot deal with our emotions until we reconnect with them. However, this can be very painful and requires a relationship in which the abused women can feel safe and accepted.

Christine's story illustrates how someone defends herself against the trauma of sexual abuse. She said that she 'switches off' her emotions; like an automaton, she merely obeys; but she trusts no-one and has no-one to whom she can turn. This is how Christine reflects on her childhood and the impact it has had on her as an adult woman:

When I was a child there was just no-one I could trust. I was so used to being told what to do, and living in an atmosphere where there are these two people that you've got to please come what may, and you never know what's going to please them. So one minute it could be one thing and the next minute something else; so you would be continually battling. And because no-one asked you what you wanted, I got the idea that all adults were like that. And it kept happening with so many different people, that I thought that all adults must be like that. So there was nobody I could approach at all. That leads you not to trust anybody; it also leads you to switch off yourself – oh it's such and such a situation so I'll react in this way; this isn't how I want to react but this is how best to react in this situation. But you almost stop thinking logically, you almost have no emotion, liberty or your independence. You don't even learn to have opinions . . . It's like the whole of your life is stifled. (Smith 1991: 77)

Lesley's emotional history was doubly complicated. She was sexually abuse by her step-father during her early teens before he eventually left the home when she was fifteen. She also recalls that she thought that she got on well with her mother until the next man appeared in her life at which point her mother's interest became entirely centred on the new relationship. At the age of 29, Lesley drank heavily, found it extremely difficult to control her temper, and was regularly in trouble with the police for being drunk or violent. She became particularly aggressive when anybody taunted her lesbian partner.

She refused to deal with male authority figures (police officers, probation officers, doctors) although she seemed to get on well with women who were in such roles. In her relationships with her partner and women professionals, Lesley appeared both vulnerable and petulant; anxious to please and yet inclined to be easily upset, with constant accusations that the other person did not like her. Typically, she would escalate her demanding and annoying behaviour until the other person either lost her temper or rejected her. It was then that Lesley felt that her suspicions about close relationships were confirmed. Her social worker described Lesley as 'wanting to be tough, completely hostile to men, often exasperating but scared of being on her own'.

## Conclusion

Internal psychological states and our ability to cope with the external demands of life have roots which reach right back into childhood.

The robustness of our early internal representations of self and others lays down the pattern of our future psychological strengths and weaknesses; it helps define the kind of person we become and feel ourselves to be. Our levels of confidence and self-esteem are sensitively linked to the way we were valued and loved in childhood. Feelings of competence and potency depend heavily on early support, recognition and encouragement. When children feel that no matter what they think or feel or do, they are not able to control what happens to them, physically or emotionally, a feeling of fatalism and helplessness sets in. Attachment relationships in which physical or sexual abuse took place often leave the individual with feelings of passivity and worthlessness. Early attachment relationships which were lost or broken leave people feeling that they cannot control the important things in their lives. Without support they remain emotionally vulnerable to setbacks and upsets. For those who feel hopeless and helpless, depression is often the psychological result.

# 11

# Relationships with society

Although not all disturbed children grow up into anti-social adults, most adults who regularly commit crimes or drink excessively or exhibit seriously unacceptable social behaviour have suffered disturbed relationships during their childhood. The complex evidence that attempts to link childhood adversity with adult social pathology is briefly reviewed in this chapter. A developmental perspective is providing psychologists with an increasingly refined outlook which is helping them throw much light on the causes of behaviours such as crime, alcohol abuse, and other conduct disorders (Le Blanc and Loeber 1993). It is broadly true that an unhappy childhood can lead to socially problematic behaviour, but the outcome is by no means inevitable or clear-cut.

**Personal feelings and public concerns**

There are types of behaviour upon which society and its agents frown. Many behaviours are defined as illegal. Individuals who break the law or behave in an anti-social manner find themselves having to relate to society in some formal way. Those who commit crimes may be sent to prison. People who drink excessively may be moved to special clinics. Anti-social, problematic adolescents and adults account for a large amount of police, welfare and health service time and money. Developmental psychologists have explored the relationship between child experiences and adult behaviour and found some interesting associations. It seems that there are both 'straight' and 'deviant' developmental pathways from childhood to adulthood (Robins and Rutter 1990a).

There are two broad categories of childhood difficulty:

1. those in which the child's behaviour is directed externally, usually with an excess of aggression and exploitation, including stealing, violence and lying; and
2. those in which emotions are directed inwards so that the child appears emotionally withdrawn and inhibited with a tendency to avoid the demands of intimacy and social relationships.

Boys are more likely than girls to respond to stress and adversity by directing their behaviour outwards. This 'externalised' response is seen in oppositional types of behaviour, including aggression, stealing and disobedience. Girls on the other hand are more likely, though not always, to react to adversity by internalising the difficulty and feeling distressed.

Conduct problems of children have been closely associated with poor quality early life experiences. They refer to a collection of anti-social behaviours including aggressiveness, truancy, disobedience, immaturity of emotional responses, temper-tantrums, non-compliance, stealing and lying. In broad terms all these behaviours describe children who are opposing the prevailing rules of either family, school or community life (Greenberg and Speltz 1988). Furthermore, children with conduct problems are at greater risk of developing into juvenile delinquents and adult criminals. However, it is more accurate to say that while not all children with conduct problems develop disorders in adulthood, nearly all adults with an anti-social personality disorder exhibited conduct problems in childhood.

In the introduction to their book on the nature and origin of 'straight and devious pathways from child to adulthood', Robins and Rutter (1990b) say:

> A syndrome of adverse outcomes, including crime, low occupational achievement, substance abuse, and marital instability, is clearly predicted by a child's antisocial, noncooperative, or confrontive behaviour combined with pathology in the family rearing, as indicated by parents' psychiatric illness, crime, and violent or erratic child-rearing practices. (Robins and Rutter 1990b: xiii)

Social environmental influences seem to account for much of the delinquent behaviour shown by children and adolescents. Poor quality relationships and insecure attachments in early childhood are closely correlated with the subsequent development of behaviour problems. Two causal mechanisms stand out in the research literature:

1.  the *lack* of personalised care-giving such as might be experienced by institution-reared children; and
2.  the *presence* of discordant and disturbed family relationships.

Boys who are hyperactive, impulsive and inattentive and who have poor relationships are also likely to show learning difficulties, and poor cognitive and academic functioning as well as criminality and delinquency during adolescence. Such boys usually have been reared in families in which there has been tension and poor quality of social relationships between family members. Reitsma-Street *et al.* (1985) found that within the same family delinquent boys experienced poorer and generally more negative relationships with their parents than their non-delinquent brothers. Moreover, if they still exhibit aggression, lack of concentration, poor peer relationships and delinquent behaviours at age thirteen, boys are highly likely to experience adjustment problems as adults, including criminality, alcohol abuse and psychiatric illness (Magnusson and Bergman 1990). It is worth mentioning that problems in peer relationships, particularly rejection by peers, is one of the most reliable predictors of later psychological disorder.

Rutter and Giller (1983) quote extensive evidence that delinquency and aggression are associated with the following (also see Patterson 1982, cited in Rutter and Rutter 1993):

1.  families who row a lot and are in a general state of discord;
2.  parents who have weak relationships with their children;
3.  parents who fail to supervise and discipline their children adequately, and where there is lack of 'house rules' so that there are no clear expectations of what can and cannot be done;
4.  parents who tend to nag and shout but who show no consistency in following through disciplinary decisions and who fail to differentiate between praising good behaviour and punishing bad;
5.  criminality in other members of the family, including parents and siblings, and;
6.  large families who live in socially deprived neighbourhoods.

The parents of aggressive delinquents often punish and threaten their children when they, as parents, feel irritable with the high levels of tension and conflict that characterise their family life. Parental coercion and physical abuse seems to produce children who try to solve their own conflicts and distress by the use of force, violence and aggression (for example, see Dodge *et al.* 1990).

More effective parents tend to show firm control as well as affection, interest and responsiveness when their children are in need. They also communicate openly, clearly and constructively with their children when they have problems to solve or difficulties to face. Several studies have examined the consequences of parents relating to their young adolescent children in a respectful and egalitarian manner. The parents show evidence of joint decision-making and a responsiveness to the child's input and point of view. Relationships which display these qualities appear to promote flexibility and autonomy in the adolescent child (Grotevant and Cooper 1985; Fleeson 1988, cited in Sroufe 1989a). Overall, low offending rates in, for example, adolescence and early adulthood, is associated with stable and high levels of attachment to parents, stable and high levels of parental supervision, commitment to school and education, low marital conflict, involvement of fathers in their sons' leisure activities, and non-conflictual intimate relationships (Le Blanc and Loeber 1993).

## Hyperactivity, impulsivity and attention deficit

McGee *et al.* (1985 and 1984, cited in Farrington *et al.* 1990) managed to refine some of the assocations between adverse early experiences and future conduct problems. They showed that while many aggressive boys had experienced rejection, family disturbance and had been separated from their parents, boys who were diagnosed as hyperactive, inattentive and impulsive had a history of poor reading and intellectual ability. Of course, many boys were both aggressive and inattentive.

Loney *et al.* (1982 cited in Farrington *et al.* 1990) who followed up 135 boys found that aggressive 9-year-olds were most likely to become aggressive and delinquent 14-year-olds, whereas hyper-activity in 9-year-olds was a good predictor of poor academic performances during adolescence. Farrington *et al.* (1990: 76–7) concluded that hyperactivity, impulsiveness and inattentiveness were 'particularly related to criminal parents, low intelligence, and large family size', while conduct problems were 'particularly related to poor supervision and poor parenting . . . and disruptions in family functioning'. Both 'hyperactivity–impulsiveness–inattentiveness' and conduct problems in childhood were strong predictors of future chronic offending, though the early background factors were different in each case. Of particular interest is the observation that the hyperactive children had been described as difficult to manage from the first two years of their life.

Farrington (1986) has also demonstrated a stepwise continuity in anti-social behaviour. Children who showed troublesome and daring behaviour between the ages of 8 and 10 were very likely to commit offences throughout their adolescence. Reviewing Farrington's work, Le Blanc and Loeber (1993: 252) write:

> Farrington identified four factors during late childhood (economic deprivation, family criminality, parental mishandling, and school failure) that were significantly associated with troublesome or daring behaviour at age 8–10. All of these factors independently predicted conviction in the juvenile years. Convictions in the young adult years (18–20) were best predicted by two former predictors, family criminality measured at age 10 and economic deprivation measured at age 14, as well as two new predictors, truancy at 12–14, and delinquent friends at age 14. Economic deprivation at age 14 continued to predict adult offending, together with two new predictors at age 18, unstable job record and anti-establishment attitude.

## Behaviour and parental absence

McCord (1990) has examined the impact of family structure and parental behaviour on children's future behaviour. She defined 'mother's competence' as efficacy of mother's efforts at discipline, her self-confidence, affection for her son, and her role as a mother. 'Father's interaction' with the family was defined as 'mother's esteem for the father, father's esteem for the mother, parental conflict, father's affection for his son, and father's aggressiveness' (McCord 1990: 120). A third dimension, 'family control', included maternal restrictiveness, supervision and expectations.

Poor child-rearing practices in respect of mother's competence, father's interaction and family control were each separately related to delinquency, juvenile deviance, crime and poor achievement.

Although poor parental behaviour and its adverse consequences on the quality of child rearing had the strongest association with juvenile delinquency, deviancy, criminality, alcoholism and poor occupational achievement, the picture is complicated by family structure. If both parents were functioning incompetently this was most likely to be associated with poor child outcome. In contrast, 'being reared by a competent mother and a father whose interactions were good seemed to reduce the risk of delinquency, deviancy, and crime, while increasing the probability for occupational achievement' (McCord 1990: 129).

Children with one competent and one incompetent parent had risk levels somewhere in-between. For children with only one parent, it was an all-or-nothing situation. The often reported higher frequency of problem children from single parent families can, in part, be accounted for by the family's history. Children of broken homes usually living with their mothers often had alcoholic or criminal fathers and had been exposed to parental conflict prior to their separation.

It seems that neither delinquency nor deviancy are related to parental absence as such. They require one of the other risk factors of mother's incompetence, poor paternal interaction and weak family control to be present. It must also be noted that the association of problem boys and single parents is further complicated when it is remembered that 'only parents' are more likely to be poor and to live in areas where levels of crime and criminal activity are high. Furthermore, the police are more inclined to search for likely offenders in the run-down and poorer parts of the community.

Newcomb and Bentler (1990) found that those who used drugs in late adolescence had experienced low social conformity, more emotional distress and less social support when tested at both 5 and 9 years of age. Many of these young children were also saying they had negative self-feelings, including low acceptance and high self-derogation. Even at the age of 5, many adult drugs users had experienced poor social integration with family and peers.


## Conclusion

A developmental perspective recognises no single or simple pathway from childhood adversity to adult conduct disorders and delinquency. There is a general belief that the more family life is disturbed or disrupted, erratic or inconsistent, coercive or unresponsive, aggressive or insensitive, the more likely it is that children will exhibit some conduct disorders in adulthood.

# 12

# Relationships with partners

The need for intimacy and attachment relationships continues into and throughout adult life. This chapter looks at how childhood attachment experiences affect the quality of relationships between adult sexual partners. The need for emotional warmth and support is seen to be very important in most adult social relationships. However, with increases in feelings of personal insecurity we see not only a decrease in mutual support but also a rise both in conflict and dependency between partners.

## Attachment and intimacy in adult relationships

The need to develop and maintain close relationships stays with us throughout life. Bowlby (1979) calls them 'affectional bonds' and we seek them 'from the cradle to the grave'. Attachment relationships in adulthood continue to foster feelings of security and self-worth. They help us to maintain emotional stability. When we lose them, we can experience helplessness and fear, pain and anger. As Bowlby (1979: 67) reminds us, we can be crushed by grief and 'a jilted lover is apt to do things that are foolish or dangerous'.

It also has to be observed that although attachments in infancy and adulthood have many similarities, there are interesting differences. In adults, attachment relationships are formed almost exclusively with sexual partners (Hazan and Shaver 1987; Hazan and Zeifman 1994). Sexual attraction brings people together and can hold them together long enough for them to form an emotional bond.

During infancy and childhood, attachment relationships are complementary (i.e., asymmetric). Infants seek security from their attachment figures but do not provide security in return; attachment figures provide care to, but do not take care from, their infants ... In contrast, adult relationships are expected to be more reciprocal (i.e., symmetric), with each member of the dyad serving both as a provider and a recipient of care, a seeker of security as well as a target of security-seeking. (Hazan and Zeifman 1994: 154)

Close relationships in adulthood, therefore, appear to involve attachment, caregiving and sexual mating. The other person is expected to provide as well as receive comfort, emotional support and sexual partnership. More specifically, according to Mattinson and Sinclair (1979: 52), marriage and finding a partner serves two psychological purposes: (i) encouraging further emotional and psychological development; and (ii) avoidance of psychological pain. Close relationships during adulthood represent an 'opportunity to reattach' and to get in touch with feelings associated with earlier attachment experiences. However, our choice of partners and friends and the way we relate to them is affected by our earlier relationship experiences:

[A] healthy personality functioning at every age reflects, first, an individual's ablity to recognize suitable figures willing and able to provide him with a secure base and, second, his ability to collaborate with such figures in mutually rewarding relationships. By contrast, many forms of disturbed personality functioning reflect an individual's impaired ability to recognize suitable and willing figures and/or an impaired ability to collaborate in rewarding relationships with any such figure when found. Such impairments can be of every degree and take many forms: they include anxious clinging, demands excessive or over-intense for age and situation, aloof non-committal, and defiant independence. (Bowlby 1979: 104–5)

There is good evidence that warm, reciprocal relationships protect us against stress but that our ability to form such close relationships is often affected by the quality of relationship we had with our own parents. In their study of romantic relationships, Hazan and Shaver (1987) found that adults show secure, avoidant and ambivalent patterns with their partners along lines very similar to those shown by infants with their parents. Franz *et al.* (1991), in their 36-year prospective study, demonstrated that warm, affectionate parenting in early childhood was likely to lead to stable, happy marriages and close friendships at 41 years of age.

Normally, we only begin to form close, loving attachments with another person outside the family once our attachments to our parents begin to loosen and fade. There is a gradual shift from total dependence on the attachment figure in early infancy to relative autonomy by the time the individual reaches adolescence. However, this natural sequence can be upset if important family relationships are disturbed. Children whose parents' marriage breaks down and who divorce often lose confidence in their parents as attachment figures. This loss of trust in one's parents can have a long-term impact on the ability to form close, intimate relationships in adult life (Wallerstein and Blakeslee 1989, cited in Weiss 1991).

Attachment experiences and the desire to be in relationships, therefore, remain as basic needs throughout life. Breakdowns and upsets in relationships generally have a pronounced emotional effect. However, people with secure patterns of attachment experience and a broad history of good quality relationships, on the whole continue to develop and strengthen the coherence and integrity of their working models of other people and social situations. They accommodate tension and conflict; upsets do not threaten the integrity and viability of their concept of self, nor do they seriously undermine feelings of self-worth and esteem.

## Co-dependent relationships

Closely related to the concept of compulsive self-reliance is the concept of compulsive care-giving and what has become known as co-dependency in relationships. In these co-dependent relationships, people become closely involved with others, but always in the role of giving care, says Bowlby (1979: 139), and never that of receiving it. Again, the absence of love or its erratic availability in childhood produces a deep need for security and care. But there are also powerful feelings of anger that occasionally rise to the surface in these relationships. These feelings may be directed either inwards and lead to depression, or outwards and lead to hostility and even violence against children or partners. For most of the time the *ambivalence* experienced in early attachment relationships is resolved in favour of wanting to be needed. The anger is defensively excluded.

The co-dependent person is described as someone who gets locked into relationships with people who are very needy and troubled –

alcoholics, depressives, addicts, abusers – people with a history of failed relationships. Throughout childhood and into adulthood, co-dependent personalities spend all their emotional energy 'dancing to the tune of others' in the hope of being loved and valued (Norwood 1985). Female sufferers have been dubbed 'women who love too much' (Norwood 1985). It has also been suggested that many people who choose careers as professional helpers, including social workers and nurses, have co-dependent tendencies.

Cermak (1990: 104) identifies five personality traits that define the co-dependent individual: (i) behaving always to please others, (ii) feeling responsible for meeting other people's needs, (iii) experiencing low self-esteem, (iv) driven by compulsions, and (v) a tendency to practise defensive denial. But anger and resentment are never far below the surface. Marlyss, described by Beattie (1987: 23), shows most of these characteristics:

> Sometimes, codependent behaviour becomes inextricably entangled with being a good wife, mother, husband, brother or Christian. Now in her forties, Marlyss is an attractive woman – when she takes care of herself. Most of the time however, she is busy taking care of of her five children and her husband, who is a recovering alcoholic. She devoted her life to making them happy, but she didn't succeed. Usually she feels angry and unappreciated for her efforts and her family feels angry at her. She had sex with her husband when ever he wants, regardless of how she feels. She spends too much of the family's budget on toys and clothing for the children . . . She chauffeurs, reads to, cooks for, cleans for, cuddles and coddles those around her. Most of the time they don't even say 'thank you'. Marlyss resents her constant giving to people in her life. She resents how her family and their needs control her life. She chose nursing as a profession, and she often resents that. 'But I feel guilty when I don't do what's asked of me. . . I feel guilty when I don't live up to other people's standards of me. I feel just plain guilty,' she said. 'In fact,' she added, 'I schedule my day, my priorities, according to guilt.'

Also typical is Rose, now in her mid-fifties and attempting to overcome her alcoholism (Edmund 1993: 103). Both her parents were alcoholics and they died in their thirties. Rose was nine when her mother died and she was looked after by her maternal grandmother. At the age of sixteen she was raped by her boyfriend. As a result she became pregnant and married him. However, he continued to abuse her and she eventually left him. Her second marriage was to a compulsive gambler and he, too, physically abused her. At the age of 27, she also left him and turned to drink.

Edmund (1993: 106) also decribes the case of Tom, a 30-year-old man trying to recover from his addiction to alcohol. He said 'I still feel totally empty inside . . . I still feel guilt and shame and anger towards my mother. She had left my father when I was six years old, taking me with her. She was a heavy drinker. I hardly ever saw my dad. I just always wanted to be wanted, so I was a 'people pleaser'. I started drinking when I was 21 and went into a phase of self-destruction.'

Kasl (1989: 31) argues that the co-dependent is 'someone whose core identity is underdeveloped or unknown and who maintains a false identity built from dependent attachments to external sources – a partner, a spouse, family, appearance, work or rules.' Without such relationships the individual fears 'she will fall into terrific emptiness because she feels she could not exist alone. Developmentally she is like a tiny child who has not left her mother's arms so she clings to forms, people and things, responsibility, security as if they were life itself . . . It is an addiction to security due to a crippling sense of powerlessness' (Kasl 1989: 31). Co-dependent relationships can be seen as cycles of enmeshment and isolation in which individuals re-enact their childhood experiences of anxiety, ambivalence and insecurity (Kellogg 1990: 8). It seems that when they were children, their parents were not available psychologically, emotionally and sometimes even physically. The legacy of such early relationships is to feel unloved and unwanted. The sense of self is poor and only seems to take shape in response to other people's needs.

Co-dependent people need to be needed. And yet they also need to be loved. By choosing very dependent and needy partners, they satisfy the need to be needed but repeat their childhood failure to be loved and cared for in return. Ultimately such relationships are doomed to failure.

## Couples in conflict

The study by Mattinson and Sinclair (1979) provides a particularly detailed and fascinating examination of the type of relationships that exist between the parents of families so often seen by social workers. These families exhibit very disturbed relationships between their members. They are extremely difficult to help and place demands on both the social and health services out of all proportion to their numbers.

Violence and threats of violence are constant between the adults and the parents and their children. Separation and threats of separation between partners and between parents and children repeatedly provoke feelings of anxiety and attachment behaviour. Within families, people come and go, as threats of leaving are carried out only to be withdrawn a short while later. Typically, one partner will leave in dramatic fashion only to return a short while later. And yet, in spite of the tension, arguments and violence, many of these couples stay together for long periods of time.

The researchers believed that a strong, but highly anxious and *ambivalent* attachment existed between many of these couples. Anger and anxiety, need and aggression follow on each other's heels in ways calculated to confuse and exasperate the outsider. Crises characterise the lives of such families.

Much of the threatening and violent behaviour was an attempt to control the other person and prevent him or her leaving the home. Women would threaten suicide. Men would control all of the household money, and in fits of acute jealousy they would forbid their partners to see anyone else, and even lock their wives in the house to try and prevent them from seeing other people in case they were tempted away to form a new relationship. If their wives went out, the men would want to know where they had been and who they had seen and spoken to. Such strategies often worked, at least in the short term, but the amount of guilt and anger in the relationship steadily rose.

Another 'coercive technique was battering':

> As one man put it, in his family asking for something was always done with fists. No wife enjoyed this treatment, but some got a wry satisfaction from it. For example, one woman, when explaining why she did not wish for a separation, announced with a note of triumph in her voice that her husband had threatened he would come to 'get her' if she moved out. He needed her too, she insisted. In most of these marriages, it was found, each party was apt to stress how much the other needed them, whilst disclaiming their own need for the partner. By need, of course, they meant a desire for a caregiving figure. What they dreaded most was loneliness. (Mattinson and Sinclair 1979: 121)

Feelings of anxiety, fear and incompleteness would produce highly inconsistent behaviour. Mrs Jafferji had two children and she wanted to leave her husband and have the social worker punish him in some way (Mattinson and Sinclair 1979: 10). After a few weeks she then told the social worker that she wanted a reconciliation. However, by this time Mr Jafferji had had enough. He wanted to end the marriage. Mrs Jafferji had difficulties in relating to her baby son and she wanted to leave him in the safety of the local hospital. The 'more she craved for herself the attention the baby needed', the more she screamed that it was her husband who needed treatment. Meanwhile, Mr Jafferji, continuing to feel inadequate and angry at his wife, could only express 'his fury with his fists'. And so things went on.

It is easy for workers with such families to feel confusion and irritation. As well as the ambivalence aroused by fears of separation, *blame*, *jealousy* and *possessiveness* also occur. These feelings are strongly associated with experiences of early social deprivation. The acute desire for attention and the competition for love in childhood produce deep-rooted needs which if not met provoke feelings of jealousy, rage and blame. A social worker described an encounter with one of her clients, saying:

> Mrs Calder said that Mr Calder had helped James with his fractions one evening. The two of them sat together while she went out to the kitchen. I asked her if she was pleased and she said she was 'quite put out'. She was used 'to being the centre of attention'. (Mattinson and Sinclair 1979: 98)

Third parties, including social workers, are quickly drawn into the psychological dynamics of the situation with the demand that they take sides. One partner might seek to ally himself or herself with the social worker against the other partner. *Trust* in others is rarely present. Separations represent confirmation that other people will, in the end, always let you down and the fear of being left alone is an ever-present prospect.

As Mattinson and Sinclair (1979: 99) observe, the clients in their study appeared to operate on the basis that 'One is terrifying, two ought to be company, three cannot possibly be.' Within the same social relationship there are feelings of helplessness and the need to be loved and supported as well as feelings of mistrust, envy, jealousy and need to control, 'all of which effectively sabotage their efforts in attachment'. Marriage offers some protection from the fear of being alone and feeling helpless and yet a lack of trust and feelings of uncertainty saturated the relationships. The couples wove an emotional tangle around each other. While one partner was in a state of anxious attachment, the other was able to express feelings of detachment and distrust. But the roles could reverse at any time. 'Together they employed a variety of strategies whereby they could control and ensure the proximity of their partner while at the same time denying their need of each other except in material terms. Their difficulties in being attached to each other were also exhibited in their difficulty in being reliable attachment figures for their children' (Mattinson and Sinclair 1979: 292).

## Support

The presence or absence of support is a theme which runs throughout the analysis and assessment of marital relationships. When the support of a partner is low or absent, the relationship is usually very poor. And when relationships between parents are discordant, the quality of parenting suffers and children exhibit upsets and disturbances. Women receive and experience little support from partners who drink heavily, abuse drugs, engage in crime, have a psychiatric disorder and show difficulties in personal relationships.

Although support can be defined along several dimensions, the level of emotional support and the availability of a warm, confiding relationship seems to be particularly important for mental health, marital harmony and the quality of parenting. The value of supportive relationships can be traced throughout the life cycle. Lack of emotional support between partners undermines not only their relationship but also the psychological wellbeing of each partner and the amount of emotional sensitivity and responsiveness they have available for their children.

## Conclusion

In practice, child and family social work often means work with parents in conflict. The parents need for intimacy and yet fear of dependency is calculated to produce turbulent partnerships in which love and care are given and taken away in a bewildering, relentless emotional drama. Anxiety and fears of losing close relationships are never far below the surface. The need for others coupled with deep-rooted feelings of insecurity and a lack of trust mean that all relationships are entered into with a high degree of ambivalence. If social workers are to keep their bearings in these highly demanding cases, it is important that they understand the psychological dynamics and emotional history of the participants.

# 13

# Relationships with children

The relationship circle is almost complete. We now consider what kind of parents people with different developmental backgrounds become. The research evidence is strong that the parents' own history of social relationships influences the quality of relationships they have with their children as well as each other. Many studies note the irony that the parents' own childhood experiences are repeated as the parents treat their children as they were treated themselves. The quality of social experience created by mothers and fathers increases the likelihood of the developmental torch being passed down through the generations.

For example, Kaufman and Zigler (1989) calculate that the risk of a child being abused if the parents had suffered abuse in childhood is at least 30 per cent. Rutter *et al.* (1983) compared the early childhood experiences of parents who had family difficulties and at least one child in local authority care with families of a similar socio-economic status. The mothers of the disordered and disturbed families were much more likely to have suffered adversity in their own childhood, with many of them experiencing separation from one or both of their parents as a result of family conflict and rejection. And in similar mood, Belsky and Pensky (1988: 195) conclude their review of 'the intergenerational transmission of family relationships' by saying that it would seem that whether we consider child maltreatment, spouse abuse or divorce, dysfunction appears to be transmitted across generations, though they add that this is by no means inevitable. 'Across the life course and across successive generations,' conclude Caspi and Elder (1988: 220), 'problems beget problems.'

We shall consider a number of research studies dealing with children of different ages which look at the family environment created by the interplay of four important dimensions: (i) the relationship history of the parents; (ii) the parents' personality; (iii) the quality of the relationship between parent and partner; and (iv) the quality of the parenting relationship between mothers and fathers and their children. These dimensions, therefore, define the social environments in which children develop and in which their selves form and their personalities are shaped. Parenting creates one of the most significant social environments in which children develop. According to Rutter (1989: 318):

> parenting is a task that is concerned with the rearing of children; a task that comprises the provision of an environment conducive to both cognitive and social development . . . as well as a task that is concerned with the parental response to children's distress, social approaches, demands, and disruptive behaviour . . . and with the resolution of interpesonal conflicts and difficulties . . . Thus, parenting requires "skills" of various kinds – as reflected in sensitivity to children's cues and a responsiveness to the differing needs of different phases of development; in social problem solving and coping with life stressors and adversities; in knowing how to play and talk with children; and in the use of disciplinary techniques that are effective in the triple sense of bringing about the desired child behaviour, of doing so in a way that results in harmony, and of increasing the child's self-control.

## Childhood experiences and parenting behaviour

Underlying any examination of the way caregivers relate to their children is the idea that the quality of these relationships is based largely on the caregiver's own working models of relationships. These models were generated within the caregiver's own history of relationships and child-rearing experiences with mothers, fathers and other significant people. And yet in cases where the quality of care triggers insecurity in a child, no blame should be attached to the mothers or caregivers. As well as the caregiver's own developmental history, the quality of care given to children depends on the level of social support enjoyed by the caregiver. To blame mothers and other caregivers is to blame their own mothers and caregivers and so on in an infinite regress (Sroufe 1988: 26). The 'ghosts' of unresolved childhood conflicts, as Fraiberg, Adelson and Shapiro (1975) describe it, 'do their mischief' in the present as parents bring their own vulnerabilities with them to the rearing of their own children. In one of his 1956 lectures, Bowlby (1979: 17–18) said:

The intrusion of hostility into a mother's, or a father's, feelings for the baby seems so strange and often so horrifying that some of you may find it difficult to believe . . . Though it is still difficult to explain this hostility, it seems plain that feelings which are evoked in us when we become parents have a great deal in common with the feelings that were evoked in us as children by our parents and siblings. The parent who suffered deprivation may, if she has not become incapable of feeling affection, experience an intense need to possess her child's love, and may go to great lengths to ensure that she obtains it. The parent who was jealous of a younger sibling may come to experience unreasonable hostility to the new 'little stranger' in the family, a sentiment which is particularly common in fathers. The parent whose love for his mother was shot through with antagonism for her demanding ways may come to resent and hate the demanding ways of the infant.

Mothers of securely attached children recall that when they were children they felt generally accepted, liked and well-nurtured by their own mothers. They have fond memories of childhood and identify positively with their mother. These mothers produced coherent and consistent models of their own attachment experiences. This was less likely to be the case with the mothers of insecurely attached children. These women often described feelings of rejection by their own mothers when they were children. They have fewer positive and less clear memories of childhood (Ricks 1985 and Morris 1980, both cited in Dunn 1993). Parents who did not enjoy close, warm, attentive parenting themselves find it harder to provide sensitive, responsive care with their own children who, as a result, are likely to develop insecure attachments (for example, see Greenberg *et al.* 1990).

Mothers with avoidant attachment experiences feel invaded by their children and try to control their own anxieties by keeping their children at an emotional distance. They may even reject them. The boundary between parents and children is rigidly maintained. In contrast, if the parents' experience is one of ambivalent attachments, they are liable to become both over-involved and irritable so that their children are not quite sure what to expect. Boundaries between parents and children are inconsistent and blurred.

Lieberman and Pawl (1988: 340–2) give the example of Mrs Bradley who had been abandoned by her biological mother. She was adopted at four weeks of age. However, she said she always felt misunderstood and rejected by her adoptive mother; indeed she decribed herself as 'motherless'. For the first two years of her life she suffered a minor malformation in the oral cavity. This caused problems when she ate and she recalls feeling constantly hungry. She felt physically and emotionally starved. 'Mrs Bradley felt that her needs and her feelings were of no importance to anyone, and therefore should be of no importance to herelf.' In spite of being an intelligent woman, she felt worthless and unwanted. Throughout her life she said she had no pleasure in either preparing or eating food.

She married and had a son, Andy, who was referred for non-organic failure to thrive when he was six weeks old. Mrs Bradley seemed unable, even unwilling to respond to her baby's signals and needs. She appeared not to recognise when he was hungry or sated. When she handled her son she was efficient but mechanical in her dealings with him. Little pleasure appeared to be experienced. Face-to-face interaction was slight. By the time he was three months old, Andy was beginning to avoid his mother's gaze. He had a bland facial expression and was reluctant to smile. Work with the mother helped her to recognise her own deep-rooted needs and very gradually this allowed her to become more attuned and responsive to the needs of her son.

Spieker and Booth (1988: 126–8) studied 60 mother–infant pairings. While mothers of infants whose attachment patterns showed ambivalence and resistance perceived both their own and their child's lives quite positively, nevertheless they were more depressed and less sure of themselves than other mothers. Mothers of avoidant children saw their own lives as well as the lives of their partners and babies more negatively, though they were less inclined to feel depressed.

The authors speculate that whereas the depressed women internalised negative thoughts about the self, the mothers of avoidant babies directed their negative feelings outwards. Mothers of disorganised and disorientated babies (D types) seemed to have fewer social resources. They appeared less skilled and sensitive in their relationships. Babies of these mothers seemed most at risk of neglect and physical harm. All mothers of insecurely attached children reported a general decline in the quality of marital relationships and emotional support from their partners.

In general, the study by Spieker and Booth reported that mothers who found their infants difficult were scored more highly in terms of aggression, hostility, suspicion and anxiety. They scored lower on social skills, sensitivity and an ability to understand the world from their babies' point of view.

the findings of this study have been important in engendering the speculation that the pattern of maternal negative and positive perceptions about self and others is related to the quality of the mother's interaction with her infant and, eventually, to the quality of her infant's attachment. (Spieker and Booth 1988: 131)

Grossmann and Grossmann (1991: 107) propose a relationship between a mother's own attachment history and her ability to deal with some of the demands of her own children. They argue that when a baby cries and is in distress, the mother experiences some alarm and feelings of ambivalence. If the parent has not had good experiences with her own attachment figure, she will have found and will continue to find it difficult to integrate negative feelings into her working models and inner representations of other people and her relationship with them. To this extent, she concentrates on how stressful situations affect and bother her. She is less able to see things from the baby's point of view; she lacks emotional empathy.

So, if the mother has had a history of rejection and experienced a lack of support when distressed, she 'might seek to exclude this present reminder of her own former misery from her perception by ignoring the infant's crying' (Grossmann and Grossmann 1991: 107). The authors describe this as 'low sensitivity'. Under pressure, the mother will attempt to manage her own emotional conflicts rather than the baby's distress. 'As a consequence, the infant experiences more often than not an emotional unavailability of the mother when he actually needs her most and thus develops an avoidant attachment pattern' (1991: 107). As earlier chapters have shown, the only way the child can manage the hurt of rejection is to attempt to become self-reliant and avoid those relationships which repeatedly fail to offer support and understanding and seem only to be a source of emotional pain.

Insensitivity to the baby's needs, signals and perceptions along with feelings of anxiety over one's own experiences results in situations being misread. Nezworski *et al.* (1988: 377–8) give a number of examples. In one case, the mothers of insecurely attached children were themselves suffering chronic stress. And yet they remained anxious and fearful about reaching out for help or about becoming dependent and forming close relationships with their partners, children or indeed anyone else. The mothers have a negative outlook on events. If a mother-in-law forgets a mother's birthday, the action is interpreted as intentional and hostile: 'she meant to hurt me'. A baby who cries may be perceived as trying to exert control: 'no-one gets the better of me'. A child's natural messiness is interpreted by a mother who remains uncertain about her own value as 'I know if anyone sees him doing that, they will think I am a bad mother.'

In general, the evidence suggests that women who have had disturbed childhoods engage in less interaction with their infants than women who have had more settled, happier childhoods (Bowlby 1988: 16). Women who were separated from one or both parents during their first ten years of life often experience relationship difficulties with their babies. The infants often have sleeping and eating problems (Frommer and O'Shea 1973).

The significance of early life disruptions and the quality of parenting is nicely demonstrated by Rutter and Quinton (1984a) in their long-term follow-up of 94 institutionally reared mothers. Of these ex-institutional women, 42 per cent became pregnant before the age of 19, compared with only 5 per cent of a control group. A third of the girls who were followed through into their mid-twenties experienced temporary or permanent breakdown in the parenting of their children. Another third of the ex-institutional women were rated as practising good parenting. None of the 51 women in the comparison group experienced a breakdown in their parenting. Although only 10 ex-institutional girls had spent the majority of their childhood in residential care, this group fared worst with 80 per cent of them experiencing serious difficulties with their parenting and problems with their children. This group had the fewest opportunities for attachment experiences, a disadvantage which appeared to pose a very considerable risk for the successful conduct of future social relationships, including parenting.

One of the most important predictors of poor parenting, writes Rutter (1988: 343),

> proved to be whether or not the girls had experienced disruptive parenting during the first four years of life, defined in terms of short-term admissions into institutional care, multiple separations through parental discord or disorder, persistent family discord, or admission into long-term institutional care before the age of two years . . . *The implication is that early disruption of parenting may be particularly damaging to the development of those aspects of personality concerned with social relationships.* (emphasis mine)

## Abusing and neglectful mothers

Parents who maltreat their children have been shown to (i) possess anxious and disturbed personality structures which are the result of their own disturbed relationship histories, (ii) lack social and emotional support, and (iii) suffer severe material and environmental stresses. The interplay of these three factors severely impairs their psychological and social functioning and reduces their ability to be emotionally available for their children.

Main and Goldwyn (1984) also furnish evidence that abusive mothers tend to be unsympathetic to other people's distress, show poor control over their own aggression, and are often socially isolated. They have inner working models tied to issues of conflict, control and rejection (Crittenden and Ainsworth 1989: 446). Anxiety is experienced when others appear to dominate and demand that their needs be met. But there is also the fear of rejection by the other if the mother wants the other to meet her own needs. As children, many of them experienced rejection by their own parents.

> Their model of themselves will be tied to the idea that others have, and will not willingly give up, needed psychological or physical resources. Consequently, coercion and victimization will be central to the mothers' perceptions of themselves. (Crittenden and Ainsworth 1989: 446)

Crittenden (1988) regarded both maltreating mothers and neglecting mothers as equally insensitive to the signals and emotional state of their babies. It seems as if abusive mothers find it difficult to be socially empathetic with their children; they cannot see the world from their child's point of view (Pianta *et al.* 1989). But Crittenden also makes a distinction between abusing mothers who show more control and hostility when dealing with their children than neglecting mothers who tend to be more withdrawn, unresponsive and display an air of helplessness. While abusive mothers relate with their children in an active, interfering and often punitive way, neglectful mothers tend to be less involved and more passive (Crittenden and Bonvillian 1984).

> Neglecting mothers are expected to have models centering around helplessness. They will not perceive others as having, or being able to give them, what they need. Neither will they see themselves as effective at eliciting the help and support of others. The affect accompanying their relationships will be one of emptiness and depression. (Crittenden and Ainsworth 1989: 446)

Frodi and Lamb (1980) observed that abusive mothers responded with less sympathy to a crying child than non-abusive mothers. Indeed, they tended to show more annoyance and anger. Threats and other 'power-assertive' techniques characterised the abusive parents' interactive style with their children (Oldershaw *et al.* 1986). In general, abusive mothers seemed to dislike the prospect of close interaction with infants. So, conclude Pianta *et al.* (1989: 207): 'Women who have not resolved their own interpersonal issues of trust, dependency, and autonomy are likely to be considerably stressed when faced with the demands of a highly dependent child.'

Mothers who, as children, were made to feel responsible for looking after their own parents, often demand care and attention from their own children. This, too, can generate a very disturbed interpersonal environment for young children which sometimes leads to physical abuse (various studies cited in Bowlby 1988: 16). However, in spite of the hostility shown by many abusing mothers, it is the infants of withdrawn, neglectful mothers who suffer the greatest developmental disturbance.

Generally, the more sensitive, responsive and interactive the mother, the more trusting and co-operative will be the child. In her study, Crittenden (1988) found that:

1. abused children of controlling mothers were generally seen to be either more behaviourally difficult or more *compulsively compliant* as they went out of their way to keep on the right side of their parent;
2. neglected children of unresponsive mothers were inclined to be passive and dull, showing an attachment pattern of anxious-ambivalence. The children of particularly withdrawn mothers 'sensed their ultimate isolation and made no effort to seek any comfort from adults' (Crittenden 1988: 159); but that
3. as the neglected children of unresponsive mothers grew older, there was a tendency to become less passive and more aggressive. It is not clear whether this is in protest to the mother's unresponsiveness or an increased demand for attention. The danger is that increased aggressiveness by the child may provoke a previously neglectful parent into an abusing parent as the stresses and strains mount (cf. Parton 1985).

Combining these insights suggests that securely attached children tend to have sensitive mothers; anxious–ambivalent children tend to have unresponsive mothers; anxious–avoidant children tend to have mothers who are both controlling and unresponsive; and children who experience avoidant–ambivalent attachments (A/C or D types) have mothers who are highly controlling (Crittenden 1988: 159).

Crittenden also speculates that maltreated children can and do form attachments with their parents. Some will show a complusive compliance as they attempt to pre-empt hostile attacks and placate their parents. This may be read as a form of anxious attachment in which the child sees brief and infrequent incidents of abuse as better than total rejection and abandonment. Psychologically at least, nurturance and a semblance of protection are better than nothing. A compulsive compliant defensive strategy, therefore, may consist of (i) excessive social vigilance; (ii) superficial compliance in the presence of seemingly dominant, threatening or powerful others; and (iii) inhibited anger.

> Such a behavior pattern is often labeled as manipulative and may describe the defensive response of both some abused children and many abusing parents. It is consistent with the development of representational models of others as powerful and hostile, the self as as lovable only when compliant, and an emotional overtone of anxiety and repressed anger. (Crittenden and Ainsworth 1989: 454)

Crittenden concludes her study by noting that both abused children and maltreating adults 'appear to experience unusually high levels of stress on a daily basis. This stress is seen as contributing to the anger, hostility and/or withdrawal of parents. Their children tend to respond with negative signals, passivity, avoidance, and/or resistance' (Crittenden 1988: 162).

But the researcher recognises one further step. When both parent and child experience even greater stress, there is a recognition that the relationship is in danger of breaking down altogether. This considerably increases the level of anxiety. The stressed child increases his or her attachment behaviour in the form of an exaggerated and compulsive compliance. This is consistent with Bowlby's proximity-seeking to the attachment figure when the child is under threat. 'The most severely abusing mothers,' writes Crittenden (1988: 163), 'were not openly hostile; they were pseudo-sensitive. The most severely abused children were not difficult; they were compulsively compliant.'

Moreover, children who inhibit any expression of their internal feelings become confused about the source, nature and character of both their own and other people's emotions. The child does not indicate how he or she feels to the mother. Therefore, the mother cannot respond to the actual emotional condition of the child. Empathy and understanding, mutuality and accurate dialogue between mother and child are therefore not possible. The child feels impotent in his or her attempts to resolve feelings of anger or fear or joy. Such experiences make it difficult for children to understand and learn how to handle the demands of future intimate relationships.

Pitcairn *et al.* (1993) examined 43 cases of child abuse in three Scottish departments of social work. The researchers report that half of the fathers and 40 per cent of the mothers involved in such cases had themselves been involved with social workers as children. The same 50 per cent of fathers (and 30 per cent of the mothers) had appeared in juvenile court. Altogether, as adults and children, 'eighty three percent of the fathers had been in trouble with the law, with 50 per cent going to prison, borstal or both (35% and 13% for mothers) . . . It is also important to note that the parents began bringing up children fairly young, with the median age at the birth of their first child being 18 for the mothers and 22 for the fathers' (Pitcairn *et al.* 1993: 76–7).

In the case of perpetrators of child sexual abuse, the evidence is that the majority of offenders are men, often biologically related (fathers, uncles, brothers, grandfathers) to the abused girl or boy. Disturbed behaviour and unhappy experiences were a feature of both the childhoods and adulthoods of many of these men. In their examination of 213 cases, Dobash *et al.* (1993) found that 23 per cent had been the victims of sexual and/or physical abuse themselves as children. A further 7 per cent had suffered emotional abuse, and 3 per cent were reported to have experienced physical neglect. As adults, about half of the perpetrators were involved in some kind of substance abuse. Using a slightly higher number of known cases (300), the researchers also found that 22 per cent of the perpetrators had been convicted of property offences, 19 per cent of violent offences, 12 per cent of sexual offences, and 8 per cent of both property and sexual offences (Dobash *et al.* 1993: 120).

Burkett (1985 cited in Sroufe 1989b) studied relationships between mothers who had been sexually abused as children by men in their family, and their own 5-to-10-year-old children. Compared with a control group of mothers, these women focused more on themselves than on their children. They offered fewer messages which suggested they understood, valued or acknowledged their children's needs or thoughts and feelings. On the other hand, they were more likely to belittle or blame their children. There was also evidence of role reversal in which the mothers showed submission, appeasement and deferment. Their children were more anxious about their mother's needs and feelings, though the children were also inclined to try and keep their distance whenever possible.

There is equally compelling evidence to link poor childhood experiences, particularly a profound lack of love and care, with parents who physically abuse their children. As adults such parents show higher than normal rates of anxiety and anger; they can be impulsive and behave immaturely; they can show high levels of dependency; they are often distrustful and unwilling to form close relationships with people; and they suffer social isolation. Rejected by other adults, such parents may turn to their own children for companionship, care and attention.

DeLozier (1982) studied 18 working-class mothers who had physically abused their children. The majority of the women had been threatened with abandonment and severe beatings by their own parents when they were children. This, we know, produces feelings of extreme anxiety and anger along with an inability to trust other people in relationships. These abusing mothers also said that their own mothers were not the people they turned to as children when they were in distress. The women displayed extreme sensitivity to any event in which there was an element or possibility of separation. Such situations provoked high levels of anxiety and anger consonant with those who have experienced histories of anxious attachments. The women wanted love and care but expected rejection.

> Thus, whilst constantly yearning for the love and care she has never had, she has no confidence she will ever receive it; and she will mistrust any offer she may receive. Small wonder therefore, if when a woman with this background becomes a mother, that there are times when, instead of being ready to mother her child, she looks to her child to mother her. Small wonder too if when her child fails to oblige and starts crying, demanding care and attention, she gets impatient and angry with it. (Bowlby 1988: 86)

However, although being maltreated as a child puts a parent at risk of being an abuser, 'the path between these two points is far from direct or inevitable' (Kaufman and Zigler 1989: 129). It is not simply being a victim of abuse that increases the risk of being an abusive parent, for much depends on the quality of subsequent life experience. The stresses of poverty, social isolation and conflict also enter into the relationship equation. It is the combination of childhood abuse and continued poor life experience which increase the chances of an individual becoming an abusive parent. Individuals emotionally damaged because they have been in a disturbed relationship with an abusive parent and who then find themselves in highly stressful and disadvantaged situations, are in danger of becoming those parents who have the weakest emotional resources to cope with the most difficult physical and interpersonal environments (Belsky and Vondra 1989).

Equally important to remember, and developmentally just as interesting, are all those parents (possibly as high as 70 per cent, according to Kaufman and Zigler 1989: 135) who were themselves abused in childhood but who do not become abusive. One powerful factor in breaking the 'intergenerational' cycle of transmission is for abused parents to find and enter into a loving and supportive relationship, say with a foster mother or a caring spouse. Lack of social support, social isolation and highly disorganised life-styles are a characteristic feature of many parents who maltreat their children (Pianta *et al.* 1989: 236).

## Stress and support

Main and Hesse (1989, cited in Main 1991) studied mothers whose children experienced insecure–disorganised attachments (type D). Many of these women had lost an attachment figure through death before they had reached mid-adolescence. However, the authors recognise that it is not so much the loss of the attachment figure that produces insensitive parenting. What seems more important is whether or not the mother has resolved and adjusted to the loss. Failure to mourn the loss of an attachment figure during childhood has potentially serious consequences for the quality of parents' relationships with their children.

Ainsworth and Eichberg (1991: 176) found in a small sample that all mothers whose mourning was unresolved had 'babies whose attachment to them was disorganized/disoriented'. Furthermore, if mothers themselves were in receipt of social and emotional support from partners or friends, this reduced the likelihood of their children feeling insecure in their attachment relationships (Crockenberg 1981).

This research points to other studies which, yet again, identify benign and vicious developmental circles. Belsky and Isabella (1988: 86–7) report that mothers who were more interpersonally sensitive and emotionally stable prior to the birth of their babies experienced less marital stress as the partnership entered parenthood. Their babies tended to show more secure patterns of attachment. Positive relationships were maintained with both husbands and babies over the first few years of parenthood. Conversely, mothers who are psychologically vulnerable and lack sensitivity when dealing with their infants are more likely to live with partners with similar emotional weaknesses. The partners fail to provide the kind of support that any mother needs when she has a baby. Babies of such couples are more likely to be insecure.

Stresses (including having and looking after a baby) therefore can be buffered by good support. However, it is women with the greatest psychological resources to cope with stress who are most likely to have partners who are supportive. Women with weaker psychological resources to cope with stress are most likely to have partners who are not very supportive. Indeed, the arrival of babies often puts an additional stress on these marital relationships. The deteriorating relationship not only reduces the level of support available but also becomes an extra source of stress in itself. Babies in such situations have parents whose level of stress has increased on two fronts (looking after a baby and worrying about the marital relationship) and whose sources of support in the process are further diminished. Poorly integrated personality structures, high levels of stress, and a lack of emotional support are the classic ingredients for producing disturbed relationships and insecurely attached children.

In their studies of ex-institutional women, Rutter and Quinton (1984a) found that marital support was a key factor in the parents' child-rearing skills. Women valued a confiding relationship which also possessed warmth and harmony. Partners who drank heavily or abused drugs, who were criminals or had a psychiatric disorder, provided little support, and this adversely affected the quality of child care in the family. Equally important in terms of mothers' experiences of support was the quality of the material environment.

In their comparative studies of ex-institutional mothers and a control group, Rutter and Quinton 'found that poor parenting was substantially more likely to occur when the women were living in poor social circumstances (operationally defined in terms of variables such as the children sharing a bed, a lack of washing machine or telephone, and the presence of housing defects such as severe damp). This effect was roughly of similar degree in both the institution and comparison groups' (Rutter 1988: 339).

## Overcoming adversity and reflections on childhood

Quinton and Rutter (1988) note that women raised in group foster homes often showed serious impairment in conducting close relationships in adult life. Although this was generally true for the women's relationships with their own children, there was evidence of some improvement in the mothers' quality of relationships with their second children compared to their first. Parenting of second children was often found to be better. Furthermore, raising children of one's own appeared to have some reparative value for those socially damaged by early life relationships.

A series of fascinating studies by Main and her colleagues (Main *et al.* 1985 cited in Bretherton 1991) examined the long-term effects of the ability to form or failure to form well-integrated representational models of social relationships during early childhood. Parents were asked about the quality of their attachment relationships with their own parents when they were children. The interviewers identified three types of respondent (Bretherton 1991: 26):

1. *Autonomous–secure individuals* who were able to give clear and coherent accounts of their early relationships with their parents *whether or not* they had been satisfying. Even in essentially positive relationships, these mothers were realistic and could recognise parental imperfections. In less satisfactory childhoods, mothers could acknowledge the deprivation and reflect on its possible impact on their development.
2. *Preoccupied–entangled individuals* who described many confused and confusing childhood memories about their attachments which could never be drawn together into a coherent or consistent picture or narrative. They remained enmeshed in and

preoccupied with past relationship struggles with their parents, did not have a strong personal identity, and continued to see themselves in terms of their parents and past relationships. Once into the recollection process, not only does the individual become preoccupied in a rambling, often agitated manner, they also simmer with anger and unresolved conflict. Clinical populations produce high numbers of 'preoccupied' individuals.

3. *Dismissing–detached individuals* who often claimed that they could not remember much about relationships with their parents in childhood. Although they tended to idealise their parents on a general level, when it came down to specific memories about attachment, they remained hazy. Idealisation prevented the individual using realistic and flexible working models of self, others and relationships. Negative feelings and information simply were not processed by the model. People in this group dismissed the influence of attachment relationships on their own development. They denied that negative childhood experiences had any impact on them personally even though most of them had experienced rejection and a lack of love. They described childhood incidents and relationships in rather neutral tones; there were few expressions of strong feeling or affect. Past losses and traumas appear not to have been mourned.

The parents in these 'Adult Attachment Interview' classifications were empirically shown to have a child whose attachment behaviour corresponded with the parents' own experience: secure individuals tended to have securely attached children; preoccupied individuals produced insecurely attached children who were anxious and ambivalent in their behaviour towards their parents; and dismissing individuals had insecurely attached children who displayed avoidant patterns of behaviour. The women with securely attached children tended to enjoy higher self-esteem, while mothers of insecurely attached children often experienced depression and low self-worth (Lyons-Ruth *et al.* 1984). These studies suggest that particular attachment patterns can be transmitted across the generations, affecting both children's developmental experiences and adults' style of parenting (Steele and Steele 1994).

For example, Richard, now aged 15, is in constant trouble at school, cannot maintain eye contact, 'is a bit of a loner', and is increasingly aggressive with his parents and his peers. Recently he had attempted suicide, albeit not very convincingly. He said life was not worth living and that his parents had no interest in him. His father is a remote figure and over the years has taken no active interest in his children or family life. Richard's mother is an obsessionally tidy woman who cannot tolerate disorder or mess. She keeps herself constantly busy and occupied. When the children were babies she had tried, whenever possible, to get friends or local child-minders to look after the children. Her own parents were in the military and they spent most of her childhood touring various parts of the world leaving her behind in a series of boarding schools. She adopts a stoical attitude and feels that as far as life is concerned you have to 'grin and bear it'. She refused to complain or get upset when her husband had several desultory affairs with other women, although she resents the children and the demands they make on her. The social worker felt that Richard's mother can 'neither love nor be loved' and that the only reason she had the children was out of a sense of duty.

Results similar to those described by Bretherton have been confirmed by Grossmann *et al.* (1988), who interviewed 65 mothers in the German towns of Bielefeld and Regensburg. The study showed that 80 per cent of the mothers who had positive, non-defensive recollections of their own childhood relationships with their mothers, had securely attached infants. 'Maternal sensitivity and acceptance of her infant during the first year of life,' write Grossmann *et al.* (1988: 258), 'and her acceptance of the individuality of her toddler, correlated significantly with the amount of attachment-relevant contents and stories during the interview, with the mother's readiness to recall childhood experiences including her feelings as a child, and with the mother's lack of defensiveness.'

Of particular interest are the high levels of empathy and social understanding shown by the mothers of the securely attached children. These mothers *reflected* more on attachment issues: 'they looked for reasons for someone's behaviour, compared behaviours and motives of themselves and their attachment figures, and saw the influence of their attachment experiences on their personality' (Grossmann *et al.* 1988: 251). They could also appraise their own children's strengths and weaknesses and still accept them as thoroughly lovable!

The converse was true for 80 per cent of the mothers who recalled their own childhood experiences in less positive terms. They had infants who were insecurely attached to them. These mothers were also less likely to analyse or reflect on their own childhood experiences.

The evidence therefore suggests that there is a transmission across the generations of inner working models derived from particular types of attachment experience, including both secure and insecure attachment patterns. The interesting exceptions were those women who did experience problematic and insecure childhoods but who were able to recognise the poor quality of their relationships with their mothers. It appeared that they had psychologically worked through their childhood experiences. They were often angry about their neglect or rejection. And most important, their children tended to show secure patterns of attachment (Main and Goldwyn 1984).

## Depressed mothers

In her studies of depressed mothers, Radke-Yarrow (1989) wondered what kind of affective environments they created for their children. Mothers who generate sensitive, responsive relationships with their children and who are emotionally available tend to produce secure attachments. But we know that people who are depressed feel a sense of hopelessness; they lack energy, suffer low self-esteem and seem psychologically unavailable for other people. They find it difficult to show emotional empathy and interest in the feelings and concerns of others.

We might speculate, therefore, that mothers who are depressed will not have a relationship with their children which is either sensitive or responsive. And indeed, the evidence seems to be that depressed mothers are more likely to have children who exhibit various kinds of relationship disturbance (for a useful review of this topic, see Sheppard 1994). There is evidence that depressed mothers are more likely to be ineffective in controlling their children (Kochanska et al. 1987); less able to handle stress involving their children; and more likely to view their children in negative terms (Radke-Yarrow 1989: 64). Williams and Carmichael (1991, cited in Sheppard 1994) found that depressed mothers perceived more behavioural problems in their 4-year-olds than mothers who were not depressed, even though the children were in fact no worse behaved than their contemporaries.

In the studies by Radke-Yarrow, mothers diagnosed as manic-depressive were most likely to have insecurely attached children. Mothers who were extremely sad and anxious presented their children with an environment of unrelieved distress. The young children appeared to adopt one of two adaptive strategies. One group were drawn into a close relationship with their mothers. Although the children achieve proximity they also found themselves experiencing and sharing the full affect of their mother's sadness and anxiety. The second strategy was to avoid the mother and her pain and sadness. The children lost closeness and they were forced to live with their own anxiety. Whichever strategy the children adopted, within these extreme environments it was difficult for them to feel secure. 'Good feelings about self may be hard to achieve. Mother's and child's abilities to relate positively and intimately with others seem endangered' (Radke-Yarrow 1991: 124).

Depressed mothers from lower socio-economic backgrounds appear to express more negativity and anger towards their children than similarly depressed mothers from middle-class backgrounds (Radke-Yarrow 1989: 55). The mixture of a depressed, angry mother and the stresses and strains of poverty presents the child with a very distressed and disturbed emotional environment.

## Conclusion

The transmission of representational models, attachment experiences and relationship patterns across the generations occurs when parents re-create the relationship experiences they had in childhood with their own children. Research evidence reveals both intergenerational continuities and discontinuities in parenting problems and childhood experiences. However, the transmission of problems across the generations is by no means inevitable. Many children show psychological resilience in the face of adversity.

# 14

# Resilience and the development of protective mechanisms

There is growing evidence that some people are able to develop reasonably well-integrated personality structures in spite of experiencing adverse environments and poor quality relationships in childhood. Poor developmental outcome has been associated with marital disharmony, institutionalisation, hostile and rejecting parenting, economic deprivation, maltreatment and war. But in spite of early adversity, the resilient individual goes on to cope appropriately and competently with social relationships, including those with partners and children.

When the overall evidence is strong that those who suffer severe life stresses are likely to develop psychological difficulties, what are the characteristics of those children who survive, and survive well? How do they manage to develop sound social understanding? What factors *protect* them from being psychologically impaired by disturbed relationships? How do they build up *resistance* to the risks experienced in their social environment? How can we understand their *resilience* in the face of adversity? A few answers are beginning to emerge.

Fonagy *et al.* (1994) provide a most useful review of the research literature. They identify a large number of defining attributes of resilient children, including (i) good social and economic environment, (ii) absence of organic deficits, (iii) easy temperament, (iv) younger age for those who have suffered a traumatic experience, (v) absence of early separation or losses, (vi) a good, warm relationship with at least one caregiver, (vii) availability in adulthood of good social support, (viii) positive school experience, (ix) involvement with organised religious activity and faith, (x) high IQ, (xi) superior coping styles, (xii) higher sense of autonomy and self-worth, (xiii) interpersonal awareness and empathy, (xiv) willingness to plan, and (xv) a sense of humour. One example comes from the work of Werner and Smith (1982), whose studies of resilient children at risk of developing behaviour problems showed that children who were very sociable and able to form strong relationships with people outside the immediate family, could reach adulthood without psychological or behavioural mishap.

In short, 'resilience is *normal* development under difficult conditions' (Fonagy *et al.* 1994: 233). Certainly, secure attachment histories help children cope with traumatic experiences such as living in a war zone or suffering a natural disaster. We therefore have to remind ourselves that the association between poor quality insecure relationships in childhood and later social and behavioural difficulties is not inevitable, only probabalistic (Belsky and Nezworski 1988b: 13). The exceptions to the rule are every bit as interesting. They throw much light on the dynamic relationship that takes place between biology and experience in human development. We shall consider three protective mechanisms and strategies that appear to be particularly effective in promoting resilience:

1. Intelligence and the ability to reflect on one's self.
2. Alternative psychological supports.
3. Removal from the risk environment.

### (1) Intelligence and the reflective self

Good levels of intelligence and cognitive ability can give people a powerful boost in their natural desire to make sense of social relationships, including even the most difficult and disturbed relationship experiences. The current wisdom is that levels of intelligence are the result of both genetic and environmental factors (Rutter and Rutter 1993: 210).

There is a strong genetic base to intellectual development which the environment may help or hinder. Identical twins are more alike in intelligence than non-identical twins, even when reared apart. 'The IQs of adopted children show higher correlations with those of their biological parents than with those of their adoptive parents'

(Rutter and Rutter 1993: 211). But nevertheless, the quality of the family environment can influence the level of cognitive functioning attained. Using control groups, it has been shown that adopted children reared in socially advantaged homes can achieve a 12-point advantage in IQ scores over children with similar biological parents raised in socially disadvantaged families (Capron and Duyme 1989). And conversely, it seems that there is a deleterious effect on cognitive development when the child suffers an adverse, disadvantaged social environment. But of course, what is also often associated with socially disadvantaged environments is an absence of good, active learning opportunities. It may be that cognitive development is impaired more by a lack of intellectual stimulation rather than poor quality and discordant personal relationships, although the two often go together.

Nevertheless, the research is telling us that even if children in socially or emotionally disadvantaged homes are not realising their full intellectual potential, there will be children in some disturbed families who have a naturally high level of intelligence. And if intelligence increases a person's ability to organise and model experience, including social experience, there is the prospect of making some sense of even disturbed relationships. The ability to make sense is closely tied to the level of integration and organisation that personality structures achieve. Intelligence, therefore, may protect some people, to a degree, from suffering severe psychological impairment as the result of disturbed relationship experiences.

What is being detected here, is the child's ability to generate sound inner working models of the self, of others, and of the relationship between them. From an early age the resilient individual appears able to *reflect* on both her own experience and the feelings and thoughts of other people, including her primary caregivers. Such an ability allows her to make sense of difficult feelings and locate herself within the relationship matrix. Mothers who are able to reflect on both their own experience and their parents' psychological strengths and weaknesses are able to achieve a 'narrative coherence'; they can make some working sense of the past and its possible effects on their own development (Fonagy *et al.* 1994: 241).

As we have seen, Main and Goldwyn (1984; Main 1991: 142–3) found that mothers who experienced their own mothers as rejecting, were in turn rejected by their own infants. These mothers had poor or idealised memories of their past. However, mothers who had been rejected by their own mothers and who were either *angry* about this or who could describe and perceive the relationship coherently, tended to have infants who were more securely attached. Similarly, mothers who could reflect on their own deprived experiences and the mental state of their parents also tended to have children who were securely attached (Fonagy *et al.* 1994). Associations have also been found between reflective fathers and securely attached children (Fonagy *et al.* 1994: 244).

Mains's findings have been confirmed by Grossmann *et al.* (1988). The researchers studied 65 mothers in two German towns. Mothers who had secure childhoods themselves tended to have securely attached children of their own. The mothers showed high levels of empathy as well as the ability to analyse their own and other people's experience and behaviour. However, perhaps the most interesting subgroup were the 18 per cent of mothers who did not receive supportive parenting themselves and yet had securely attached children. These women 'broke the cycle of unsupportive parenting by their willingness to be open and constructively regretful of their unhappy attachment experiences' (Grossmann *et al.* 1988: 256). Mothers who had insecure attachment experiences with their parents but were unwilling or unable to reflect on and analyse that unsupportive experience, were much more likely to have insecurely attached children of their own.

In Fonagy *et al.*'s (1994) study, it appeared that 'resilient' mothers could *accurately conceptualise* the nature of the relationship they had with their mother. They possessed 'autobiographical competence' in strong measure. They generated more effective models of self, other people and social relationships and so operated at a more socially competent level and therefore experienced less social stress. Social skills and cognitive ability are often closely associated. Mothers who hold coherent and consistent models of their own attachment history, whether that history was favourable or unfavourable, are more likely to develop integrated models of self and personality structures as well as enjoy secure attachments with their own children. Main and her colleagues believe that those who can access, process and organise all aspects of their relationship history, whether pleasant or painful, are likely to develop more fully integrated personality structures (Main 1991). In turn this allows them to respond accurately and sensitively to the emotional condition of others, including their own children. Fonagy *et al.* (1994: 245) also add that reflective mothers with a deprived childhood appear capable of more effective planning, finding a supportive partner, and learning from experience.

As Fonagy *et al.* (1994) argue, the mothers' strong reflective ability suggested that they possessed good social understanding and social empathy, abilities heavily associated with possessing effective 'mentalising' skills and a good 'theory of other minds'. These mentalising abilities work not only retrospectively in terms of making sense of their own parents' personalities, but also contemporaneously in terms of accurately and sensitively understanding their own babies. These resilient mothers seem able to reflect on the possible mental states of other people to a naturally high degree. This increases their empathy, sensitivity and responsiveness, all factors positively associated with the generation of secure attachment experiences. Conversely, a 'history of lack of love and neglect predicted infant insecurity only in mothers with low reflective self function ratings' (Fonagy *et al.* 1994: 245).

The ability to reflect on one's own and other people's mental states underpins a number of other attributes associated with resilience – imagination, the abilty to play and fantasise, and a sense of humour. 'But even more important,' conclude Fonagy *et al.* (1994: 250), 'is the feedback aspect of reflection. The opportunity of reflection upon intention allows for the modification of unhelpful internal models of relationships through encounters with new significant figures; it equips the individual with ballast, a self-righting capacity.'

### (2) Psychological supports

During their development, children often reach a 'turning point'. A new experience may open up or close down opportunities. For example, going to college and meeting new, socially competent people will offer a different set of relationship prospects from those which may lie in wait for the individual who drops out of school or becomes pregnant. In these ways, children may be able to build up psychological resistance to some of the risks in their social environment by enjoying strong *support* and sound experiences which enhance a positive concept of self outside the risk environment. For example, if the children of parents who quarrel and fight can develop a close relationship with an adult outside the family, they can protect themselves against some of the psychological stresses of home life. Children may get this support from teachers who encouraged them at school or uncles and aunts who recognise and appreciate their strengths and likeable qualities.

Women raised in an institutional setting showed resistance to some of the potentially damaging aspects of a life in residential care by finding a good partner. The emotional support of a reasonably stable and non-deviant spouse with whom the women had a close, confiding, harmonious relationship acted as a powerful protective mechanism against the upsets and disturbances experienced during childhood (Rutter *et al.* 1990: 137). In the absence of support, none of the ex-institutional women showed good parenting (Rutter 1988: 337).

One of the factors that seemed to help some girls develop a degree of protection against the psychological disadvantages of group-home life was a positive school experience. Success in drama or sports, practical subjects or art produced pleasure and an increased sense of self-worth and competence. Some of the group-home girls also learned to *plan* aspects of their working and relationship life in a more constructive and clear-sighted fashion. They could experience themselves as *potent*, able to *control* what was happening to them. This helped them overcome feelings of fatalism and reduced the tendency apparent in the other group-home girls to be impulsive. They tended to take action and not sit back and passively accept what life threw at them. This often extended to 'planning' relationships, careers and marriage. The girls did not rush into relationships, work or motherhood. They did not marry young. They stayed longer in education and work, continued to extend their experiences, meeting a wider range of people, who like themselves had developed a more planned and less impulsive approach to their lives. Therefore, if they did develop a love relationship, it was more likely to be with someone who was relatively stable and supporting, which further reduced their vulnerability to risk factors in their environment.

These young women provide another example of how individual qualities can influence the social environment, in this case benignly. To an extent we all select and shape our own social world (Scarr and McCartney 1983). Those who are hostile provoke aggression; people who smile engender cheerfulness; the helpful and generous trigger feelings of mutuality and co-operativeness.

Harris and Bifulco (1991: 263) offer an example of a 51-year-old woman who had suffered severe lack of care and depression over a long period but eventually formed a good, supportive relationship with her third husband. For the last nine years she had remained well. When she was seven her father had died. Her mother was unable to cope and sent her and her brother and sister to an institution until they were in their teens. She married young, had children quickly and found that her husband had been having affairs with other women. After her divorce she suffered a breakdown. Some of her children were adopted. A second husband drank and beat her up. She suffered another bout of depression, left her husband and came to live in London with her baby. She then met her current partner:

> 'He says he wishes he'd met me years ago. He's a very stabilizing person: I rely on him a lot. We talk and talk about everything, and sometimes we can't stop. He's so good for me – he's just like my Dad.' At the end of the interview she told us: 'I used to expect everything to go wrong and it did . . . I used to be a terrible pessimist and I'm not any more.' The perspective of attachment theory not only gives us an account of how early relationships can set us on a downward spiral, but also gives us hope that secure attachments in later life can help us climb up once more. (Harris and Bifulco 1991: 263)

Belsky and Pensky (1988: 208), in their review of the research which examined the transmission of dysfunctional behaviour across the generations, were equally struck by those who seemed to escape any serious psychological damage even though their childhood experiences were adverse. They cite several studies which show that women who were maltreated and abused as children could break the abusive cycle if they found a stable and emotionally supportive partner. Although the evidence suggests that the children of many abused mothers develop avoidant or disorganised patterns of attachment, the abused mothers who entered supportive relationships produced children with secure patterns of attachment behaviour. Supportive marriages and partnerships seem able to act as a buffer and interrupt the transmission of dysfunctional behaviour across the generations.

## (3) Removal

The third protective mechanism is total removal from the adverse environment. Adoption represents the most common and successful route out of seriously disturbed relationships with parents and biological families. Although there are inherent risk factors and extra developmental hurdles present in adoption (see Brodzinsky 1987; Howe 1992), on average adopted children fare better than children from similar social and family backgrounds who remain with at least one of their biological parents.

Several studies flesh out this picture. Maughan and Pickles (1990) were able to study some of the data generated by the National Child Development Study. This is a prospective study of the 17,000 children born in Britain during a week in March in 1958. The researchers were able to compare (i) illegitimately born children who were subsequently adopted, (ii) other illegitimate children who remained with their natural parents, and (iii) the large majority of legimate children.

The adopted children joined families in which there were few economic difficulties and many were described as middle class. Both the earlier and present studies of these children had shown that at age 7, 11 and 16, the illegitimate children who remained with their biological parents displayed the highest levels of behaviour problems. At 11 and 16, the adopted children exhibited an average level of behavioural problems somewhere between the illegitimate and legitimate group. At 16, the adopted children on average, like many of the illegitimate children, also showed greater problems in their relationships with peers than legitimate chidren. However, at age 23 comparisons with the illegitimate group showed that the adopted children, like the legitimate children, performed well educationally, though adopted men along with illegitimate men tended to have more job changes than their legitimate counterparts. Women in the illegitimate group were much more likely to become pregnant as teenagers than either their adopted or legitimate peers.

Tienari *et al.* (1990) studied the adopted children of schizophrenic birth mothers. Earlier work had suggested that a strong genetic component in the transmission of schizophrenia explained the finding that there was more schizophrenia found in the biological parents of schizophrenic adoptees than occurred in a control group.

More detailed investigations revealed that the quality of child rearing and interpersonal relationships in the adoptive home were critical in the emergence of schizophrenic symptoms in the adopted children of schizophrenic birth mothers. In 'healthy-rearing families the adoptees have little serious mental illness *whether or not their biological mothers were schizophrenic*' (Tienari *et al.* 1990: 373; emphasis in original). In contrast, adoptive homes in which child-rearing practices were not good produced a greater number of disturbed adoptees whatever the psychiatric condition of the their biological mothers. However, it was the adopted children of schizophrenic mothers who were most likely to become psychiatrically ill if they also found themselves with adopters whose parenting and relationship skills appeared poor. Of course, it may simply be that a dispositionally difficult child adversely affects the quality of parenting and family relationships:

> Genetically transmitted vulnerability, to be expected in only a portion of those at risk, may be a necessary precondition for schizophrenia, but a disturbing environment may also be significant in transforming the vulnerability into clinically overt schizophrenia. Being reared in a healthy family may also be a protective factor for a child at risk. Finally, there is the possibility that the genetic vulnerability of the offspring manifest itself in a way that includes dysfunction in the adoptive family . . . The question of the direction of control between adoptive parents and adoptees must remain open . . . This issue can be expressed as a question of whether illness in the adoptees induces dysfunction in the adoptive parents, or whether parental dysfunction contributes to pathology in the adoptees, and parental healthy functioning promotes health in the adoptees despite the genetic risk associated with illness in a biological parent. (Tienari *et al.* 1990: 377)

These results are fascinating insofar as they point yet again to the complex interplay between genes and experience. On the whole, adoption helped many illegitimately born children avoid some, though not quite all, of the developmental risks which they might have suffered if they had remained with their biological parents. What this research was not able to disaggregate was the relative weight of inherited personality characteristics, the influence of good quality parenting, and the risk factor associated with the actual psychological experience of being adopted.

Nevertheless, these studies do point to the conclusion that there are potential developmental advantages for many children if they are removed from family and community environments which are heavily disadvantaged and psychologically damaging and placed in high quality social environments. This is not necessarily an argument for removal. Equally powerful in many cases is the argument to improve the quality of family and community life for those children born into disadvantaged homes and run-down neighbourhoods. The concept of family support as well as material aid for disadvantaged families is receiving renewed recognition in the arguments for promoting less stressful social environments and more secure attachment experiences. We shall return to these ideas in the final chapter.

# 15

# Assessment

There is a tendency in the practice of many professionals to jump from problem to solution, without pausing to wonder what is actually going on. A failure to reflect on seemingly familiar situations leads to routine responses; professional habits whose origins have become obscured with time. Patients who tell their doctor that they feel a bit depressed might routinely be prescribed valium. Young mothers who complain of the stresses of looking after babies and toddlers might be directed towards a playgroup or nursery for a break. Clients who miss appointments and yet who continue to make demands of the service might have their cases closed.

Such responses often misunderstand the nature of the problem. In social work, such misunderstandings do not necessarily become recognised as bad practice. If the car mechanic makes a poor diagnosis and carries out the wrong repair, the car will still not start. Only occasionally will a poor assessment and inappropriate practice be immediately apparent in social work. Indeed, clients who fail to respond to the services offered or the 'treatments' proposed may themselves be blamed for the failure. Families who do not return for therapy are said not to be ready to change. A depressed mother who fails to respond to the efforts of the social worker may find that her case is closed. Clients who break 'partnership' agreements may be seen as irresponsible or confrontational.

There are many practices in social work which conspire to subdue a practitioner's interest in people. Procedures replace the struggle to make sense; performance matters more than percipience; the rational seeks to deny the emotional; politics triumphs over psychology; and the market place rides rudely over the personal and the intimate. But the control that the procedural, the political and the market appear to bring to the management and understanding of human relationship is ultimately illusory. They merely impose an order out of which the more demanding, disturbed and dysfunctional clients repeatedly break. Such clients and those who work with the distressed and delinquent often play by a different set of rules. These rules involve the emotions and they tend to be governed more by feelings than rational thought.

If we are to make sense of our clients and ourselves and respond appropriately and effectively, we need to understand how and why people behave as they do under stress and difficulty. We need to assess the character and quality of other people's relationships as well as our own. We have to know how to respond. The assessment phase of the social work process is of fundamental importance if the social worker is to practise sensitively, think intelligently, manage effectively and treat appropriately. The *social work process* has five basic steps (Howe 1987: 7):

1. Identification of *problem* or *need*: 'What is the matter?'
2. *Assessment* or *analysis* of people and their situations: 'What is going on?'
3. Statement of *goals*, plans and intentions: 'What is to be done?'
4. The *methods* by which the goals are to be achieved and the problem solved or need met: 'How is it to be done?'
5. Periodic *review* and *evaluation* of problem, assessment, goals and methods: 'Has it been done?'

The assessment, in which the social worker analyses what is going on, remains the central element in this process. The social worker seeks to make sense of what people are doing and saying, feeling and thinking. Her own feelings and reactions are not exempt from this analysis.

As social workers are concerned with the quality and character of interpersonal relationships and their effect on individuals and their experience, the focus of attention here is on the assessment of people and their relationships with others. The social worker has to wonder, puzzle and pose questions. 'What is the connection between the quality of early relationships and the quality of later relationships?' (Emde and Sameroff 1989: 13). Why is this fourteen-year-old boy behaving so aggressively and recklessly? What are the developmental consequences for a young girl whose mother constantly makes her feel guilty, claiming that it is the child's bad behaviour that is making the parent so ill? And what can possibly explain why this couple went out, taking their four young children with them, and bought an expensive freezer on hire purchase knowing full well that they already have serious rent arrears and are in heavy debt to another finance company?

For practical assessment purposes, we need to consider the interaction between an individual's developmental history; his or her personality; and the quality of his or her current social relationships and material environment. An assessment along these lines will help us to understand people's behaviour and feelings.

We also need to remind ourselves of the various types of relationship that might invite our attention and to which we might wish to apply the above assessment formula. In Chapters 8 to 13 we recognised six significant types of relationship and the kinds of behaviours and emotions that go with them: relationships with (i) parents and family, (ii) peers, (iii) self, (iv) society, (v) partners, and (vi) children. Recognising the nature of these relationships and understanding their past and present character marks the beginning of the assessment phase. Our claim throughout this book has been that if we can understand someone's history of attachment relationships and developmental experiences we can make sense of their behaviour in current relationships in each of the six categories.

There is a seventh category which we have touched upon from time to time. The social worker, with his or her own history of relationships, forms *professional relationships* with clients. These relationships affect assessments as well as practice and it is right and proper that the social worker reflect on these, preferably with another who is outside the relationship and who can hear what is being said with a dispassionate ear. Mattinson (1975) has considered how disturbed clients can affect social workers and how practitioners bring many of the characterstics of their relationship with the client into the supervision process. A good supervisor will be able to help the practitioner recognise and reflect on this process in a way that throws light on what is going on. The way social workers feel about particular clients and the effect clients have on them can act as a 'diagnostic' indicator.

In practice, the social worker may find herself working with any one or a combination of the six types of relationship. Relationships might be seen as disturbed, disrupted or disordered. Sameroff and Emde (1989: 230) describe a three-stage sequence in which the level of upset escalates from *perturbation* through *disturbance* to *disorder*.

(1) *Perturbations* include the normal range of upsets that affect an individual or family. A child or parent may fall ill, a grandparent may die, or a young teenage daughter may become pregnant. Although the event can be experienced as upsetting and disruptive, most people cope with and adjust to the new demands.

(2) *Disturbance* in relationships represents a slowness or a failure to cope with and adjust to changes in role, behaviour or social demands. 'Whereas a perturbation may resolve itself relatively quickly,' write Sameroff and Emde (1989: 230), 'a disturbance results when a problem in regulation persists over time.' The disturbance is not necessarily indicative of any pathology in the quality of the relationship, but it does represent a *risk*. If a mother is psychiatrically ill for a long time or a child has to remain in hospital for many months, not only are relationships temporarily disturbed, they are at risk of becoming disordered. Other environmental risk factors include such things as low income, poor housing, absence of social support and emotionally unavailable parents.

(3) *Disorder* is indicated 'when the relationship disturbance begins to restrict developmental processes' (Sameroff and Emde 1989: 230). A depressed mother's continued failure to be sensitive and responsive to her baby's signals and attempts at communication initially represents a disturbance in the mother–child relationship. However, if the neglect continues, the relationship is likely to deteriorate. The lack of reciprocity, mutuality and sensitivity means that the relationship is no longer coherent – it is disordered. Disordered relationships, in which availability and consistency are increasingly absent, threaten the baby's developmental prospects and, as we have seen, this can lead to insecure and anxious patterns of attachment. When disturbed relationships begin to affect the internal organisation and mental modelling of social experience, the individual's psychological structures beome disordered. The ability to cope sensibly and effectively with social situations becomes seriously impaired. Coping with the normal demands of daily life can become difficult and problematic.

This simple tripartite classification of perturbation, disturbance and disorder suggests a first step in assessing the quality of a relationship. It also hints at some of the different sites at which we might look for information (Emde and Sameroff 1989: 6). For example, if a child's behaviour is disturbed, the cause might be located (i) within the child (temperament, disposition, physiology), (ii) in the child's current relationships with others, or (iii) in the child's personality which is a product of past relationships. The authors further note that each diagnostic focus has a different implication for intervention and treatment.

The example recognises a basic division between the quality of past and present relationship experiences. But we have already argued that the individual's self, personality and level of social competence formed and developed within the context of earlier social relationships. Different qualities of relationship experience have a profound impact on the coherence of the selves which form and the levels of integration achieved by different personalities. Depending on the quality of these earlier relationship experiences, an individual will therefore find himself or herself more or less socially competent. Thus, his or her ability to deal competently with *present* social relationships and other contemporary environmental demands can only be fully understood in terms of his or her *past* experiences. So, for example, we might want to 'explore relevant life events, notably departures, serious illness, or death, and also arrivals, and the degree to which the presenting symptoms can be understood as recent or belated responses to them' (Bowlby 1979: 143).

In problematic and needful situations there is, therefore, a need to assess and analyse an individual's current behaviour and level of social competence within one or more of the six relationship categories described in Chapters 8 to 13. In making an assessment of one or more individuals, we need to consider:

1. *Present Relationships*. The quality and character of current relationship experiences and their effect on behaviour.
2. *Relationship History*. The quality and character of past relationship experiences and their implications for personality formation and present behaviour.
3. *Context*. The quality and character of the material environment, the level of social support, the number of stresses being experienced and the effect of all these on behaviour and experience, both in the present and the past.

## (1) Present relationships

In many cases, the character and quality of a client's current relationships both defines the concern and points to a possible understanding of the origins and nature of that concern. Does this child direct his anxieties and anger outward in the form of aggression and violence or inwards in the form of social withdrawal? Who is on the receiving end of the aggression? What is the current state of the parents' marriage? If relationships are poor and hostile between a mother and a father, what is the impact on their children's behaviour? What is the nature of a daughter's hostile feelings about the prospect of caring for her elderly, infirm mother?

The interest in relationships is based on the recognition that whereas some relationships appear to promote healthy adaptation and a general social competence, other relationships seem to lead to poor functioning and social difficulties. More fundamentally, relationship experiences become internalised and are essential to the formation of the self and the personality structures that emerge during development. Relationships are not only internalised, they are also carried forward to influence the way we handle later relationships. For example, people who exploit others and appear unable to empathise with their distress have often been found to have had punitive, rejecting and emotionally cold parenting experiences (Troy and Sroufe 1987).

When looking at a relationship, we need to consider both *what* each partner does, and *how* they do it (Sroufe 1989b: 98). For example, how well regulated and in-tune is the behaviour of each partner in terms of the behaviour and feelings of the other? What degree of empathy does a mother show when her baby is distressed? Sroufe (1989b: 104–9) believes that an assessment should describe three features of a relationship:

1. Content and quality.
2. Function.
3. Structure.

*(i) Content and quality*

A description of how people behave in a relationship and what they do to each other is the first step in trying to understand what is going on. But perhaps more revealing are the qualitative aspects of what goes on in the relationship. Looking at *motivation* invites us to consider how involved and committed is each partner to the relationship. What is the level of *interest* in the other? What is the level of emotional investment in the wellbeing of the partner, the child or the friend? How affected is the individual when the partner is upset, unavailable, or unresponsive? More generally, how *involved* are the partners in each other's experiences, outlooks and feelings? 'These are powerful variables,' says Sroufe (1989b: 105), 'in assessing the vitality and depth of a relationship.'

*Affective tone* refers to the feelings associated with and triggered by a relationship. Hostility between a parent and child invariably damages a child's psychological development. On the other hand, enjoyment, shared feelings and friendliness usually indicate a mutual confidence and satisfaction with the relationship. There is a common ground of emotion and understanding between the partners. We have already seen the importance of the quality of affective tone in relationships between parents and children and between adult partners.

*Operational style* is defined by Sroufe (1989b) as all those activities which regulate or fail to regulate the relationship. The style used means that either people find the relationship satisfies their emotional and social needs or they find it fails to satisfy and instead frustrates and bothers. Under operational style, Sroufe mentions such things as sensitivity and reciprocity; directness and clarity of communication; mutual support; and flexibility, especially when conflicts have to be resolved; and tolerance, particularly when there are disagreements. The more people are flexible, open, tolerant, adaptable and respectful of other people's autonomy and point of view, the more constructive, rewarding and pleasurable will they find their relationships with others to be.

Other observers, too, have described the various types and qualities of interaction and they, too, have noted their effect on relationships and development. Crittenden (1988: 142) has decribed the interacting styles of parent-to-children and children-to-parents. She recognises five types of adult interactions with children:

1. *Controlling* behaviour achieved by being *overtly hostile*. This behaviour includes such things as being physically abrupt, rough, glaring, angry and impatient.
2. *Controlling* behaviour achieved by being *covertly hostile*. The parent might ignore or override the child's mood or wishes by teasing or being inappropriately playful. There is a 'pseudo-sensitivity'. Activities might be changed abruptly, even if the

child is thoroughly absorbed in a piece of play. Such interventions irritate the child. It seems that his or her feelings are not important and easily devalued by the parent.

3. *Unresponsive* behaviour which sees the parent sitting in silence or perhaps showing no interest in what the child is doing. The parent remains distant and seemingly unavailable.

4. *Sensitive* patterns of behaviour describe parents whose responses are alert and attuned to the child's actions and feelings. Parents and child exhibit a kind of behavioural and emotional synchrony.

5. *Inept* patterns show behaviours from all four categories, although there is a liberal sprinkling of sensitivity. It is just that the parent either cannot maintain a coherent pattern of sensitivity at any one time, or sustain such a pattern over a period of time.

Crittenden also recognises a similar range of possible behaviours on the child's part. Children can be difficult, passive, or co-operative. *Difficult* behaviour includes crying, grimacing, wincing, rejecting proffered toys or refusing to engage with the parent. *Passive* patterns function to reduce contact with the mother and the child. Crittenden mentions such tactics as vacant facial expressions, reluctance to play, and failing to respond to adult overtures. *Co-operative* behaviour witnesses delight at social intercourse, turn-taking, and a general willingness to respond to adult interest.

These behavioural patterns have been used by Crittenden to study the interactions that take place between mothers and children. In three samples, she looked at relationships between low-income mothers and their children whose ages ranged from birth to 24 months. These are her findings:

the controlling interaction pattern was associated with abusing mothers, the unresponsive pattern with neglecting mothers, the inept pattern with marginally maltreating mothers, and the sensitive pattern with adequate mothers . . . Moreover, the infants of these mothers behaved in predictable ways: abused children were generally difficult, neglected children passive, and both marginally maltreated and adequately reared children cooperative. In other words, abusing mothers seemed to expect a dominant role in a coercive relationship; their infants seemed to expect the need for overt resistance to that control. Neglecting mothers appeared not to expect that a relationship with their babies would be established, and their infants' passivity suggested similar expectations. Marginally maltreating and adequate mothers were generally sensitively responsive to infant signals, suggesting that they expected engaging, noncoercive, reciprocal relationships. Their infants' cooperativeness, in turn, suggested that they expected their mothers to be responsive to their needs and wishes. (Crittenden 1988: 142–3)

Sroufe (1989b: 122), too, feels that these parent-child interactions can be mapped along a number of axes. Parenting behaviour can be seen as (i) warm and supporting *or* rejecting and hostile; (ii) permissive and mutual *or* restrictive, controlling and dominating; and (iii) anxious and overinvolved *or* calm and detached. In the manner of Crittenden he observes that particular clusters of parental behaviours are usually associated with certain patterns of behaviour in the child. He gives several examples of complementary relationships. In one he describes a parent who is affirming and understanding and a child who is disclosing and expressive (Sroufe 1989b: 122).

### (ii) Function

This aspect refers to how well the relationship is meeting the needs of the partners. Sroufe (1989b: 106) identifies the two main functions of the family as: '(1) nurturing (rearing) of children and (2) meeting of adult intimacy needs'. Failure of one or both of these functions threatens a child's healthy psychological development. Feeling understood, supported, cared for and valued are what most of us are looking for in our personal relationships. Their absence leads to anxiety, sadness, low self-esteem or anger. Relationships are the social environment in which our emotions and needs find expression and receive definition. They help us to regulate our feelings. If our relationships fail to regulate our affect, we are left frustrated, anxious, confused and angry. These are not constructive feelings and they are likely to leave us psychologically frustrated, socially incompetent and emotionally diverted from the business of everyday life and work.

### (iii) Structure

Most of the ideas about structure derive from the work of family analysts and family therapists (for a good introduction, see Burnham

1986). To some degree, relationship functions imply relationship structures, and vice versa. Distort one and you distort the other. For example, parents should parent their children. Even though they may not be having their intimacy needs met by their adult partner, they should not attempt to meet these needs through their children by treating them like siblings or lovers. This compromises the child's need to be nurtured and disturbs their psychological development. Most families have rules and these define the way things are done and handled in their family. Structural rules which promote the healthy functioning of relationships within the family (for both adults and children) can be contrasted with family rules which inhibit open, accurate and flexible exchanges between family members. Families which have an unspoken rule which says that strong feelings and conflict are never to be expressed may find that powerful emotions have nowhere to go except inwards (in the form of a 'symptom') or, in some cases, outwards (in the form of a member leaving, escaping or acting delinquently).

Several of the parameters identified in this section have been studied by Cohen *et al.* (1990). Amongst their more specific findings, the researchers noted that parents who tried to control their children using 'power-assertive punishments' (threatening, bullying, hitting, isolating, shouting) often found themselves with a child who was aggressive and delinquent. Parents who were inconsistent in enforcing rules and decisions were associated with children who were more socially withdrawn. Mothers who were 'inattentive', lacked concern and showed little 'investment' in their children (for example, failed to take them to the dentist and were negligent about vaccinations and inoculations) had children who were at risk of substance abuse.

Several of these assessment dimensions crop up in Mattinson and Sinclair's (1979) study of families being visited by social workers. Their work, in fact, predates the codes and classifications developed by researchers such as Sroufe, but their approach anticipates the kind of thinking developed by more recent analysts and observers of family relationships. Mattinson and Sinclair (1979: 31) identified four characteristics which were shared by most of the families seen by the social workers: (i) ambivalent marital bonds, (ii) lack of success in parental roles, (iii) lack of constructive support from families of origin, and (iv) continual threat of separation from one or other members of the family.

*Ambivalent marital bonds* was the most important feature of the life of the families studies. The researchers convey the essence of this assessment characteristic by quoting a social worker:

> The parents are locked in a kind of marriage where they can't live without each other and yet their interaction isn't satisfying and doesn't meet each other's needs. They're deprived as people, so they haven't very much to offer. She was one of fifteen and he spent long periods in care. Neither has much affection to give. (Mattinson and Sinclair 1979: 32)

The parents need each other though each one finds it difficult to meet the other's needs. Needing people who are not very good at meeting your needs produces feeling of anger. Such relationships are wracked with conflict and emotional ambivalence.

*Lack of success in parental roles* was most evident in the way the women talked about their inabilities and failings as mothers. Some had, at one time or another, abandoned their children; some had been neglectful; while yet others had requested that their children be received into the care of the local authority. The families also experienced serious financial problems. Debt and material deprivation were common. Few of the fathers were successful bread-winners.

*Lack of alternative sources of support* arose when families were cut off from their families of origin. There were two ways in which this might happen. In some cases the children's grandparents were geographically distant (for example, they were living in another country). In other cases, the parents' own family of origin had either cut off ties or were in difficulties themselves and so unable to provide emotional and practical support. If a parents' marriage broke up, there was no obvious source of support for either the separated parents or their children.

*Continual threats of separation* occurred in most of the families. The knock-on effect of separation was to consider who should be living with whom. Again, Mattinson and Sinclair (1979: 34) use quotes from social workers to illustrate the phenomenon: 'The department has a history of involvement with this case. The mother buggered off to Ireland and for two years they tried to reconstitute the family under the father. Then it became obvious that this wasn't going to work and they sent out a telegram to the mother asking her to come back.'

## (2) Relationship history

The assessor is interested in all those experiences which might have had an impact on a person's emotional and psychological development and which have helped to form his or her personality. Although the assessment concentrates on the quality of interpersonal experiences, it does not deny the existence or significance of genetic dispositions and biologically-given temperaments in the individual's makeup. The social worker is generally not in a good position to tease out or make discrete measurements of such things, although occasionally he or she will be able to note the impact on social relationships of babies who have feeding difficulties, children who are autistic, adults who have learning disabilities, or people who seem constitutionally bright and cheerful.

The most common starting point, particularly in the assessment of children, but of equal relevance to the assessment and understanding of adult functioning, is the type of parenting the individual received during his or her childhood. Cohen *et al.* (1990: 255) identify three *risk* factors associated with parent characteristics and family structure:

1. Parents who have had treatment for and a history of a psychiatric illness.
2. Parents who have had a history of problem behaviour, including alcoholism and criminality.
3. Remarriage.

Each of these risks can be often associated with disturbed and disordered family environments. One of the most consistent and powerful observations reported by researchers is that it is the upset in and disorderliness of social relationships within families that disturbs psychological and emotional development. The risk factors described above either create the disorder (mental illness) or they are caused by the disorder (remarriage after breakdown and conflict in the first marriage).

Severe upsets, disturbances and disorders in social relationships between parents and children are associated with insecure patterns of attachment behaviour, poorly integrated personality structures and social incompetence. It is within the matrix of particular social relationships that the pattern of a child's attachment behaviour forms. As we have seen, in broad terms, attachment patterns can be classified as either ordered (secure) or disordered (absent or insecure). We have seen that the different patterns of attachment behaviour are also associated with different developmental pathways, a range of personality types, and various behavioural characteristics. These behaviours and personality traits will often be carried through into adulthood, particularly if the social environment remains unchanged throughout childhood. However, the concept of resilience discussed in Chapter 14 may explain why some people manage to become socially competent adults in spite of adverse relationship experiences during their childhood years.

An assessment of past relationship experiences may help the social worker understand a client's current behavioural and relationship difficulties. These may become particularly pronounced at times of increased stress. Stress levels may increase as a result of social incompetence within the conduct of a relationship. Equally important, stress levels may rise as a result of socio-economic difficulties. A good guide to understanding current relationship and coping abilities is indicated by the pattern of childhood attachment patterns experienced by the client. Chapter 6 provides detailed descriptions of the main patterns of attachment behaviour experienced in early childhood. We now consider how these early experiences can affect the behaviour and relationship styles of older children and adults. As we have seen, each attachment pattern is associated with a particular personality structure and level of social competence expressed in terms of the ability to relate to others appropriately and effectively:

1.  Secure attachments.
2.  Insecure–anxious–ambivalent–resistant attachments.
3.  Insecure–anxious–avoidant attachments.
4.  Insecure–anxious–disorganised attachments.
5.  Nonattachments.

*(i) Secure attachment experiences*

This individual is capable of forming and sustaining close, intimate, stable, responsive and reciprocal social relationships. Personality structures and coping mechanisms stay intact under moderate levels of conflict, anxiety, stress and frustration. There are strong feelings of self-confidence and self-worth. The individual regards himself or herself as socially competent and acceptable. Trust in others and the ability and desire to empathise are readily present. There is a relaxed assuredness and general confidence about social relationships. Other people represent a potential source of interest, pleasure and mutuality. There is a general 'moving towards' people.

## (ii) Insecure–anxious–ambivalent–resistant attachments

The need for closeness and intimacy is recognised, but their availability cannot be taken for granted. In the past, close relationships have proved to be inconsistent and unreliable. All seems to be going well so long as the other person is available, but the closeness and responsiveness do not last. Therefore, other people with whom one seeks an intimate relationship can never quite be trusted. The world of relationships and other people never feels entirely under the control of the ambivalent personality. This produces feelings of anxiety. Such feelings are most heightened at times of separation. A lack of confidence and self-doubt about one's lovability raise old fears of being abandoned, unwanted and unloved.

The ambivalent character is possessed of a deep insecurity. Feelings of anxiety and emotional tension are never very far below the surface. In terms of relationships, there is a fear of letting go; emotionally speaking, there is a need to cling and hang on. Other people cannot be trusted to return and be available once they are out of sight. A lot of emotional energy may be spent on keeping the other person in sight and to hand. Jealousy and possessiveness result in frequent rows, feelings of hurt and fears of abandonment. Feelings of anger are easily roused as threats of separation or loss are flung into most quarrels and upsets. And yet to feel dependent on another also produces feelings of anger, resistance and resentment: 'I want to be close to you and to need you but all my past experience has taught me that although you love me now, sooner or later you will leave me and I shall be alone, desperate and hurt. I am therefore confused and angry that I have to need you and want you to need me. I am therefore in a constant state of anxiety knowing that you have the power to hurt me.' Thus, other people are experienced with a profound ambivalence.

Unlike the avoidant personality who defends himself or herself by trying to switch off strong emotions, the ambivalent personality mounts defences which see him or her either clinging on to the relationship or pre-empting the perceived separation by walking out or threatening to leave first. The preferred defence mechanisms include denial of strong feelings, projection of one's own emotional state onto other people or objects and blaming them for one's difficulties, and anti-social acting out. There is a desperate need for intimacy, love and attention, but those who might provide these things cannot be trusted to supply them constantly and unconditionally. There is a fretful, even neurotic quality to the character of the ambivalent person's close relationships with others. Conflict is the main characteristic of ambivalent relationships. There is a proneness to be attention-seeking. Life is often lived at an emotionally heightened level with much drama. The individual is liable to behave impulsively and things seem to be in a perpetual state of crisis. Actions indicate feelings. There is a need to ward of feelings of loneliness and emptiness which leads to a constant demand that the world take note and become involved. Not to take note and not to become involved feel like rejection and abandonment. Relationships which do break down produce powerful feelings of anger and anxiety. At such times there is much physical and emotional thrashing about as yet again one feels that one is essentially impotent and helpless when it comes to controlling other people's emotional availablity and reliability. In relationship terms, there is a 'moving against' people; the ambivalent personality is constantly drawn to other people but fights against the dependency and anxiety that such relationships arouse.

*(iii) Insecure–anxious–avoidant attachment experiences*

The avoidant individual finds it difficult to form and sustain intimate relationships. In the past the need to be loved and valued resulted only in hurt and rejection. There is therefore a tendency to avoid emotional closeness; it is potentially dangerous. There is a deep-rooted hesitancy, reluctance and even fear of allowing oneself to become emotionally involved. Compulsive self-reliance and attempts to be emotionally independent are therefore common characteristics. However, the structure of the personality is such that even moderate levels of anxiety, emotional tension or conflict cause upset and breakdown. There is emotional brittleness and fragility beneath the apparent indifference. Relationships are indiscriminate and conducted on a relatively shallow plane. There is little emotional investment in other people. The ability to be interested in others and empathise is low. The avoidant personality can be rejecting and hostile when faced with other people's emotions and feelings. In spite of a cool, often rigid persona, there is underlying emotional uncertainty. Unsure about loving and uncertain about being loved, feelings of self-worth are low. Hints of despair and depression lie behind the stiff upper lip. Lacking self-confidence, the avoidant personality expects rejection. In emotional terms, there is tendency to 'move away' from people.

### (iv) Insecure–anxious–disorganised attachments

Infants who have a caretaker who is available and actively involved in their care but who is, at the same time, hostile, violent and a cause of fear, find themselves in a dilemma. Normally, fear triggers attachment behaviour. But for the child whose parent or caregiver is both the attachment figure and the cause of the fear, there is no resolvable course of action. The only thing to do is freeze, either physically, emotionally or both. The anxiety and confusion is too great to handle. The only way to defend oneself against such deep conflict is to attempt some psychological opt-out; simply try not to be there. All emotional feelings are shut down. The resulting attachment pattern is therefore disorganised. Relationships with other people are a source of confusion. The result is not an attempt at emotional independence, characteristic of the avoidant personality, nor the emotional ambivalence shown by the resistant personality, but a halfway defensive strategy of emotional neutrality. The child or the adult is neither distant nor involved. They are present but unavailable; complaisant but incapable of showing reciprocity. In relationship terms, there is a 'standing still'.

### (v) Nonattachments

The absence of any opportunity to form close affectional bonds with other people during early childhood denies the child the chance to express attachment behaviour. Children raised in caring but essentially impersonal institutions are most likely to develop the behaviours associated with disorders of nonattachment, though in theory any profoundly unresponsive environment could deny the infant the opportunity to form an attachment relationship. Individuals who have not had attachment experiences handle social relationships in a superficial manner and they lack notions of reciprocity and mutuality. Other people are valued only insofar as they meet certain basic needs – food, sex, money, opportunities. Relationships with others are simply a means to an end and may well be abruptly abandoned once the end has been met. Often, there is little long-term satisfaction for those who find themselves involved in such relationships. For those who have not experienced a strong attachment relationship, there is no great sense of loss or anxiety when relationships disappear or break down. They are simply replaced. There is a lack of discrimination in the friendliness expressed towards others – anyone, it appears, will do. There is a tendency to be impulsive. Conflict, frustration and situations that deny access to things which would meet felt needs lead to anger and aggression.

## The Carr family

Mrs Carr has four children. The pattern of ambivalent, anxious and insecure attachments, and the relationships they sponsor, are typical of many of the families seen by social workers. Throughout her own childhood, Mrs Carr was repeatedly locked in the family's apartment with her younger sister while their prostitute mother went out looking for clients. When her mother had money she spent it quickly and extravagantly on drink, food and luxuries. The girls would be bought frilly dresses and boxes of chocolates, but these good times were short-lived. Although food was left for the children when their mother went out, they suffered many periods of serious neglect. Mrs Carr would return home from school and often find no-one at home. When she was seven, the two sisters were placed in foster care. Mrs Carr's difficult and testing behaviour as a child resulted in frequent changes of foster parent.

Shortly after leaving school at sixteen, Mrs Carr became pregnant. She lived with a young man but the relationship did not last long. Just before her nineteenth birthday, Mrs Carr met her husband. He was unemployed, impulsive and immature. They rowed a great deal, and after particularly stormy arguments he would return to his mother. Mr and Mrs Carr had three children in quick succession. Mr Carr resented the children and seemed jealous of the attention they received from his wife who taunted him saying he was just a 'big baby' and dared him to leave. He began to drink a lot. He also became involved with a gang of men and joined them in a series of warehouse burglaries. The gang were actually caught after their stolen truck had run out of petrol. Mr Carr received a nine-month prison sentence.

Mrs Carr is overweight. Her moods swing between excitement and depression. She often complains to her social worker that the children 'get her down'. Nevertheless, the older ones are often to be found at home even though the school makes frequent complaints about their non-attendance. Most nights the younger children end up sleeping with their mother in her large bed. There are times when Mrs Carr is almost a daily visitor to the social work department: she wants to know whether or not she should have the baby immunised; she would like to move house because the neighbours are making her life a misery with their foul language which she says is not good for the children to hear; she wants to make a complaint to the head of the agency about the incompetence of her regular social worker; she gives this same social worker a tin of biscuits that she has won at a raffle. The social worker never knows when Mrs Carr is about to describe her as wonderful or awful, 'for her or against her', although she can guarantee that hardly a week would pass by without some crisis or other befalling the mother and her family. Mrs Carr seems to test the social worker's patience and goodwill to the limit. Appointments are broken, school teachers are insulted, and confessions are made in which, for example, Mrs Carr tells the social worker that she had drunk so much vodka the night before that she failed to wake up in the morning and send the children to school.

When the social worker visits Mrs Carr's home, she is expected to be 'one of the family'. Cups of tea appear and the children climb all over their visitor, while Mrs Carr tells the worker about a man she had met in the pub the previous night who 'really fancied' her and that she would like to go to bed with him 'because he was very cuddly and kept buying me expensive cocktails'. Sex seems to represent closeness rather than eroticism in Mrs Carr's accounts. She says that she misses her husband even though they quarrelled endlessly when he was at home. On very bad days, Mrs Carr slumps into a deep apathy. No food is prepared, the children whine and cry and she threatens to kill herself if they do not keep quiet and behave.

Her usual way out of this low, irritable mood is to go out and treat herself even though she cannot afford the item. On this basis, an ice-cream maker, a large framed picture of a cat and its kittens, and an enormous freezer have been acquired.

Although Mrs Carr copes reasonably well while the children are babies, she is less tolerant of them when they grow older. Not only do they continue to make demands of her, they seem less prepared to take any notice of their mother's increasingly impatient harangues. She feels helpless, frustrated and angry when faced with the children's wild and uncontrollable behaviour. Twice in recent months, Mrs Carr has asked her social worker to take Alan, her eldest son, away. On one occasion he had set fire to the rabbit hutch while Mrs Carr's sister and her young children were visiting the family. Although none of the rabbits died, two of them had their fur badly singed. It was only the excited barking of the family's two dogs that alerted Mrs Carr to the incident. It seems only a matter of time before Alan, already well-known to the police over a number of minor criminal episodes, will be in more serious trouble.

## (3) Context

The quality of the social and physical environment respresents the most visible and pervasive element in the assessment process. A poor quality environment may be a cause of stress in its own right. Bad housing, violent and criminal neighbourhoods, and low income can cause and compound relationship difficulties.

If the physical and material environment is stressful, this can adversely affect the way parents relate to each other and to their children. If relationships become strained and conflictual, this merely adds to the stresses already being experienced. People under stress and experiencing anxiety benefit from and respond positively to social support. But poor quality environments are not rich in sources of social support. Most people living in such environments are too absorbed by the demands of their own concerns to have the emotional time and energy to help others. And finally, many families who do not function well – interpersonally, socially or economically – are particularly likely to end up living in the poorest, most physically deprived neighbourhoods, thus adding to their already existing difficulties. Perversely, the families already under stress and least able to cope with the added burdens of a low quality environment are the familes most likely to find themselves living in the poorest housing, on the lowest incomes, and in the most deprived parts of the community.

This picture illustrates some of the problems of teasing out the direction of causal relationships when trying to understand the problems experienced by those living in low socio-economic conditions. Do people who are socially inept inevitably end up living in the poorest environments or do poor environments undermine and tax people's social competence? Does poverty lead to crime or do the police mainly search out criminals in poor areas? Is drug use and abuse high in run-down neighbourhoods because adolescents are more disturbed and less well adjusted or are drugs just more available in such communities?

The research evidence certainly correlates low socio-economic status with teenage problem behaviour and family breakdown, but it cannot be argued that poverty simply causes delinquency and family problems. The picture is complicated and difficult to unravel. However, what is not in doubt is that environmental stresses increase as incomes fall, housing standards drop, local crime rates rise, community resources stretch, and social support networks fragment, break down and disappear. Assessments need to take the material and social contexts of people's lives into full account if behaviour and relationships are to be fairly and comprehensively understood.

# 16

# Responses

An assessment should lead to an understanding and not a judgement. Using the insights of attachment theorists and developmental psychologists, the assessment is not designed to establish who did what to whom or to apportion blame. It is not an investigation. The assessment encourages analysis rather than accountability, compassion rather than condemnation. In this final chapter we look at three broad types of social work responses which appear in the wake of the assessment process.

**Past, present and future practice orientations**

Over the years, social workers have tended to direct more of their energies towards work which is supportive and understanding and away from techniques which are psychotherapeutic and interpretive. The shift is based on more than simple doubts about the effectiveness of psychotherapy in a social work context. If the quality of social relationships in childhood affect the formation of personality, social competence and behaviour, it might be appropriate (and cost-effective) to help parents provide a good quality social environment so that their children's psychological development might take place under more propitious conditions. Within this perspective, family support work and professional patience become the basis of sound policy and practice.

We also know that some of the most demanding, difficult and time-consuming clients are those who experience constant conflict and anxiety in their social relationships. Procedural responses and task-orientated, time-limited techniques have little impact on such cases. Psychologically speaking, these methods miss the point.

Developmentally oriented assessments suggest that social services need to take a longer-term view when working with families and individuals who are both demanding and time-consuming.

For example, the basic aim of family support, long-term involvement and benign guidance is to alter the quality of care provided to children. However small the success, it means a child's developmental pathway is shifted, if only a little, in the direction of a more coherent and consistent psychological experience. As a result, the child's and the adult's working models of self and of relationships are modified (Belsky and Nezworski 1988b: 14). But the implications of a developmentally orientated practice go beyond even this. Belsky and Isabella (1988: 87) remind us that a whole host of factors affect the quality of a child's relationship experiences: the parents' relationship history, the personalities involved, the quality of relationships, the degree of social support, the level of income, and the stressfulness of the neighbourhood. The risk is greatest when two or more of these factors are running in the direction of adversity. Stress levels rise. Therefore, the implications of any full and rounded assessment are that a range of interventions and responses is probably necessary. Three types of response will be outlined:

1. Understanding.
2. Support.
3. Psychotherapy.

### (1) Understanding

Perhaps the most underestimated social work skill is that of understanding. The attempt to make sense of other people's feelings and behaviour is more than an intellectual event. It is an act of compassion. Rather than feel exasperated or confused with difficult and demanding clients, the social worker who tries to understand what is happening is more likely to show patience and develop humane practices. With distressed and disturbed people, the social worker 'must be warm without being seductive, firm without being punitive, and accepting without having to identify with his mode of behavior' (Reiner and Kaufman 1959: 14).

When we feel anxious and uncertain in a relationship, various emotions and courses of action present themselves. We might want to stop the relationship; cases are closed or neglected. If we feel angry, the temptation might be to punish the client. Help might be denied or court action might be threatened. Attempts are sometimes made to simplify confusing and troublesome relationships by trying to fit them into some rational plan. Agreements are made; objectives are set; tasks are prescribed. Such rationally based approaches work with many clients but by no means all. When clients repeatedly fail to carry out tasks or seem wilfully to ignore agreements, the social worker needs to ask why. There is little point in feeling cross, let down or punitive.

Distressed and disturbed people evoke and provoke strong feelings in others. The social worker, of course, is no exception. If practitioners are to work successfully with people who are in distress and if they do not want to feel constantly blown off course, they will need to make good sense of turbulent relationships. Tolerance and a capacity not to be too surprised or hurt are most important. Understanding what is going on allows the social worker to 'stay with' the client and not to give up. Many of social work's most difficult clients will have had a long history of rejections and failed relationships. This is why the social worker needs to stick with 'hard' cases. If she gives up and rejects demanding people and hard cases, she will be behaving like everyone else with whom clients have been in relationship. An assessment based on a developmental perspective provides a powerful intellectual base on which the social worker might stand firm and stay involved. Even though the client feels that he or she may never emerge from the distress, the social worker, by keeping her bearings can maintain her presence. She can be someone who is steady, reliable and available when the emotional drama is high and the levels of upset are great.

Understanding others not only helps social workers keep their bearings, but *being understood* also helps clients feel acknowledged and valued. Being understood is reassuring; it shows care and interest; and it can clear confusion. Understanding and empathy have long been recognised as core elements in the helping relationship (Rogers 1961; Truax and Carkhuff 1967). In their study of clients' views, Mayer and Timms (1970: 84) quote one respondent who said 'I sort of felt, well, somebody understands and they're interested and they want to help and they don't think it's silly.'

In contrast, clients who feel that their social worker does not understand them or shows no interest in their situation feel resentment and hostility and they may terminate contact. 'I know I'm not perfect,' reflected a mother of a difficult and disturbed son, '*I* know that, but they've never got down to how any of us was . . . I felt misunderstood. Even now I feel upset about everything' (Howe 1989: 72).

Understanding clients is less appealing to those who wish to quantify practice and package responses. And yet the absence of an understanding relationship is capable of undermining the most efficient care packages and the most standardised of procedural responses. To understand and be understood are powerful features of all human relationships (Howe 1993). They are particularly important at times of stress and difficulty. Successful relationships meet our needs for intimacy and offer us emotional support, care and understanding as well as protect us against stress and adversity.

## (2) Support

The research evidence shows that the absence of support contributes to feelings of loneliness, depression and despair. Its presence raises self-esteem and lightens the burden of daily life. Support can come in two forms: practical and emotional (Gibbons 1992c: 27).

*Practical support* can include help with looking after the children, help with the shopping, more money, loans of money, and obtaining better housing. *Emotional support* describes such things as the opportunity to confide in someone, knowing that other people are available when needed, and being recognised, accepted and valued by another person. It can also include motivational features such as providing encouragement and acknowledgement.

Cohen and Syme (1985) recognise three other kinds of support. *Status* recognition helps to boost confidence and may be achieved through marriage, gaining a job or acquiring a social position. *Information* can be supportive; it gives people knowledge and the resources to develop some control over their experiences. Informational support can include giving advice and helping people to make decisions. *Social companionship* includes the rewards of friendship and gaining pleasure and relaxation through shared leisure pursuits.

Again and again, research highlights the powerful role that support plays in people's ability to cope with the stresses and strains of everyday life. A close, intimate and confiding relationship with a caring partner appears to provide the most effective and potent kind of emotional support. It is no surprise, therefore, to discover that many of those who are not coping well with social relationships, who suffer poor mental health and find living in disadvantaged neighbourhoods particularly stressful also lack emotional support. Even if they have a partner, their difficulties probably mean that he or she is failing to give help, care and support. Indeed, in many cases the quality of the relationship with the partner is probably part of the problem.

Attempts to improve relationships between partners is a familiar aim in social work and counselling, not just because it is a worthwhile goal in itself but because strong mutual support between people improves personal wellbeing, mental health and the quality of parenting. For example, many studies have found that the stronger the marital relationship the better the quality of the partners' parenting (Belsky and Vondra 1989: 174–8). But conversely, if relationships between parents are poor, they not only reduce the strong positives, they begin to introduce strong negatives into the quality of child rearing. In other words, the quality of the relationship between parents tends to move the quality of parenting in either a clear positive or negative direction; from the child's point of view it rarely remains neutral.

Mothers who do not enjoy a supportive marital relationship can sometimes find support from family or female friends. In their review of social networks, Belsky and Vondra (1989: 178–85) report that in the absence of marital support, good and supportive relationships with other women helped some mothers maintain their confidence, self-esteem and sense of competence both in themselves and in their ability to rear their children.

Social workers can help promote each of these different kinds of support, although they may not always be the best people to deliver them. Support locks people into the social fabric. The presence of support means that people feel that they belong, that they are cared for and valued. Support reduces stress and decreases anxiety. Stress and anxiety, as we know, undermine self-control and disturb relationships – with partners, parents and children. Support, therefore, represents an attempt to improve the quality of social as well as material experience.

The most effective kind of support comes from intimate partners, followed by family and close friends. But support can also be found at the level of neighbourhood resources and within professional relationships. Without emotional and practical support marriages are at risk of falling apart, parenting can become poor, and children may grow up disturbed and disruptive. Rutter (1988: 340–1) speculates:

It is well established that attachment relationships in infancy have a powerful anxiety-reducing function. Young children are more ready to explore their environment in the presence of an attachment figure and they seek proximity to such figures when faced with stressful circumstances. Does the protective effect of a warm confiding marital relationship work in the same fashion? . . . it could still be that attachment components constitute the crucial elements in the provision of support. It seems from the studies in adult life that confiding is an essential part of a supportive relationship . . . It is clear that that at all ages from infancy onwards human beings develop committed relationships that share many similar qualities.

## Support within the relationship between social worker and client

In its basic emotional form, support has *nurturing* qualities. The social worker's relationship with clients who have had a history of emotional deprivation must show consistency and care. Promises must be kept and the social worker must be reliable. Being attentive and responsive are important. However, the client, though attracted to the nurturing qualities of the relationship, will be reluctant to trust its continued availability. The client's experience is one of always being let down and ultimately abandoned. The social worker will have to learn to live with (and understand) anger, rejection, ambivalence and indifference. The developmental base to this type of work is also recognised by Nezworksi *et al.* (1988: 360):

We agree with Bowlby, Mahoney and other cognitive therapists that the deep structural change we are targeting is most likely to occur in the context of an emotionally significant relationship that challenges and disconfirms early unconscious assumptions (e.g., 'I am unworthy of nurturance, the world is dangerous') or their coping derivatives (e.g. 'Don't trust anyone, I don't need help'). In this view, a significant ingredient for change involves the nurturing actions of the therapist. The therapist strives to establish a secure, safe, and caring relationship.

It is to be doubted, though, that social workers could or should engage in such undiluted psychotherapy. They can never provide the attachment experiences that clients need and probably never had.

Social workers should simply be 'good enough'. Workers who are sucked into meeting every need soon discover that the client is the source of a seemingly endless stream of demands. All too often, the worker ends up feeling drained and angry. 'More therapeutic,' found Mattinson and Sinclair (1979: 211), '. . . was to say "No" when this seemed inappropriate, and to face facts which, at times, included the awfulness of the clients' behaviour, and then say, "I'll come again next week".'

Nevertheless, a good relationship is capable of providing a 'corrective emotional experience' (Alexander and French 1946 cited in Neworski *et al.* 1988). This can be particularly important for mothers of young children whose parenting skills need to be developed and supported. If the social worker can be consistent, caring and reliable, this allows the client to improve her level of social functioning within a reasonably predictable relationship. It might also boost feelings of trust and self-worth. All of these will contribute in some small measure to better parenting.

For more focused and expert attention on matters of parenting, the social worker might consider referring the client to a psychologist or other child guidance professional who runs skills training classes. Bowlby (1988: 20) was in no doubt that help with parenting and teaching mothers and fathers how to understand their baby, and how to respond appropriately and accurately, had long-term value. He believed that skilled help given to parents during the first few months or years of the baby's life went far in assisting parents to develop an affectionate and understanding relationship with their child. These are important years for the infant and any improvements in the quality of early social relationships will have lifelong benefits for personality development and social competence.

*Social support of the family*

The principles which guide the social worker's relationship with clients also underpin the idea of family support seen at a community level. Families, says Fahlberg (1991: 68), provide:

> safety and security, stimulation and encouragement, and reasonable expectations and limits. Children need both emotional support and structure as they meet each developmental challenge and cope with inevitable frustration in the process. Children who do not receive support become bewildered, insecure, and lacking in self-esteem.

If children and their parents experience less stress, fewer conflicts and more support, the quality of their lives will be improved. Good support enhances optimism, feelings of self-worth and a sense of control over one's own experience. Social relationships between adults and between parents and their children will be less conflictual. The quality of family life affects nurturing experiences, development and safety. This is why social workers should be constantly mindful of the significance and importance of the quality of:

> interpersonal relationships, the necessity of building alliances with children and adults by enhancing communication skills, increasing the individual's knowledge of self, and the importance of developing a plan for continuity of relationships throughout a lifetime. (Fahlberg 1991: 12–13)

Social policy and practice should aim to strengthen relationships and improve the quality of family life. This outlook challenges the idea that children are best protected by investigation, detection, rescue and removal. The welfare of children and the wellbeing of parents is best promoted by supporting the family. Whittaker (1993: 6) identifies a number of ideas which encourage family support:

- the idea of the family as the ideal developmental context for the child.
- the notion of services as first and foremost family supportive and family strengthening.
- a primary focus on meeting basic developmental needs of children in culturally acceptable ways as opposed to identifying and treating child or family pathology.
- more focus on what might be termed an ecological perspective . . . moving from changing children and families from the 'inside out' to the 'outside in', e.g. by working to create more supportive environments as well as improving individual coping skills.

The studies carried out by Brown and Harris (see Harris 1993) identify the important role that support plays in people's ability to cope with stresses and difficulties. It appears that it is the quality of emotional support rather than the frequency of social contact that helps people cope. Mothers who suffered depression were found to have experienced a lack of care during childhood. This undermined their confidence and feelings of self-worth. Their lives seemed to be one long series of unsupportive relationships from childhood to adulthood. However, good quality supportive relationships could help overcome some of the effects of these childhood adversities. Harris (1993: 103) describes how one woman managed to escape the downward spiral of worthlessness, hopelessness and despair by finding strong supportive relationships in an adoptive mother and a caring husband:

> One of our respondents was removed from her mother at the age of three on grounds of abuse and neglect; and until the age of 11 she was variously in institutions and some seven foster homes, usually for about three months, after which she would be sent back into local authority care. From her descriptions these rejections were often associated with her refusing to polish the floors in her new 'homes'. When nearly 12 she was sent to a more tenacious foster mother: 'Only when she had proved that she wasn't just going to send me back to the home because I was naughty, only then could I begin to trust her,' she told us. She settled down at 13 when she was offically adopted, and her foster mother's neighbour later traced her younger sister and adopted her so that they met up again after a decade. She married a considerate young man at 22, had two daughters, and never suffered depression. She was at no point rated helpless.

Although acknowledging a wide range of family support services, in her review of the topic, Gibbons (1992b: 2) recognised three particular types of provision: (i) 'services more specifically geared to parents who are identified by others or themselves as in some way falling below acceptable standards of care of their children'; (ii) locally-based projects and family centres designed to provide a supportive service to families in neighbourhoods of high social need; and (iii) services for families with a child who has a disablity.

Home-start began in Leicester as a home visiting scheme to families experiencing various practical and relationship difficulties (Harrison 1981). Typically the parents of such families are young, sometimes impulsive and often socially isolated. Volunteers offer the families support and friendship as well as practical help. The families are visited with their full agreement. The purpose and nature of the visits are determined by the families. There are no time limits. The volunteers are mothers with older children who, with some professional support and training, seek to establish a relationship with one or two families. There is an egalitarian quality to the relationships established. Practical assistance along with conversations, advice and help by example form part of the visits. The volunteers have gained knowledge through their own parenting and to that extent they can play the part of a mother to the mother. They offer support on the visit and can also be available at night or weekends if there is a strong need. The project was evaluated by an independent researcher (van der Eyken 1982). The results were encouraging. The families' level of functioning in many cases improved and there was a high rate of satisfaction reported by the families themselves.

The project described by Jones *et al.* (1976) and Jones (1985) looked at services aimed at families who were struggling to look after and control their children. The study took place in a poor, disadvantaged part of New York state. In terms of keeping children out of public care, the most successful kind of work was carried out by committed but unqualified social workers, often recruited from the local community. They tended to visit the families regularly but without the high psychotherapeutic and casework focus preferred by the professionally qualified, highly trained social workers. The unqualified workers became involved in ways which were practical, emotionally supportive and low in technical sophistication. The frequent, accessible support given to the parents helped them keep their children at home and in the family. The emphasis was on long-term support, availability and 'being there' when needed. Less effective in keeping vulnerable children out of public care were short-term, time-limited and goal-orientated techniques mainly practised by qualified practitioners (Jones 1985: 143).

In family welfare work, primary preventive measures are best targeted on neighbourhoods where stress levels are high, families are young, poverty is common and child rearing is difficult (Gibbons 1992c: 24). Supportive provisions should be available to all families in such areas and not just those who are recognised as problematic by formal agencies. One way in which local authorities develop family support provisions is through the sponsorship of independently run voluntary and informal neighbourhood groups. Gibbons *et al.* (1990) studied the impact of family support provisions in two geographical areas. It seemed that the family projects were successful in attracting parents and families with the highest levels of need. Most parents reported some gain. Indeed, the parents who lived in the neighbourhood where family support policies and provisions were particularly strong seemed to gain the most and appeared to be coping better. Gibbons concludes (1992c: 32): 'The research provided some reasons to think that parents under stress more easily overcome family problems when there are many sources of family support available in local communities. The most useful form of provision may be good quality day care.'

Family centres have established themselves as a key resource in many communities experiencing high social need. They offer a range of services from intensive casework to out-of-school clubs, from parenting skills classes to playgroup sessions. Smith (1992) studied six family projects established by the Children's Society in different parts of the United Kingdom. She paid particular attention to what the users had to say about the centres. Most of the users lived in disadvantaged neighbourhoods where life was felt to be a struggle. For some, the environment was poor: heavy traffic, high rates of violence and crime, drug dealing, hostile neighbours. Many of the children and the adults had health problems. Incomes were generally low. There were high numbers of single parent households. Not a few of the mothers said they suffered from depression.

The family centres were viewed as a positive resource by nearly all the parents. The two main benefits revolved around the social opportunities available for children and for parents. 'Learning to mix' and 'learning to share' were seen as helping the children's social development. The parents also saw themselves benefiting:

> Seven out of ten parents (72 per cent) thought that the projects had given them time off – 'you can leave him there while you do a bit of shopping'. There was also a very positive view of the opportunities to share problems and experiences with other parents: 66 per cent thought the projects had helped with 'having other adults to talk to' – 'you find you're not on your own', 'I've made some good friends', 'you don't feel so isolated' were frequent comments . . . Here are some examples of parents' comments about the impact of the family centres for them and their children . . . 'I've made some friends through the centre – and it's changed my child . . .' 'It's calmed me down a bit, I think. It's made me look at things a bit more in perspective instead of getting so wound up.' (Smith 1992: 19)

By relieving some of the considerable pressures that many of these parents experience and by providing social support, the aim is to lessen the conflict and the despair that can all too easily disturb family life and social relationships. Even innately competent infants can display disordered functioning when placed in social environments which are characterised by high levels of stress.

And beyond the provision of family support and neighbourhood resources lie arguments for even wider and deeper environmental and economic changes. Poverty and stress go hand in hand. Stress increases the likelihood of social relationships in the family becoming disturbed and disordered. Disturbed relationships in childhood upset psychological development and the formation of well-integrated personality structures. Disturbed developmental pathways and poorly integrated personalities undermine social competence. A lack of relationship skills and social empathy can lead to a variety of difficult behaviours including aggression, inability to concentrate and persist, withdrawal, depression, crime, self-abuse, incompetent parenting and repeated 'marital' breakdown. In social and economic terms, these are costly behaviours for both the individuals concerned and society.

Improved housing, higher levels of income support, low unemployment and greater child-care provisions all help to reduce stress. Every little reduction in the pressures and demands which afflict the lives of those who live in the poorest parts of the country on the lowest incomes helps to nudge family life and social relationships in the direction of co-operation and mutuality and away from conflict and distrust.

### (3) Psychotherapy

Historically, psychotherapeutically based casework has played an important part in social work's development. Up until the 1960s, individual and family casework was largely informed by theories which owed a lot to the psychodynamic and psychoanalytic traditions. In social work, these approaches have largely fallen out of favour and out of fashion. They fell prey to two disparate forces. Empirical researchers sought to measure social work's effectiveness and ability to bring about behavioural change: they found casework wanting. Radicals of the 1960s poured scorn on any practice which appeared to pathologise the poor and subdue the difficult and disgruntled: they found traditional social work guilty on both counts.

It is to be doubted that social workers should behave like peripatetic psychotherapists. Clients who might need more concentrated and specialist attention are better referred to a psychologist, psychiatrist or counsellor. It also has to be noted that the kind of theories and psychotherapeutic practices derived from attachment theory and other developmental psychologies are far removed from traditional psychoanalytic techniques. The empirical and ideological critiques so easily mounted in the 1960s against casework now have a much tougher time trying to dismiss the highly sophisticated theories and findings being generated by modern developmental perspectives which are heavily rooted in the scientific method and which recognise clear links between the quality of personal experience and the quality of the material environment.

A full-blown psychotherapeutic encounter would see the relationship as the vehicle for bringing about change in the client's perception and understanding of both the self and others. 'Reforming the self' requires the therapist or counsellor to understand how the self was formed in the first place. If the self first forms in relationship with others, the self can only re-form in the context of new relationship experiences (Howe 1993). In the language of attachment theory, the new experiences generated within the psychotherapeutic relationship allow the client to modify old representational patterns, to change old inner working models of the self and its relationship with other people. By offering the client a relationship, the therapist or counsellor then uses this relationship to help the client examine and modify his or her relationship with others. In its most basic form, the therapeutic relationship simply offers a nurturing experience. There is no explicit examination of what is going on. Security and trust, availability and care reduce anxiety and increase feelings of self-worth.

Of course, this is Bowlby's description of a developmentally secure environment from which we explore translated directly into a psychotherapeutic context. An attachment-like relationship with the therapist allows the client to develop trust. He or she can then venture slowly and with caution beyond the safety of the relationship and explore feelings and relationships with other people. Past and present representations of the self and others can be recognised and examined. The caring, nurturing, safe relationship with the therapist by its constancy and consistency attempts to contradict the client's negative core beliefs about self and others.

For example, the avoidant individual has learned to defend himself by denying that he feels any hurt when others reject him. The defence is increased by avoiding intimate relationships and the person becoming compulsively self-reliant. If the therapist can build a secure relationship with her client, it may be possible for him to acknowledge and communicate painful feelings and learn how to handle them.

Nezworski *et al.* (1988: 365) mention work with a mother who found her child's clinginess a problem. As the relationship with the therapist became established, the mother acknowledged that she felt very angry when the child behaved in this clinging way. She saw it as an unfair attempt to restrict her movements and prevent her from leaving. The more the child was inclined to cling, the more promptly the mother put him down, which, of course, increased the clinging behaviour. 'I can't let him control me,' she said. It was not until she could articulate her strong negative feelings that the mother could begin to move forward.

Beyond nurturing relationships, security and exploration lies the world of therapeutic interpretation. Why does a client feel so much anger in his relationship with his partner? What are the origins of a mother's feelings of profound anxiety for her baby daughter and why is physical contact with her so difficult? The therapist as interpreter will want to help the client discover what links exist between present feelings and past experiences. If the client can discover the relationship between past and present, he or she can then consider how the past might still be influencing current feelings, thoughts and behaviour. The next step is to help the client attempt some cognitive reconstruction of the way the world of self and others is modelled and understood. Improvements in cognitive modelling allow clients to handle people and relationships in a more accurate and competent manner. Summarising the process, Bowlby (1979: 145–6; 1988: 138–9) identifies five therapeutic tasks:

1. The client is provided with a secure base from which to explore unhappy and painful events. The therapist remains available and attentive.
2. The therapist assists the client in his or her explorations. The feelings and behaviours that certain relationships trigger (say with partners, children, parents) are identified and acknowledged. The therapist may want to ask clients which are the relationships in which they typically find themselves and how do they typically feel and react.
3. The therapist and client will need to recognise how the therapeutic relationship is being used by the client. What feelings, expectations and models of previous attachment experiences is the client importing into the current relationship? These may reveal how the client typically handles his self or her self in relationship with others.

4.  This leads to the fourth step in which the client is encouraged cognitively to link past relationship experiences (particularly with parents and other significant people) with current behaviour and emotions. This can be a painful thing to do as the past is revived and relived. One's parents, for example, might be recognised as unloving or hostile.

5.  The client is finally helped to understand how his or her current representational models of self and relationship with others is a product of past, often painful relationship experiences. This offers the opportunity to re-construct the models, re-form the self and to learn to cope better with social relationships.

Social workers would not normally expect to work with people as undiluted psychotherapists. Nevertheless, elements of the process will be ever-present in their dealings with clients. Once social workers have formed any kind of *relationship* with their clients, representational models, defences and attachment experiences are bound to crop up. Feelings of anger, dependency, anxiety, avoidance and ambivalence will constantly colour the relationship. The nature and origins of these feelings (both in the client and in the social worker) have to be understood if the character of the relationship is to make sense. We are back with the need for the social worker to understand what is going on if he or she is to remain patient and available and not give up on the case and not be provoked into acting rigidly and bureaucratically because of feelings of fear and anxiety, uncertainty and intolerance.

**Conclusion: straight and devious pathways**

Whatever the response, policies and practices based on developmental perspectives are designed to help families create social environments which are less damaging and more sensitive to the cognitive and emotional needs of growing children. The intention of such responses is to recover children from 'devious' developmental pathways and return them to the road of 'straight' social and psychological experiences (see Robins and Rutter 1990a). The same theoretical and empirical base informs the way social workers help adults with high levels of need and severe social difficulties. Understanding, emotional support, practical support and a reliable, responsive relationship are each capable of providing a humane social service and an improved emotional environment. If the aim is to improve the quality of people's relationship experiences, the social worker, along with all the other professional workers who have dealings with the heavy users of the health and welfare services, has no choice but to understand the intricate dynamics between people's relationship history, their personality and the character of their current environment, both social and material.

The words of John Bowlby (1988: 136) are both an appropriate and a fitting way to end this book. They sum up beautifully the essence of attachment, theories of the relationship, social development, and all those theories based upon them:

> The model of developmental pathways regards an infant at birth as having an array of pathways potentially open to him, the one along which he will in fact proceed being determined at every moment by the interaction of the individual as he now is with the environment in which he happens to be. Each infant is held to have his own individual array of potential pathways for personality development which, except for infants born with certain types of neurological damage, include many that are compatible with mental health and also many that are incompatible. Which particular pathway he proceeds along is determined by the environment he meets with, especially the way his parents (or parent substitutes) treat him, and how he responds to them. Children who have parents who are sensitive and responsive are enabled to develop along a healthy pathway. Those who have insensitive, unresponsive, neglectful, or rejecting parents are likely to develop along a deviant pathway which is in some degree incompatible with mental health and which renders them vulnerable to breakdown, should they meet seriously adverse events. Even so, since the course of subsequent events is not fixed, changes in the way a child is treated can shift his pathway in either a more favourable direction or a less favourable one. Although the capacity for developmental change diminishes with age, change continues throughout the life cycle so that changes for the better or for the worse are always possible. It is this continuing potential for change that means that at no time of life is a person invulnerable to every possible adversity and also that at no time of life is a person impermeable to favourable influence.

# Bibliography

Ainsworth, M. D. S. (1967) *Infancy in Uganda: Infant Care and the Growth of Attachment* (Baltimore: Johns Hopkins University Press).

Ainsworth, M. D. S. (1973) 'The development of infant–mother attachment', in Caldwell, B. M. and Riccuiti, H. N. (eds), *Review of Child Development, Volume 3* (Chicago: University of Chicago Press).

Ainsworth, M. D. S. (1991) 'Attachments and other affectional bonds across the life cycle', in Parkes, Stevenson-Hinde and Marris (1991) pp. 33–51.

Ainsworth, M. D. S. and Bowlby, J. (1991) 'An ethological approach to personality development', *American Psychologist*, April, pp. 333–41.

Ainsworth, M. D. S. and Eichberg, C. (1991) 'Effects on infant–mother attachment of mother's unresolved loss of an attachment figure, or other traumatic experience' in Parkes, Stevenson-Hinde and Marris (1991).

Ainsworth, M. D. S. and Wittig, B. (1969) 'Attachment and exploratory behavior of one year olds in a strange situation', in Foss, B. M. (ed.), *Determinants of Infant Behavior, Volume 4* (New York: Wiley) pp. 111–36.

Ainsworth, M. D., Blehar, M. C., Waters, E. and Wall, S. (1978) *Patterns of Attachment* (New Jersey: Erlbaum).

Anderson, J. (1972) 'Attachment out of doors', in Blurton-Jones, N. (ed.), *Ethological Studies of Child Behaviour* (Cambridge: Cambridge University Press).

Baron-Cohen, S., Leslie, A. M. and Frith, U. (1985) 'Does the autistic child have a "theory of mind"?', *Cognition*, vol. 21, pp. 37–46.

Bartholomew, K. and Perlman, D. (1994) *Attachment Processes in Adulthood, Volume 5: Advances in Personal Relationships* (London: Jessica Kingsley).

Bates, J. E. and Bayles, K. (1988) 'Attachment and the development of behavior problems', in Belsky and Nezworski (1988) pp. 253–99.

Bateson, P. (ed.) (1991) *The Development and Integration of Behaviour* (Cambridge: Cambridge University Press).

BBC 2 (1994) *Life Stories: A Mother's Love*, 24 May.

Beattie, M. (1987) *Codependent No More* (New York: Harper & Row).

Belsky, J. and Isabella, R. (1988) 'Maternal, infant, and social-contextual determinants of attachment security', in Belsky and Nezworski (1991) (eds.) pp. 41–94.

Belsky, J. and Nezworski, T. (eds) (1988a) *Clinical Implications of Attachment* (New Jersey: Lawrence Erlbaum).

Belsky, J. and Nezworski, T. (1988b) 'Clinical implications of attachment', in Belsky and Nezworski (1988a) pp. 3–17.

Belsky, J. and Pensky, E. (1988) 'Developmental history, personality, and family relationships', in Hinde, R. A. and Stevenson-Hinde (1988) pp. 193–217.

Belsky, J. and Vondra, J. (1989) 'Lessons from child abuse: the determinants of parenting', in Cicchetti and Carlson (1989) pp. 153–202.

Bowlby, J. (1951) *Maternal Care and Mental Health* (Geneva: World Health Organization).

Bowlby, J. (1969) *Attachment and Loss, Volume I: Attachment* (London: Hogarth Press).

Bowlby, J. (1973) *Attachment and Loss, Volume II: Separation, Anxiety and Anger* (London: Hogarth Press).

Bowlby, J. (1979) *The Making and Breaking of Affectional Bonds* (London: Tavistock).

Bowlby, J. (1980) *Attachment and Loss, Volume III: Loss, Sadness and Depression* (London: Hogarth Press).

Bowlby, J. (1988) *A Secure Base: Clinical Applications of Attachment Theory* (London: Routledge).

Bowlby, J. (1991a) 'Postscript', in Parkes, Stevenson-Hinde and Marris (1991) pp. 293–7.

Bowlby, J. (1991b) 'Ethological light on psychoanalytical problems' in Bateson (1991) pp. 301–14.

Bretherton, I. (1991) 'The roots and growing points of attachment theory', in Parkes, Stevenson-Hinde and Marris (1991) pp. 9–32.

Brodzinsky, D. M. (1987) 'Adjustment to adoption: a psychosocial perspective', *Clinical Psychological Review*, vol. 7, pp. 25–47.

Brown, G. and Harris, T. (1978) *Social Origins of Depression: A Study of Psychiatric Disorder in Women* (London: Tavistock).

Brown, G. and Harris, T. (1986) 'Stressor, vulnerability and depression', *Psychological Medicine*, vol. 16, pp. 739–44.

Brown, G. and Harris. T. (1989) *Life Events and Illness* (New York: Guilford).

Brown, G., Harris, T. and Bifulco, A. (1986) 'Long term effects of early loss of parent', in Rutter, M., Izard, P. and Read, P. (eds), *Depression in Young People* (New York: Guilford Press) pp. 251–96.

Brown, J. and Dunn, J. (1991) ' "You can cry, Mom": the social and developmental implications of talk about internal states', *The British Journal of Developmental Psychology*, vol. 9, pp. 237–56.

Browne, A. and Finkelhor, D. (1986) 'Impact of child sexual abuse: a review of the research', *Psychological Bulletin*, vol. 99, no. 1, pp. 66–77.

Bruner, J. (1983) *Child's Talk* (New York: Norton).

Burkitt, I. (1991) *Social Selves: Theories of the Formation of the Personality* (London: Sage).

Burnham, J. (1986) *Family Therapy: First Steps Towards a Systemic Approach* (London: Tavistock).

Cadoret, R. J. (1986) 'Adoption studies: historical and methodological critique', *Psychiatric Development*, vol. 1, pp. 45–64.

Cadoret, R. J., O'Gorman, T. W., Heywood, E. and Troughton, E. (1985a) 'Genetic and environmental factors in major depression', *Journal of Affective Disorders*, vol. 9, pp. 155–64.

Cadoret, R. J., Troughton, E., O'Gorman, T.W. and Heywood, E. (1985b) 'Alcoholism and antisocial personality: inter-relationships, genetic and environmental factors', *Archives of General Psychiatry*, vol. 42, pp. 161–7.

Cadoret, R. J., Troughton, E., Merchant, L. M. and Whitters, A. (1990) 'Early life psychosocial events and adult affective symptoms', in Robins and Rutter (1990a) pp. 300–13.

Capron, C. and Duyme, M. (1989) 'Assessment of effects of socio-economic status on IQ in a full cross-fostering study', *Nature*, vol. 340, pp. 552–4.

Carlson, V., Cicchetti, D., Barnett, D. and Braunwald, K. (1989) 'Disorganized/disoriented attachment relationships in maltreated infants', *Developmental Psychology*, vol. 25, pp. 525–31.

Caspi, A. and Elder, G. H. (1988) 'Emergent family patterns: the intergenerational construction of problem behaviour and relationships', in Hinde and Stevenson-Hinde (1988) pp. 218–40.

Caspi, A., Elder, G. H. and Herbener, E. S. (1990) 'Childhood personality and the prediction of life-course patterns', in Robins and Rutter (1990a) pp. 13–35.

Cassidy, J. and Kobak, R. R. (1988) 'Avoidance and its relation to other defensive processes', in Belsky and Nezworski (1988) pp. 300–25.

Cermak, T. L. (1990) *Evaluating and Treating Adults* (Minneapolis: Johnson Institute Books).

Chess, S. and Thomas, A. (1990) 'Continuities and discontinuities in temperament' in Robins and Rutter (1990a) pp. 205–20.

Cicchetti, D. and Carlson, V. (eds) (1989) *Child Maltreatment: Theory and Research on the Causes of Child Abuse and Neglect* (Cambridge: Cambridge University Press).

Cohen, P., Brook., J., Cohen, J., Velez, C. N. and Garcia, M. (1990) 'Common and uncommon pathways to adolescent psychopathology and problem behaviour', in Robins and Rutter (1990a) pp. 242–58.

Cohen, S. and Syme, S. L. (eds) (1985) *Social Support and Health* (New York: Academic Press).

Collins, N. L. and Read, S. J. (1990) 'Adult attachment, working models, and relationship quality in dating couples', *Journal of Personality and Social Psychology*, vol. 58, pp. 644–63.

Coons, P. M. and Milstein, V. (1986) 'Psychosexual disturbances in multiple personality, *Journal of Clinical Psychiatry*, vol. 47, pp. 106–10.

Corrigan, P. and Leonard, P. (1978) *Social Work Under Capitalism: A Marxist Approach* (London: Macmillan).

Cotterill, R. (1989) *No Ghosts in the Machine* (London: Heinemann).

Crittenden, P. M. (1988) 'Relationships at risk', in Belsky and Nezworski (1988a) pp. 136–74.

Crittenden, P. M. and Ainsworth, M. (1989) 'Child maltreatment and attachment theory', in Cicchetti and Carlson (1989).

Crittenden, P.M. and Bonvillian, J. (1984) 'The relationship between material risk status and maternal sensitivity', *American Journal of Orthopsychiatry*, vol. 54, pp. 250–62.

Crockenberg, S. (1981) 'Infant irritability, mother responsiveness, and social support influences on the security of infant–mother attachment', *Child Development*, vol. 52, pp. 857–69.

Cummings, E.M. and Davies, P.T. (1994) 'Maternal depression and child development', *Journal of Child Psychology and Psychiatry*, vol. 35, no. 1, pp. 73–112.

Cummings, E.M., Lanott, R.J. and Zahn-Waxler, C. (1985) 'Influence of conflict between adults on the emotions and aggression of young children', *Developmental Psychology*, vol. 21, pp. 495–507.

Daniels, D. and Plomin, R. (1985) 'Origins of individual differences in infant shyness', *Developmental Psychology*, vol. 21, pp. 118–21.

DeLozier, P.P. (1982) 'Attachment theory and child abuse' in Parkes and Stevenson-Hinde (1982) pp. 95–117.

Dobash, R.P., Carnie, J. and Waterhouse, L. (1993) 'Child sexual abusers: recognition and response', in Waterhouse (1993) pp. 113–35.

Dodge, K.A., Bates, J.E. and Pettit, G.S. (1990) 'Mechanisms in the cycle of violence', *Science*, vol. 250, pp. 1678–83.

Donaldson, M. (1992), *Human Minds: An Exploration* (London:Penguin).

Dunn, J. (1986) 'Growing up in a family world', in Richards and Light (1986) pp. 98–115.

Dunn, J. (1988) *The Beginnings of Social Understanding* (Oxford: Blackwell).

Dunn, J. (1991) 'Relationships and behaviour: the significance of Robert Hinde's work for developmental psychology', in Bateson (1991) pp. 375–87.

Dunn, J. (1993) *Young Children's Close Relationships: Beyond Attachment* (Newbury Park, California: Sage).

Dunn, J. and Brown, J. (1992) 'Early conversations about causality', *British Journal of Developmental Psychology*, vol. 10.

Dunn, J. and Plomin, R. (1990) *Separate Lives: Why Siblings Are So Different* (New York: Basic Books).

Dunn, J., Brown, J. and Beardsall, L. (1991) 'Family talk about feeling states and children's later understanding of others' emotions', *Developmental Psychology*, vol. 27, pp. 448–55.

Edmund, M. (1993) 'Twelve people's experience of being codependent and having treatment', unpublished MSW, University of East Anglia, Norwich.

Egeland, B. and Farber, E.A. (1984) 'Infant–mother attachment: factors related to its development and changes over time', *Child Development*, vol. 55, no. 3, pp. 753–71.

Emde, R.N. (1989) 'The infant's relationship experience: developmental and affective aspects', in Sameroff and Emde (1989) pp. 33–51.

Emde, R.N. and Sameroff, A.J. (1989) 'Understanding early relationship disturbances', in Sameroff and Emde (1989) pp. 3–14.

Erikson, E.H. (1959) *Identity and the Life Cycle* (New York: International Universities Press).

Fahlberg, V. I. (1991) *A Child's Journey Through Placement* (Indianapolis: Perspectives Press).

Farrington, D. P. (1986) 'Stepping stones to adult criminal careers', in J. Q. Olweus, J. Black and M. R. Yarrow (eds) *Development of Antisocial and Prosocial Behaviour* (New York: Academic Press).

Farrington, D. P, Loeber, R. and van Kammen, W. B. (1990) 'Long-term criminal outcomes of hyperactivity-impulsivity-attention deficit and conduct problems in childhood', in Robins and Rutter (1990a) pp. 62–81.

Feeney, J. A., Noller, P. and Patty, J. (1993) 'Adolescents' interactions with the opposite sex: influence of attachment style and gender', *Journal of Adolescence*, vol. 16, pp. 169–86.

Fendrich, M., Warner, V. and Weissman, M. (1990) 'Family risk factors, parental depression and childhood psychopathology', *Developmental Psychology*, vol. 26, pp. 40–50.

Ferguson, H., Gilligan, R. and Torode, R. (eds) (1993) *Surviving Childhood Adversity: Issues for Policy and Practice* (Dublin: Social Studies Press, Trinity College).

Feshbach, N. D. (1989) 'The construct of empathy and the phenomenon of physical maltreatment of children', in Cicchetti and Carlson (1989) pp. 349–73.

Finkelhor, D. *et al.* (1986) *A Sourcebook on Childhood Sexual Abuse* (New York: The Free Press).

Fonagy, P., Steele, M., Steele, H., Higgitt, A. and Mayer, L. S. (1994) 'The Emanuel Miller Memorial Lecture 1992. The theory and practice of resilience', *Journal of Child Psychology and Psychiatry*, vol. 35, no. 2, pp. 231–58.

Fouts, G. and Atlas, P. (1979) 'Stranger distress: mother and stranger as reinforcers', *Infant Behavior and Development*, vol. 2, pp. 309–17.

Fox, N. (1994) 'Scientists suggest shyness starts in the genes', *Guardian*, 22 February.

Fraiberg, S. (1977) *Every Child's Birthright: In Defense of Mothering* (New York: Basic Books).

Fraiberg, S., Adelson, E. and Shapiro, V. (1975) 'Ghosts in the nursery: a psychoanalytic approach to the problems of impaired mother–infant relationships', *Journal of the American Academy of Child Psychiatry*, vol. 14, pp. 378–421.

Franz, C. E., McClelland, D. C. and Weinberger, T. (1991) 'Childhood antecedents of conventional social accomplishments in mid-life adults: a 36-year prospective study', *Journal of Personality and Social Psychology*, vol. 60, pp. 586–95.

Frith, U. (1989) *Autism: Explaining the Enigma* (Oxford: Blackwell).

Frodi, A. M. and Lamb, M. E. (1980) 'Child abusers' responses to infant smiles and cries', *Child Development*, vol. 51, pp. 238–41.

Frommer, E. A. and O'Shea, G. (1973) 'Antenatal identification of women liable to have problems in managing their infants', *British Journal of Psychiatry*, vol. 123, pp. 149–56.

Gibbons, J. (ed.) (1992a) *The Children Act 1989 and Family Support: Principles into Practice* (London: HMSO).

Gibbons, J. (1992b) 'Introduction to the book', in Gibbons, J. (1992a) pp. 1–8.

Gibbons, J. (1992c) 'Provisions of support through Family Projects', in Gibbons (1992a) pp. 23–33.

Gibbons, J., Thorpe, S. and Wilkinson, P. (1990) *Family Support and Prevention: Studies in Local Areas* (London: HMSO).

Greenberg, M. T. and Speltz, M. L. (1988) 'Attachment and the ontogeny of conduct problems', in Belsky and Nezworski (1988a) pp. 177–218.

Greenberg, M. T., Cicchetti, D. and Cummings, E. M. (eds) (1990) *Attachment in the Preschool Years: Theory, Research, and Intervention* (Chicago: University of Chicago Press).

Grossmann, K. E. and Grossmann, K. (1991) 'Attachment quality as an organizer of emotional and behavioral responses in a longitudinal perspective', in Parkes, Stevenson-Hinde and Marris (1991) pp. 93–114.

Grossmann, K., Fremmer-Bombik, E., Rudolph, J. and Grossmann, K. E. (1988) 'Maternal attachment representations as related to patterns of infant–mother attachment and maternal care during the first year', in Hinde and Stevenson-Hinde (1988) pp. 241–60.

Grotevant, H. and Cooper, C. R. (1985) 'Patterns of interaction in family relationships and the development of identity exploration', *Child Development*, vol. 29, pp. 82–100.

Hamlyn, D. W. (1978) *Experience and the Growth of Understanding* (London: Routledge & Kegan Paul).

Happe, F. G. E. (1994) 'Current psychological theories of autism: the "theory of mind" account and rival theories', *Journal of Child Psychology and Psychiatry*, vol. 35, no. 2, pp. 215–29.

Harris, P. (1989) *Children and Emotion: The Development of Psychological Understanding* (Oxford: Blackwell).

Harris, P. (1991) 'The work of the imagination', in Whiten (1991) pp. 283–304.

Harris, P. L. (1994) 'The child's understanding of emotion: developmental change and the family environment', *Journal of Child Psychology and Psychiatry*, vol. 35, no. 1, pp. 3–28.

Harris, T. (1993) 'Surviving childhood adversity: what can we learn from naturalistic studies?', in Ferguson, Gilligan and Torode (1993) pp. 93–107.

Harris, T. and Bifulco, A. (1991) 'Loss of parent in childhood, attachment style, and depression in adulthood', in Parkes, Stevenson-Hinde and Marris (1991) pp. 234–67.

Harris, T. O., Brown, G. W., and Bifulco, A. (1987) 'Loss of parent in childhood and adult psychiatric disorder: the role of social class position and premarital pregnancy', *Psychological Medicine*, vol. 17, pp. 163–83.

Harrison, M. (1981) 'Home-start: a voluntary home-visiting scheme for young families', *Child Abuse and Neglect*, vol. 5, pp. 441–7.

Hay, Dale F. and Angold, Adrian (eds) (1993) *Precursors and Causes in Development and Psychopathology* (Chichester: John Wiley).

Hazan, C. and Shaver, P. R. (1987) 'Romantic love conceptualized as an attachment process' *Journal of Personality and Social Psychology*, vol. 52, pp. 511–24.

Hazan, C. and Shaver, P. R. (1990) 'Love and work: an attachment theoretical perspective', *Journal of Personality and Social Structure*, vol. 59, pp. 270–80.

Hazan, C. and Zeifman, D. (1994) 'Sex and the psychological tether', in Bartholomew and Perlman (1994) pp. 151–77.

Hetherington, E. M. (1988) 'Parents, children, and siblings: six years after divorce', in Hinde and Stevenson-Hinde (1988) pp. 311–31.

Hetherington, E. M. (1989) 'Coping with family transitions: winners, losers, and survivors', *Child Development*, vol. 60, pp. 1–14.

Hinde, R. A. (1979) *Towards Understanding Human Relationships* (London: Academic Press).

Hinde, R. A. (1982) 'Attachment: some conceptual and biological issues', in Parkes and Stevenson-Hinde (1982) pp. 60–76.

Hinde, R. A. (1987) *Individuals, Relationships and Culture: Links Between Ethology and the Social Sciences* (Cambridge: Cambridge University Press).

Hinde, R. A. (1988) 'Introduction', in Hinde and Stevenson-Hinde (1988).

Hinde, R. A. (1989) 'Ethological and relationship approaches', *Annals of Child Development*, vol. 6, pp. 251–85.

Hinde, R. A. and Stevenson-Hinde, J. (1987) 'Interpersonal relationships and child development', *Developmental Review*, vol. 7, pp. 1–21.

Hinde, R. A. and Stevenson-Hinde, Joan (eds) (1988) *Relationships Within Families: Mutual Influences* (Oxford: Oxford University Press).

Hodges, J. and Tizard, B. (1989a) 'IQ and behavioural adjustment of ex-institutional adolescents', *Journal of Child Psychology and Psychiatry*, vol. 30, no. 1, pp. 53–75.

Hodges, J. and Tizard, B. (1989b) 'Social and family relationships of ex-institutional adolescents', *Journal of Child Psychology and Psychiatry*, vol. 30, no. 1, pp. 77–97.

Holmes, J. (1993) *John Bowlby and Attachment Theory* (London: Routledge).

Hood, L. and Bloom, L. (1979) 'What, when and how about why: a longitudinal study of early expressions of causality', *Monographs of the Society for the Study of Child Development*, vol. 44, p. 6.

Hopkins, J. (1991) 'Failure of the holding relationship: some effects of physical rejection on the child's attachment and inner experience', in Parkes, Stevenson-Hinde and Marris (1991) pp. 187–98.

Howe, D. (1987) *An Introduction to Social Work Theory* (Aldershot: Gower).

Howe, D. (1989) *The Consumers' View of Family Therapy* (Aldershot: Gower).

Howe, D. (1992) 'Assessing adoptions in difficulty', *British Journal of Social Work*, vol. 22, pp. 1–15.

Howe, D. (1993) *On Being a Client: Understanding the Process of Counselling and Psychotherapy* (London: Sage).

Howe, D., Sawbridge, P. and Hinings, D. (1992) *Half a Million Women: Mothers Who Lose Their Children By Adoption* (Harmondsworth: Penguin).

Humphrey, N. (1986) *The Inner Eye* (London: Faber & Faber).

Ingleby, D. (1986) 'Development in social context', in Richards and Light (1986).

Inglis, K. (1984) *Living Mistakes: Mothers Who Consented to Adoption* (Sydney: George Allen & Unwin).

Jenkins, J. M. and Smith, M. A. (1991) 'Marital disharmony and children's behaviour problems: aspects of a poor marriage that affect children adversely', *Journal of Child Psychology and Psychiatry*, vol. 32, pp. 793–810.

Jones, C. (1983) *State Social Work and the Working Class* (London: Macmillan).

Jones, M. A. (1985) *A Second Chance for Families: Five Years Later: a Follow Up Study of a Program to Prevent Foster Care* (New York: Child Welfare League of America).

Jones, M. A., Neuman, R. and Shyne, A. W. (1976) *A Second Chance for Families: Evaluation of a Program to Reduce Foster Care* (New York: Child Welfare of America).

Kagan, J. (1989) *Unstable Ideas: Temperament, Cognition and Self* (Cambridge, Ma.: Harvard University Press).

Kasl, C. D. (1989) *Women, Sex and Addiction* (New York: Mandarin).

Kaufman, J. and Zigler, E. (1989) 'The intergenerational transmission of child abuse', in Cicchetti and Carlson (1989) pp. 129–50.

Kellogg, T. (1990) *Broken Toys, Broken Dreams* (Amherst, Mass.: Brat).

Kessen, W. (1979) 'The American child and other cultural inventions', *American Psychologist*, vol. 34, pp. 815–20.

Kety, S. S., Rosenthal, D., Wender, P., Schulsinger, F. and Jacobson, B. (1978) 'The biologic and adoptive families of adoptive individuals who became schizophrenic', in Wynne, L. C., Cromwell, R. L. and Matthysse, S. (1978) (eds), *The Nature of Schizophrenia* (New York: John Wiley, 1978).

Klaus, M. H. and Kennell, J. H. (1982) *Maternal–Infant Bonding*, 2nd edn (Saint Louis: Mosby).

Klein, J. (1987) *Our Need for Others and its Roots in Infancy* (London: Tavistock).

Kochanska, G., Kuczynski, L., Radke-Yarrow, M. and Welsh, J. D. (1987) 'Resolutions of control episodes between well and affectively ill mothers and their young children', *Journal of Abnormal Child Psychology*, vol. 15, pp. 441–56.

LaFreniere, P. and Sroufe, L. A. (1985) 'Profiles of peer competence in the preschool', *Development Psychology*, vol. 21, pp. 58–68.

Le Blanc, Marc and Loeber, Rolf (1993) 'Precursors, causes and the development of criminal offending', in Hay and Angold (1993), pp. 233–63.

Lee, C. I. and Bates, J. E. (1985) 'Mother–child interaction at age two years and perceived difficult temperament', *Child Development*, vol. 56, pp. 1314–25.

Leiderman, P. H. (1989) 'Relationship disturbances and development through the life cycle', in Sameroff and Emde (1989) pp. 165–90.

Leslie, A. M. (1987) 'Pretense and representation: the origins of "theory of mind"', *Psychological Review*, vol. 94, pp. 412–26.

Leslie, A. M. (1991) 'Theory of mind impairment in autism', in Whiten (1991) pp. 63–78.

Lieberman, A. F. and Pawl, J. H. (1988) 'Clinical applications of attachment theory', in Belsky and Nezworski (1988a) pp. 327–51.

Liotti, G. (1991) 'Insecure attachment and agoraphobia', in Parkes, Stevenson-Hinde and Marris (1991) pp. 216–33.

Lyons-Ruth, K., Connell, D. B, Grunebaum, H., Botein, S. and Zoll, D. (1984) 'Maternal family history, maternal caretaking, and infant attachment in multi-problem families', *Journal of Preventive Psychiatry*, vol. 2, nos 3 and 4, pp. 403–25.

Lyons-Ruth, K., Connell, D. B., Grunebaum, H. and Botein, S. (1990) 'Infants at social risk: maternal depression and family support services as mediators of infant development and security of attachment', *Child Development*, vol. 61, pp. 85–98.

McCord, J. (1990) 'Long-term perspectives on parental absence', in Robins and Rutter (1990a) pp. 116–34.

Magnusson, D. and Bergman, L. R. (1990) 'A pattern approach to the study of pathways from childhood to adulthood', in Robins and Rutter (1990a) pp. 101–15.

Main, M. (1991) 'Metacognitive knowledge, metacognitive monitoring, and singular (coherent) vs. multiple (incoherent) model of attachment', in Parkes, Stevenson-Hinde and Marris (1991) pp. 127–59.

Main, M. and Cassidy, J. (1988) 'Categories of response to reunion with the parent at age six', *Developmental Psychology*, vol. 24, pp. 415–26.

Main, M. and George, C. (1985) 'Responses of abused and disadvantaged toddlers to distress in age-mates: a study in the day-care setting', *Developmental Psychology*, vol. 21, pp. 407–12.

Main, M. and Goldwyn, R. (1984) 'Predicting rejection of her infant from mother's representations of her own experience: implications for the abused–abusing intergenerational cycle', *Child Abuse and Neglect*, vol. 8, pp. 203–17.

Main, M., Kaplan, N. and Cassidy, J. (1985) 'Security in infancy, childhood and adulthood'. In I. Bretherton and E. Walters (eds) *Growing Points of Attachment Theory and Research: Monographs of the Society for Research in Child Development*. 50 (1–2, Serial No. 209).

Main, M. and Weston, D. (1982) 'Avoidance of the attachment figure in infancy', in Parkes and Stevenson-Hinde (1982) pp. 31–59.

Mattinson, J. (1975) *The Reflection Process in Casework Supervision* (London: Institute of Marital Studies).

Mattinson, J. and Sinclair, I. (1979) *Mate and Stalemate* (London: Institute of Marital Studies).

Maughan, B. and Pickles, A. (1990) 'Adopted and illegitimate children growing up', in Robins and Rutter (1990a) pp. 36–61.

Mayer, J. and Timms, N. (1970) *The Client Speaks* (London: Routledge).

Mead, G. H. (1934) *Mind, Self and Society* (Chicago: University of Chicago Press).

Nash, Alison and Hay, Dale F. (1993) 'Relationships in infancy as precursors and causes of later relationships and psychopathology', in Hay and Angold (1993) pp. 198–232.

Newcomb, M. D. and Bentler, P. M. (1990) 'Antecedents and consequences of cocaine use: an eight-year study from early adolescence to adulthood', in Robins and Rutter (1990a) pp. 158–81.

Nezworski, T., Tolan, W. J. and Belsky, J. (1988) 'Intervention in insecure infant attachment', in Belsky and Nezworski (1988a).

Norwood, R. (1985) *Women Who Love Too Much* (New York: Arrow Books).

Odent, M. (1984) *Birth Reborn* (New York: Pantheon).

Oldershaw, L., Walters, G. C. and Hall, D. K. (1986) 'Control strategies and noncompliance in abusive mother–child dyads: an observational study', *Child Development*, vol. 57, pp. 722–32.

Olson, D. R., Astington, J. W. and Harris, P. (1988) 'Introduction', in Astington, J. W., Harris, P. and Olson, D. R. (eds), *Developing Theories of Mind* (Cambridge: Cambridge University Press, 1988) pp. 1–15.

Park, R. D. and Waters, E. (1989) 'Security of attachment in preschool friendships', *Child Development*, vol. 60, pp. 1076–81.

Parker, J. G. and Asher, S. R. (1987) 'Peer relations and later personal adjustment: are low-accepted children at risk?', *Psychological Bulletin*, vol. 102, pp. 357–89.

Parkes, C. M. (1985) 'Bereavement', *British Journal of Psychiatry*, vol. 146, pp. 11–17.

Parkes, C. M. (1986) *Bereavement: Studies of Grief in Adult Life*, 2nd edn (Harmondsworth: Penguin).

Parkes, C. M. (1991) 'Attachment, bonding, and psychiatric problems after bereavement in adult life', in Parkes, Stevenson-Hinde and Marris (1991) pp. 268–92.

Parkes, C. M. and Stevenson-Hinde, J. (1982) *The Place of Attachment in Human Behaviour* (London: Tavistock).

Parkes, C. M. and Weiss, R. (1983) *Recovery from Bereavement* (New York: Basic Books).

Parkes, C. M., Stevenson-Hinde, J. and Marris, P. (eds) (1991) *Attachment Across the Life Cycle* (London: Tavistock/Routledge).

Parton, N. (1985) *The Politics of Child Abuse* (London: Macmillan).

Patterson, G. R. and Dishion, T. J. (1988) 'Multilevel process family models', in Hinde and Stevenson-Hinde (1988) pp. 283–310.

Perlman, D. and Bartholomew, K. (1994) 'Attachment processes in adulthood: an introduction', in Bartholomew and Perlman (1994) pp. 1–13.

Peterson, G. H. and Mehl, L. E. (1978) 'Some determinants of maternal attachment', *American Journal of Psychiatry*, vol. 135, pp. 1168–73.

Pianta, R., Egeland, B. and Erikson, M. F. (1989) 'The antecedents of maltreatment: results of the Mother–Child Interaction Research Projects', in Cicchetti and Carlson (1989) pp. 203–53.

Pitcairn, T., Waterhouse, L., McGhee, J. Secker. J., and Sullivan, C. (1993) 'Evaluating parenting in child physical abuse', in Waterhouse (1993) pp. 73–90.

Plomin, R. (1986) *Development, Genetics and Psychology* (New Jersey: Erlbaum).

Plomin, R. and Bergeman, C. S. (1991) 'The nature of nurture', *Behavioral and Brain Sciences*, vol. 14, pp. 373–427.

Quinton, D. and Rutter, M. (1988) *Parenting Breakdown: The Making and Breaking of Intergenerational Links* (Aldershot: Averbury).

Quinton, D., Rutter, M. and Gulliver, L. (1990) 'Continuities in psychiatric disorders from childhood to adulthood in the children of psychiatric patients', in Robins and Rutter (1990a) pp. 259–78.

Radke-Yarrow, M. (1989) 'Family environments of depressed and well parents and their children: issues of research methods', in Patterson, G. R. and Blechman, E. (eds) *Family Social Interactions* (New Jersey: Erlbaum, 1989).

Radke-Yarrow, M. (1991) 'Attachment patterns in children of depressed mothers', in Parkes, C. M., Stevenson-Hinde and Marris (1991) pp. 115–26.

Radke-Yarrow, M., Richters, J. and Wilson, W. E. (1988) 'Child development in a network of relationships', in Hinde and Stevenson-Hinde (1988) pp. 48–67.

Reiner, B. S. and Kaufman, I. K. (1959) *Character Disorders in Parents of Delinquents* (New York: Family Service Association of America).

Reitsma-Street, M., Offord, D. R. and Finch, T. (1985) 'Pairs of same sexed siblings discordant for anti-social behaviour', *British Journal of Psychiatry*, vol. 146, pp. 415–23.

Richards, M. (1974) *The Integration of a Child into a Social World* (Cambridge: Cambridge Univerity Press).

Richards, M. and Light, P. (eds), (1986) *Children of Social Worlds: Development in a Social Context* (Cambridge: Polity Press).

Riekar, P. and Carmen, E. (1986) 'The victim to patient process: the disconfirmation and transformation of abuse', *American Journal of Orthopsychiatry*, vol. 56, pp. 360–70.

Robins, L. (1966) *Deviant Children Growing Up* (Baltimore: Williams & Wilkins).

Robins, L. N. and Rutter, M. (eds) (1990a) *Straight and Devious Pathways from Childhood to Adulthood* (Cambridge: Cambridge University Press).

Robins, L. and Rutter, M. (1990b) 'Introduction', in Robins and Rutter (1990a) pp. xiii–xix.

Robson, K. M. and Kumar, R. (1980) 'Delayed onset of maternal affection after childbirth', *British Journal of Psychiatry*, vol. 136, pp. 347–53.

Rogers, C. (1961) *On Becoming a Person* (Boston: Houghton Mifflin).

Rosenblatt, J. S. (1991) 'A psychobiological approach to maternal behaviour among the primates', in Bateson (1991) pp. 191–222.

Rosenthal, D., Wender, P. H., Kety, S. S., Welner, J. and Schulsinger, F. (1971) 'The adopted-away offspring of schizophrenics', *American Journal of Psychiatry*, vol. 128, pp. 307–11.

Rubin, K. H. and Lollis, S. P. (1988) 'Origins and consequences of social withdrawal', in Belsky and Nezworski (1988a) pp. 221–52.

Russell, D. E. H. (1986) *The Secret Trauma: Incest in the Lives of Girls and Women* (New York: Basic Books).

Russell, D. E. H. (1988) 'The long term effects of incestuous abuse', in Wyatt, G. E. and Powell, G. J. (eds), *Lasting Effects of Child Sexual Abuse* (London: Sage, 1988).

Rutter, M. (1978) 'Early sources of security and competence' in Bruner, J. and Garton, A. (eds), *Human Growth and Development* (Oxford: Oxford University Press, 1978) pp. 33–61.

Rutter, M. (1980) 'Attachment and the development of social relations' in Rutter, M. (ed.), *Developmental Psychiatry* (Washington, DC: American Psychiatric Press, 1980).

Rutter, M. (1981) *Maternal Deprivation Reassessed*, 2nd edn (Harmondsworth: Penguin).

Rutter, M. (1988) 'Functions and consequences of relationships: some psychopathological considerations', in Hinde and Stevenson-Hinde (1988) pp. 332–53.

Rutter, M. (1989) 'Intergenerational continuities and discontinuities in serious parenting difficulties' in Cicchetti and Carlson (1989) pp. 317–48.

Rutter, M. (1991) 'A fresh look at maternal deprivation', in Bateson (1991) pp. 331–76.

Rutter, M. and Garmezy, N. (1983) 'Developmental psychopathology', in Hetherington, E. M. (ed.), *Carmichael's Manual of Child Psychology, Volume 4* (New York: Wiley, 1983).

Rutter, M. and Giller, H. (1983) *Juvenile Delinquency: Trends and Perspectives* (Harmondsworth: Penguin).

Rutter, M. and Quinton, D. (1984a) 'Long-term follow-up of women institutionalized in childhood: factors promoting good functioning in social life', *British Journal of Developmental Psychology*, vol. 2, pp. 191–204.

Rutter, M. and Quinton, D. (1984b) 'Parental psychiatric disorder: effects on children', *Psychological Medicine*, vol. 14, pp. 853–80.

Rutter, M. and Rutter, M. (1993) *Developing Minds: Challenge and Continuity Across the Life Span* (Harmondsworth: Penguin Books).

Rutter, M., Quinton, D. and Liddle, C. (1983) 'Parenting in two generations: looking backwards and looking forwards', in Madge, N. (ed.), *Families at Risk* (London: Heinemann, 1983).

Rutter, M., Quinton, D. and Hill, Jonathan (1990) 'Adult outcomes of institution-reared children: males and females compared', in Robins and Rutter (1990a) pp. 135–57.

Sable, P. (1989) 'Attachment, anxiety and loss of husband', *American Journal of Orthopsychiatry*, vol. 59, no. 4, pp. 550–6.

Sameroff, A. J. (1989) 'Principles of development and psychopathology', in Sameroff and Emde (1989).

Sameroff, A. J. and Emde, R. N. (eds) (1989) *Relationship Disturbances in Early Childhood: A Developmental Approach* (New York: Basic Books).

Scarr, S. and McCartney, K. (1983) 'How people make their own environment', *Child Development*, vol. 54, pp. 425–35.

Sheppard, M. (1994) 'Maternal depression, child care and the social work role', *British Journal of Social Work*, vol. 24, pp. 33–51.

Simpson, J. A. and Rholes, W. S. (1994) 'Stress and secure base relationships in adulthood', in Bartholomew and Perlman (1994) pp. 181–204.

Smith, D. (1991) 'The long term effects of child sexual abuse on the mental health of adult women', unpublished MSW, University of East Anglia, Norwich.

Smith, T. (1992) 'Family centres, children in need and the Children Act 1989', in Gibbons (1992a) pp. 9–22.

Sosa, R., Kennell, J., Klaus, M., Robertson, S. and Urrutia, J. (1980) 'The effect of a supportive companion on length of labour, mother–infant interaction and perinatal problems', *New England Journal of Medicine*, vol. 303, pp. 597–600.

Spieker, S. J. and Booth, C. L. (1988) 'Maternal antecedents of attachment quality', in Belsky and Nezworski (1988a) pp. 41–94.

Sroufe, L. A. (1978) 'Attachment and the roots of competence', *Human Nature*, vol. 1, no. 10, pp. 50–7.

Sroufe, L. A. (1985) 'Attachment classification from the perspective of infant–caregiver relationships and infant temperament', *Child Development*, vol. 56, pp. 1–14.

Sroufe, L. A. (1988) 'The role of infant–caregiver attachment in development', in Belsky and Nezworski (1988a) pp. 18–38.

Sroufe, L. A. (1989a) 'Relationship, self, and individual adaptation', in Sameroff and Emde (1989) pp. 70–96.

Sroufe, L. A. (1989b) 'Relationships and relationship disturbances', in Sameroff and Emde (1989) pp. 97–124.

Sroufe, L. A., Jacobvitz, J., Mangelsdorf, S., DeAngelo, E. and Ward, M. J. (1985) 'Generational boundary dissolution between mothers and their pre-school children: a relationship systems approach', *Child Development*, vol. 56, pp. 17–29.

Steele, H. and Steele, M. (1994) 'Intergenerational patterns of attachment', in Bartholomew and Perlman (1994) pp. 93–120.

Stern, D. N. (1987) *The Interpersonal World of the Infant* (New York: Basic Books).

Stevenson-Hinde, J. (1991) 'Temperament and attachment: an eclectic approach', in Bateson (1991) pp. 315–29.

Tienari, P., Lahti, I., Sorri, A., Naarala, M., Moring, J., Kaleva, M., Wahlberg, K. and Wynne, L. (1990) 'Adopted-away offspring of schizophrenics and controls', in Robins, L. N. and Rutter (1990a).

Tizard, B. and Hodges, J. (1978) 'The effects of early institutional rearing on the development of eight year-old children', *Journal of Child Psychology and Psychiatry*, vol. 19, pp. 99–118.

Trevathan, D. (1987) *Human Birth: An Evolutionary Perspective* (New York: Aldine Gruyter).

Troy, M. and Sroufe, L. A. (1987) 'Victimization among preschoolers: the role of attachment history', *Journal of the American Academy of Child and Adolescent Psychiatry*, vol. 26, pp. 166–72.

Truax, C. B. and Carkhuff, R. B. (1967) *Towards Effective Counselling and Psychotherapy* (Chicago: Aldine).

Vaillant, G. E. and Vaillant, C. D. (1981) 'Natural history of male psychological health', *American Journal of Psychiatry*, vol. 137, pp. 1433–40.

van der Eyken, W. (1982) *Home-start: a Four Year Evaluation* (Leicester: Home-Start Consultancy).

Vaughn, B., Egeland, B., Sroufe, L. A. and Waters, E. (1979) 'Individual differences in infant–mother attachment at twelve and eighteen months: stability and change in families under stress', *Child Development*, vol. 50, pp. 971–5.

Waterhouse, L. (ed.) (1993) *Child Abuse and Child Abusers: Protection and Prevention* (London: Jessica Kingsley).

Weiss, R. S. (1991) 'The attachment bond in childhood and adulthood', in Parkes, Stevenson-Hinde and Marris (1991) pp. 66–76.

Werner, E. E. and Smith, R. S. (1982) *Vulnerable But Invincible: A Longitudinal Study of Resilient Children* (New York: McGraw-Hill).

Whiten, A. (ed.) (1991) *Natural Theories of the Mind: Evolution, Development and Simulation in Everyday Mindreading* (Oxford: Blackwell).

Whittaker, J. (1993) 'Changing paradigms in child and family services: challenges for practice, policy and research', in Ferguson, Gilligan and Torode (1993) pp. 3–13.

Wing, L. and Gould, J. (1979) 'Severe impairments of social interaction and associated abnormalities in children: epidemiology and classification' *Journal of Autism and Developmental Disorders*, vol. 9, pp. 11–29.

# Author index

Adelson, E. 161
Ainsworth, M. 51–3, 63–4, 68, 78–9, 86, 89, 166, 168, 171
Anderson, J. 55
Asher, S. 124
Atlas, P. 62

Baron-Cohen, S. 41
Bartholomew, K. 102
Bates, J. 67, 90–1
Bayles, K. 90–1
BBC 111
Beattie, M. 154
Belsky, J. 66, 75, 90, 113, 132, 160, 171–2, 179, 184, 209, 211
Bentler, P. 149
Bergeman, C. 67
Bergman, L. 146
Bifulco, A. 135, 184
Bloom, L. 32
Bonvillian, J. 166
Booth, C. 163–4
Bowlby, J. 23, 45–7, 49–51, 53–6, 63–5, 67, 72, 76, 78, 82–3, 87–8, 91, 93, 98, 103, 139, 151–3, 161, 165, 167, 170, 192, 214, 221, 223
Bretherton, I. 65–6, 173, 175
Brodzinsky, D. 133, 185
Brown, G. 133–5, 215
Brown, J. 33
Browne, A. 140
Bruner, J. 3
Burkett, L. 4, 169
Burkitt, I. 19
Burnham, J. 196

Cadoret, R. J. 10–11, 106
Capron, C. 180
Carkhuff, R. 210
Carlson, V. 89
Carmen, E. 140
Caspi, A. 13, 102–3, 160
Cassidy, J. 91–2, 109, 120
Cermak, T. 154
Chess, S. 67
Cohen, P. 113, 197, 199
Cohen, S. 211
Collins, N. 126–9
Coons, P. 141
Cooper, C. 147
Cotterill, R. 20
Crittenden, P. 86, 166–8, 194–6
Crockenberg, S. 172
Cummings, E. 114–15

Daniels, D. 68
Davies, P. 115
DeLozier, P. 170
Dishion, T. J. 24
Dobash, R. 169
Dodge, K. 147
Donaldson, M. 35
Dunn, J. 3, 6, 11, 25, 29, 30, 33–5, 61, 65, 68, 85, 92, 113, 117, 162
Duyme, M. 180

Edmund, M. 154–5
Egeland, B. 88
Eichberg, C. 89, 171
Elder, G. 102–3, 160
Emde, R. 62, 64, 100, 189–91
Erikson, E. 132

Fahlberg, V. 20, 52–4, 57–8, 81–3, 132, 135, 214–15
Farber, E. 88
Farrington, D. 147–8
Feeney, J. 122
Fendrich, M. 114
Feshbach, N. 38
Finkelhor, D. 140
Fonagy, P. 178–82
Fouts, G. 62
Fox, N. 68
Fraiberg, S. 3, 57, 161
Franz, C. 152
Frith, U. 30–2, 40, 42–3
Frodi, A. 167
Frommer, E. 165
Fury, G. 37, 118

Garmezy, N. 24
George, C. 118
Gibbons, J. 211, 216–17
Giller, H. 146
Goldwyn, R. 166, 176, 180
Gould, J. 40
Greenberg, M. 145, 162
Grossmann, K. 82, 85, 106–7, 109–10, 118–20, 164, 175, 181
Grossmann, K. E. 82, 106–7, 109, 110, 118–20, 164
Grotevant, H. 147

Hamlyn, D. W. 10
Happe, F. 41
Harris, P. 33, 35–6, 38–40
Harris, T. 133–5, 184, 215–16
Harrison, M. 216
Hay, D. 53
Hazan, C. 86, 116, 126–7, 151–2
Hetherington, E. 114
Hinde, R. A. 12–4, 16, 67, 92
Hinings, D. 59
Hodges, J. 122–5
Holmes, J. 51, 98
Hood, L. 32
Hopkins, J. 108–9
Horney, K. 90

Howe, D. 19, 58–9, 133, 185, 189, 211, 220
Humphrey, N. 28

Ingleby, D. 15
Inglis, K. 59
Isabella, R. 172, 209

Jones, M. 217

Kagan, J. 67–8, 85
Kasl, C. 155
Kaufman, I. 209
Kaufman, J. 160, 171
Kellogg, T. 155
Kennell, J. 52
Kessen, W. 16
Kety, S. S. 10
Klaus, M. 52
Klein, J. 20
Kobak, R. 91–2, 120
Kochanska, G. 176
Kumar, R. 52

LaFreniere, P. 118
Lamb, M. 167
Le Blanc, M. 144, 147–8
Lee, C. 67
Leiderman, P. 61, 85
Leslie, A.M. 20, 42
Lieberman, A. 81, 162
Loeber, R. 144, 147–8
Lollis, S. 117
Lorenz, K. 51
Lyons-Ruth, K. 89, 174

McCartney, K. 183
McCord, J. 148–9
Magnusson, D. 146
Main, M. 21, 23, 75–7, 79, 81, 107–9, 118, 166, 171, 173, 176, 180–1
Mattinson, J. 55, 87, 94–5, 152, 155–8, 190, 197, 198, 214
Maughan, B. 185
Mayer, J. 210

Mead, G. H.   19
Mehl, L.   52
Milstein, V.   141

Nash, A.   53
Nezworski, T.   66, 75, 90, 164, 170, 209, 213–14, 221
Newcombe, M.   149
Norwood, R.   154

Odent, M.   52
Oldershaw, L.   167
Olson, D.   33
O'Shea, G.   165

Park, R.   69
Parker, J.   124
Parkes, M.   58, 60, 135, 137
Parton, N.   167
Patterson, G.   24
Pawl, J.   81, 162
Pensky, E.   132, 160, 184
Perlman, P.   102
Peterson, G.   52
Pianta, R.   166–7, 171
Pickles, A.   185
Pitcairn, T.   88, 169
Plomin, R.   25, 67–8

Quinton, D.   114, 126, 165, 172–3

Radke-Yarrow, M.   105, 114, 176–7
Read, S.   126–9
Reiner, B.   209
Reitsma-Street, M.   146
Rholes, W.   52, 83, 97, 127
Richards, M.   66
Ricks, M.   24
Riekar, P.   140
Robson, K.   52
Robertson, J.   46, 56
Robins, L.   13–15, 144–5, 222
Rogers, C.   210
Rosenblatt, D.   53
Rosenthal, D.   10
Rubin, K.   117

Rutter, Marjorie   10–14, 22–3, 25, 43–4, 56–7, 66, 74, 96, 114, 119, 126, 134, 138–9, 146, 179, 180
Rutter, Michael   10–15, 18, 22–5, 43–4, 46–9, 56–7, 61, 66–7, 74, 89, 96, 99–102, 114, 119, 126, 134, 138, 139, 144–6, 160–1, 165, 172–3, 179–80, 183, 213, 222

Sable, P.   135
Sameroff, A.   3, 71, 189–91
Sawbridge, P.   59
Scarr, S.   183
Shaver, P.   86, 126–7, 151–2
Shapiro, V.   161
Sheppard, M.   176
Simpson, J.   52, 83, 97, 127
Sinclair, I.   55, 87, 94–5, 152, 155–8, 197–8, 214
Smith, D.   4, 141–2
Smith, R.   179
Smith, T.   218
Speltz, M.   145
Spieker, S.   163–4
Sroufe, L.   4, 14, 22, 24–5, 37, 65, 68, 70, 81, 89–90, 118, 125, 131–2, 147, 161, 193–4, 196
Steele, H.   82, 174
Steele, M.   82, 174
Stern, D.   62, 64
Stevenson-Hinde, J.   16, 85
Syme, S.   211

Thomas, A.   67
Tienari, P.   10, 185–6
Timms, N.   210
Tizzard, B.   122–5
Tolan, W.   75
Trevathan, D.   52
Troy, M.   193
Truax, C.   210

Vaillant, C.   132
Vaillant, G.   132
van der Eyken, W.   217
Vaughn, B.   97
Vondra, J.   171, 212

Waters, E.   69
Weiss, R.   52, 135, 153
Werner, E.   179
Weston, D.   108
Whittaker, J.   215
Wing, L.   40

Winnicott, D.   73
Wittig, B.   53

Zeifman, D.   116, 151–2
Zigler, E.   160, 171

# Subject index

abandonment 87, 170, 201
abuse of children 88, 92, 118, 126, 160, 166–71, 184, 195–6
abusing parents 166–71, 195–6
acceptance 25
adaptive responses 89–95
adolescence 23, 86, 122, 132–3
adoption 10–11, 52–3, 58–9, 110–12, 123–5, 133, 162–3, 179–80, 185–7, 216
Adult Attachment Interview 174
adversity in childhood 8, 14, 96, 99
ambivalent attachments, description of 80, 83, 210–12
anger and loss 56–60
anorexia nervosa 139
anti-social behaviour 13, 44, 144–50
anxiety 12, 23, 25, 47, 50, 53–6, 60–1, 89–95
anxiety and loss 56–60
anxiety and separation 86–95
assessments, making of 6, 8, 188–207
asymmetric attachments 152
attachment behaviour 23, 54, 64
attachment classification system 78–95
attachment, continuity of 109–10
attachment experiences 78–95
attachment and anxiety 53–6
attachment and culture 84–5
attachment relationships 22, 25
attachment theory, origins of 45–51
attachment, types of 78–95

attachments, forming new 110–12
attention deficit 147–8
attention seeking 202
autism 10, 40–3, 78
autonomous individuals 173
avoidance 90–1, 93, 202–3
avoidant attachments, description of 80, 82

babies, responses of 61–6
being understood 210
beliefs 15, 31, 33
beyond attachment 25, 45–6, 61, 65
birth-mothers of adopted children 58–9
blame 157
bonding 52, 151
Bowlby and attachment theory 45–51
brain 14–15, 17, 20,
brain development 17–18, 20

care, lack of 134–5, 146
cats, brain development of 17, 41
cheerfulness 10, 13
children, relationship with 160–72
conflict, couples in 155–8
conflict, parental 113–14, 129, 146, 155–8
consciousness of self 15
communication 31–2, 63–6, 76–7, 107
compliance 167–8

compulsive self-reliance 91, 139, 153, 164
conduct disorders 144–50
conscientiousness 44
controlling parents 25
co-dependent relationships 153–5
co-operation 36, 40
coping 23, 26, 37, 38, 44, 89, 96, 100, 122–5, 191
counselling 219–22
criminal behaviour 144–50
culture 15–16, 19, 41
culture and attachment 84–5
culture and emotion 38–40
cultural context 3, 9, 29, 32, 38–40, 61
cultural differences 13, 84

deception 43
defence mechanisms 89–95, 202, 220
defensive strategies 89–95, 98, 128
delinquency 46–7, 144–50
denial 93, 154, 202
depression 23, 25, 47, 56–60, 114–15, 133–5, 139, 153, 163, 176–7, 203
deprivation 47
desires 15, 31, 33
despair 56–60, 75, 203
developmental psychology 4, 7
dismissing individuals 174
disorganised attachments, description of 80–1, 203
divorce 13–14, 48, 113–14, 153
Down's syndrome 42

emotion and culture 38–40
emotion theorists 38
emotional development 32–40
emotional support 158, 166, 182–4, 198, 211, 215–19
emotions 32–40
empathy 25, 27, 64, 70, 169, 175, 182, 210
ethology 46, 50–1
evolution and attachment 51–3
exclusion 90

expectations 19–21, 24, 38, 72, 97
experience, organisation of 71–7
exploration 53–6
extroversion 13, 44, 68

family centres 218
family, relationships with 105–15
family structure 196–8
family support 209, 211–19
fantasy play 36–7
feminism 48
fostering 110–12
freezing 89, 92
Freud 50
friendship 119–22, 124, 126, 212
frozen child 92, 108–9, 203

gender 22, 29–30, 32
genes 9–15, 41, 63–6, 68, 185–6
genes and experience 9–15
Genie 16
grief 56–60, 135–7
grief, chronic 137
grief, delayed 136
grief, unexpected 136
guilt 39, 56–60, 87, 140, 156

Harlow's monkeys 51
helplessness 22, 56–60, 135, 157, 176
Home-start 216–17
hopelessness 56–60, 135, 176
human face 62–3
human voice 62–3
humour 65, 179
hyperactivity 147–8

identity 132
imagination 35–7
impulsivity 147–8
insecure attachment, description of 80–1
institutional care 98, 102, 106, 122–6, 146, 165–6, 172–3, 183, 204
intelligence 11, 13, 179–82

intergenerational
    continuities   102–3, 160, 171,
    175, 177
intergenerational
    discontinuities   179–82
internal working models   12, 17–23,
    38, 54, 62–3, 71–7, 86, 161, 166
interpretation   19–21, 32, 38–40
intersubjectivity   66
intimacy   16, 25, 151–9, 196–7,
    211–12
IQ   11, 123, 179

jealousy   25, 127, 156–7, 162, 201

language   4–6, 16, 19, 65–6, 86
laughing   12
libido   50
life cycle   23, 56, 58, 102–3
Lorenz   51
loss   46–7, 56–60, 98, 135–7, 171
loss and anxiety   56–60

make-believe   35–6, 42
making sense   17–9, 23, 29, 62, 71,
    74
maternal deprivation   45, 49–50
maternal sensitivity   63
meaning   16, 24, 38–40
mental illness   101, 140–2, 146, 199
mental models   12, 17–23, 38, 54,
    71–7
mental representations   19–23, 38,
    54, 62–32, 71–7, 161, 166, 173–6
mentalising   31, 35–6, 43, 182
meta-representations   20–1
mind, development of   14
minds, theory of other   14, 21,
    27–32, 41, 43, 182
monkeys   51, 92
moral development   27–44
mother–infant relationship   52,
    164–5
mothers, responses of   63–6
multiple models   75, 77
mutuality   25, 64, 68, 86, 169

natural characteristics   3
nature   17
nature–nurture debate   9–15, 63–6,
    101
neglect of children   166–71, 195–6
neglecting parents   166–71, 195–6
neuroticism   68
nonattachments   106
nonattachments, description
    of   81, 84, 203–4
novelty   54
nurture–nature debate   9–15, 63–6,
    101

other minds   21, 39

parent–child interaction   63–6
parental conflict   113–14, 126, 146,
    155–8
parental death   76
parental responses   12
parenting, ideal   107–8
parenting, quality of   160–77, 196,
    214
parenting styles, continuities
    in   160–77
parents, relationships with   105–15
partners, relationships with   151–9,
    198, 212
peer rejection   118–19
peers   25, 102, 116–30
peers, relationship with   116–30,
    146
perceptual discrimination   62
personality disorder   44
personality, formation of   2, 3, 6,
    26, 43–4, 48, 57, 73, 76–7
play   33, 36–7, 40, 42–3, 55, 65, 69,
    74, 107–8, 117–18
possessiveness   127, 157, 201
potency   183, 216
poverty   97, 167, 171–3, 177, 200,
    206–7, 219
powerlessness   155
premature births   52
preoccupied individuals   173–4
pretend play   33, 36–7, 40, 42–3
pride   39

primary representations 20
privation 47
projection 93–4
proximity-seeking 52–6, 103
psychoanalytic theory 46, 49, 219
psychotherapy 219–22

quality of experience 21

race 32
reattachments 152
reciprocity 29, 40, 64–5, 68
reflective self 179–82
relationship history 6, 24
relationship styles 4, 38
relationship styles, continuities
 in 160–77
relationships, assessment
 of 192–206
relationships, past and present 6–7,
 22, 44, 96–100, 192
relationships, quality of 21, 24–6,
 40, 43–4, 60–8
repression 93
resilience 140, 178–87
resistant attachment, description
 of 80, 83
Robertson, James 56–60
romantic relationships 152–3

Sally-Anne experiment 42–3
schizophrenia 10, 185–6
school 117–18, 123, 125, 131–2,
 147–8, 183
secure attachment, description of
 79–82, 200–1
secure base 52–56, 98
selective attachment 53, 62
self and social environment 3,
 100–1
self, consciousness of 15, 21, 73
self, formation of 2, 5–6, 15–17,
 19, 24–6, 43–4, 57, 62, 73, 77
self, representation of 143
self-awareness 21, 73
self-confidence 139–40
self-disclosure 16, 35, 65

self-esteem 22, 68–9, 84, 131–2,
 134, 139–40, 149, 154, 174, 176,
 182–3
self-knowledge 37, 39
self-understanding 39, 179–82
self-worth 131–2, 134, 179, 215,
 220
separation 46–7, 86–95, 198
separation anxiety 56–60, 86–95
separation protest 52
sex 22
sex differences 29–30
sexual abuse 4, 140–2, 169–70
sexual relationships 122, 126–9,
 133, 151–9
sexuality 50, 102
shame 39, 140
shock 56–60
shyness 10, 13, 44, 68
siblings 25, 61
smiling 12, 63, 66
social being 2, 9–25
social being, becoming a 9–25
social competence 24, 26–45, 55,
 63, 66, 68–9, 96, 101, 119, 192
social empathy 27–44, 85–6
social environment 3
social experience 17–9
social intelligence 28–44
social meaning 39
social relationships, quality of 2,
 4, 12, 15–19
social understanding, development
 of 27–44
social work process, the 189
social work responses 8, 208–23
social work support 213–14
social worker's
 understanding 209–11
society, relationships with 144–50
splitting 93–4
strange situation test 79
stress 6, 23, 26, 51–3, 97, 127, 145,
 152, 164, 167–8, 171–3, 177,
 200, 206–7, 212, 215, 219
supervision, social work 95, 190
support 158, 171–3, 182–4, 198,
 209, 211–19

support, lack of 171–3
survivors 178–87
symmetric attachments 152

*tabula rasa* 14
teachers' views 117–18, 125, 131–2
temperament 3, 14, 66–8, 101, 191
temperamental differences 66–8
theory of other minds 14, 21,
    27–32, 41, 43, 182
threat 51–3, 87
truancy 145

trust 157
trust, lack of 84
twins 179–80

understanding other people 19,
    21, 27–44, 66, 71–7, 209–11
unemployment 13
uniqueness, individual 14–15, 25

violent parenting 109
visual experience 17

withdrawal 68